Teacher Unions
in Schools

Teacher Unions in Schools

Susan Moore Johnson

Temple University Press / Philadelphia

Library of Congress Cataloging in Publication Data

Johnson, Susan Moore.
  Teacher unions in schools.

  Bibliography: p.
  Includes index.
  1. Teachers' unions—United States.   I. Title.
LB2844.53.U6J63 1984   331.88'11371100973   83-18067
ISBN 0-87722-327-0

Temple University Press, Philadelphia 19122
© 1984 by Temple University. All rights reserved
Published 1984
Printed in the United States of America

An earlier version of Chapter Six
appears in Harvard Educational Review 53
(1983): 309–326. Copyright © 1983 by
President and Fellows of Harvard College.
All rights reserved.

To Glenn

Contents

Acknowledgments

I wish to thank the many unnamed teachers, principals, union leaders, and district administrators who participated in this study. They were cordial, frank, and insightful, making my work both pleasant and productive. Since they must remain anonymous, my only public gesture of gratitude must be this effort to report their views accurately.

I am indebted to Edward Meade and the Ford Foundation. They generously supported this research, but bear no responsibility for its conclusions. I am also grateful for the institutional support provided by the Institute for Educational Policy Studies, directed by Jerome T. Murphy, and the Harvard Graduate School of Education, headed by Dean Paul Ylvisaker.

There are many whose example, suggestions, criticisms, reassurances, and proddings moved this work along. More than any other, I am indebted to Jerry Murphy, who taught me most of what I know about qualitative research and generously offered direction, encouragement, and thoughtful responses to many drafts. David K. Cohen brought to this research his soothsayer's insight for the right issues and taught me to think in new ways. David Kuechle, whose outstanding teaching engaged my interest in collective bargaining, provided me with a broad and knowledgeable perspective on educational labor relations. Barbara Neufeld, the best of friends and colleagues, was generous with her time, support, and clear thinking throughout this project.

Laura Bachman, Rhonda Htoo, Mary Fasenmeyer, and Genny Dunne accurately transcribed the field notes. Peg Egan assisted me in coding the data. Darcy Marshall and Gail Taylor provided ongoing administrative support. Tina Hansar patiently typed earlier drafts, and Markie Trottenberg prepared the final manuscript with speed and care. I am truly grateful to each of them.

My family endured this project as families do. Krister and Erika kept academic work in its place with their "knock-knock" jokes and splinters. Glenn, who did his best to be patient, regularly reminded me that my life had more meaning than the current draft, and sustained me with varied, welcomed distractions over the course of three years.

Teacher Unions
in Schools

Introduction

Nearly forty years after negotiation of the first teachers' contract,[1] controversy persists over the impact of collective bargaining on public education. Advocates contend that teacher unions[2] are reforming the schools; critics argue that they are laying waste to them.[3] The one point of agreement is that the effects of collective bargaining are both big and important. Stephen K. Bailey characterized the popular and professional debates:

> Few issues in the field of American education have been more controversial in the past two decades than the rise of teachers' unions. Struggles over appropriate bargaining agents, what issues are negotiable, grievance procedures, the right to strike, and even the underlying compatibility of unions and the educating professions have divided faculty, outraged administrators, politicized schools and colleges, entangled the courts, and roiled public opinion.[4]

Although public attention has been drawn to the expansion of teacher unionism, until recently there has been scant empirical research to inform public opinion about its effects. Do teacher contracts reduce teacher services or enhance professional commitment? Are routine school practices more adversarial or simply more equitable as a result of collective bargaining? Do teacher unions undermine administrative authority and divert teacher loyalties or ensure better management and promote teacher participation in policymaking? The answers put forth have been shaped more by dogma than by data. It is important to consider these questions carefully because collective bargaining practices are widespread and apparently robust. Currently, more than 75 percent of the nation's teachers belong to unions, and over 1,400 local districts bargain collectively.[5]

I came to this research as a defender of neither labor nor management, but with a commitment to good schools. Although I had little direct experience with unions or bargaining, nine years as a teacher and administrator led me to expect few unequivocal answers to these questions about the organizational effects of unionism. The evidence from the schools promised to be complex, just as schools are complex. I knew that I would not settle the ongoing controversy with this research, but believed that I might at least complicate the debate and was convinced that there are others who share my interest in such data and analysis. Citizens want to know what collective bargaining is doing to their schools. Practitioners want to know how to make collective bargaining work—or, at least, how to work with collective bargaining. Policymakers want to know how legislative action might change the impact of teacher unionism. Policy analysts want to understand how collective bargaining, as one of a number of educational policies, works. Therefore, with these varied interests in mind, I set out to determine the extent to which unions and contracts have affected school practices, to characterize the nature of those effects, and to try to account for different outcomes in different places.

What Is Known and Not Known

Despite its presumed importance, educational labor relations has received little systematic research attention. Personal experience has been the primary source of what is known and believed about teacher unionism in the schools, with professional journals typically reporting the labor experiences of one school district or presenting the advice of one school administrator or teacher.[6] The empirical research centers largely on salary scales rather than on school practices and attempts to measure the effects of collective bargaining on teacher salary levels by comparing salary increases in unionized and nonunionized districts.[7]

There are a small number of empirical studies, however, that do examine the organizational effects of collective bargaining. Although the perspectives and methods of these studies vary, there is general consensus among them about the dominant effects of teacher unionism on the schools. Collective bargaining has, various authors conclude, increased the formal authority of teachers and restricted the formal authority of principals, centralized and standardized school practices, redefined and reduced teachers' work obligations, and increased teachers' job protections. For example, in one of the earliest such studies, Perry and Wildman concluded:

> [N]egotiations on "working conditions" in the schools has to some extent substituted centralized decision-making for decentralized decision-making on the management side. School principals *have* lost significant discretion in this process.[8]

In an update of the study, Perry concludes that, in addition to improving teacher salaries, collective bargaining has substantially expanded "the job rights of teachers in terms of both protection from arbitrary treatment and participation in decision-making."[9] In a more recent study, McDonnell and Pascal argue that the greatest nonbudgetary effects of collective bargaining are at the school level, largely with the reduction of administrative discretion.[10] Kerchner and Mitchell conclude that collective bargaining has been a principal cause of changes in work responsibilities, the control of teacher performance, and the authority available to principals.[11] The effects that have been identified by these authors are consistent with the fact that collective bargaining, by its very nature, enhances the rights of teachers, constrains the prerogatives of management, and requires centralized contract negotiation and administration.

Many practitioners and educational commentators are disturbed by these effects, each of which has generated some concern. The reallocation of authority is said by some to have left principals without sufficient power to run effective schools.[12] The increased centralization of the school district is thought by others to have excessively and unwisely formalized, standardized, and rationalized school operations. Defining teachers' work obligations may, some say, reduce school services to unsatisfactory levels. Moreover, the job protections won by teachers through collective bargaining are blamed for maintaining incompetent teachers in the schools. Each of these is a serious charge that warrants close attention. In order to assess the claims of union advocates and the complaints of union critics, we need to ask additional questions about the extent of the identified effects. How much authority have principals lost? To what degree has the school district been centralized? How much or how little responsibility do teachers now assume? How secure, in fact, are their positions?

In addition, we must know whether these effects are, as much of the literature seems to imply, consistent from district to district and from school to school.[13] If the effects are consistent, one might well conclude that local actors have no control over the outcomes and that all labor relations are moving inexorably toward the regimented, hostile practices thought to typify big city school districts. In fact, this is not the case.

Many acknowledge that the picture of educational labor practices is as varied as that in the industrial sector described twenty years ago by Slichter, Healy, and Livernash.[14] In reporting his recent findings, Perry noted, "First, collective bargaining relationships in public education, as in the private sector have become incredibly diverse in almost every respect."[15] Similarly, Kerchner cautions about diversity:

> Perhaps, however, the most significant qualification about school labor relations is that there are extreme variations in impacts. Indeed, this may be the most important single conclusion about governance impacts, because it challenges the assumption that there is a single "industrial model" of labor relations that has been imposed on education.[16]

The qualifications made by these researchers suggest that it is important to go beyond the generalizations about collective bargaining effects and to explore the variation in those effects both among districts and among schools within districts. How diverse are labor relationships, contract language, and contract administration under collective bargaining? Are contract provisions similarly enforced in all settings? Do principals exercise different levels of influence over the role of the union and the contract in their schools?

I decided to investigate each of these concerns by conducting field research in the schools. I was skeptical about certain assumptions that were implicit in much of the literature about labor relations. It seemed that many researchers and commentators were unfamiliar with the unique features of schools, teachers, and principals and might, therefore, be inattentive to the particular ways in which collective bargaining would be played out in the schools.

There were three assumptions embedded in much of the commentary and research that seemed problematic. The first was that the contract provisions, once negotiated, were, in fact, implemented in the schools. If true, this would allow researchers to remain at some distance and to infer school practices from contract language. For example, if a contract included provisions for the establishment of a school advisory committee, one might assume its establishment. However, I had seen many district office policy statements sit unheeded in the filing cabinets of the schools. Moreover, my previous research about performance-based layoff practices illustrated that, once negotiated, the implementation of these practices was at best uncertain.[17] My experience and research had confirmed that school districts are not the hierarchical, "tightly coupled" systems they would have to be if the contract were to be fully and literally implemented in all schools.[18]

Second, the collective bargaining literature often treats principals as neutral functionaries who routinely carry out the orders of district officials and abide by the restrictions and requirements of the teachers' contract. Again, my experience with principals of varying administrative effectiveness and style suggested that this was misleading. Some principals enforce rules; others do not. Some command faculty loyalty; others foster dissent. How these principals work and how they are regarded by teachers might well be expected to influence the activity of the union and the role of the contract in the schools.[19] I hypothesized that differences in principals' attitudes and administrative styles would produce differences in labor relations practices from school to school, even within the same district.

Third, there is little acknowledgment in the literature that the school differs from the industrial workplace, where skills and responsibilities are defined, where employees work in an explicitly hierarchical relationship with their supervisors, and where the product of their efforts is tangible and appraisable. Schools are, in fact, very different places. The process of education is as yet poorly defined, and the responsibilities of teachers and administrators are broad and diffuse.[20] While hierarchical on paper, the relationship between teachers and administrators is in many ways reciprocal and their work interdependent.[21] Finally, because schools are designed to educate children rather than to manufacture widgets, teachers hold different views about the character and social value of their work.[22] Educational practice is not easily rationalized[23] and therefore may not readily adapt to the rationalized format of collective bargaining agreements. For all of these reasons, I decided to look at collective bargaining from the perspective of the schools rather than the negotiating table.

A Method of Inquiry

Recognizing the varied forms that labor relations practices take, I selected a diverse sample of six school districts for consideration. Media attention is typically focused on a few urban districts that are simultaneously contending with declining resources and declining enrollments. I wanted to consider labor relations in a range of settings. In order to better sort out the effects of collective bargaining from the effects of other economic and demographic variables, it seemed important to document how teacher unionism affects rural, suburban, and urban districts, to consider districts with expanding resources and enrollments as well as those experiencing decline, and to view labor practices in the context of both cooperative and adversarial labor relations.

On the basis of preliminary data, I had hypothesized that the effects of teacher unionism at school sites might be less extensive, formal, and fixed than they are generally thought to be. Consequently, I intentionally sought out three districts reputed to have militant unions and/or experience with multiple teacher strikes. In addition, the six sample districts are diverse in size, controlling state statute, AFT/NEA affiliation, region, urban/suburban/rural character, racial and ethnic composition, enrollment and economic trends, strength and activity of the union, and strength of the contract. Table I summarizes these district features.

I selected the school districts sequentially to ensure that the balance of variables would be maintained. There were many combinations of districts that might have comprised this sample. The districts chosen were recommended by SEA administrators, union leaders, community leaders, and other schools officials as ones that matched the combinations of characteristics I was seeking. I requested entrée into eight districts; two refused my request and the remaining six made up the final sample. I assumed that an examination of these six districts would make it possible to map the range and variation of public school labor practices.

Data collection, which extended from July 1979 to November 1980, proceded similarly in each district, with interviews being conducted at the district, school site, and classroom levels of the school organizations. I first conducted in-depth interviews with all central office administrators and all union leaders who were identified locally as relevant to the research. They provided general information about the districts, descriptions of the labor relationships, orientation to the contract, and retrospective accounts of negotiation, settlements, and strikes. (Interview protocols and a summary of the respondents by district are included in Appendix A.)

On the recommendations of these central office administrators and union leaders, I selected a group of principals varying in age and experience, gender, school level and location, labor attitudes, and administrative style. I repeatedly asked those interviewed whether the sample was "balanced and representative of the range of principals in the district." My questions to principals focused on both district-wide and school site labor relations. I sought to understand their styles and strategies as school managers and to gather specific information about the role and influence of the union and contract in their schools.

On the basis of these interviews with principals, I selected three to five schools in each district that represented the range of

Table I *Characteristics of Sample School Districts*

District	Region	Type	Enrollment	Economy	Student Composition	Affiliation	Number of strikes
Plantville	Northeast	Urban	9,800 Declining	Declining	White	AFT	None
Shady Heights	Northeast	Suburban	18,000 Declining	Declining	White	AFT	4
Vista	Southwest	Suburban consolidated	17,600 Expanding	Expanding	White, small % Hispanic	NEA	None
Metropolis	Northeast	Urban	240,000 Declining	Declining	62% black, 32% white, 6% Hispanic,	AFT	3
Mill City	Midwest	Urban	17,000 Declining	Declining	Predominantly black	NEA	5
Northwood	Northwest	Rural	850 Expanding	Stable	White	NEA	None

grade level, location, administrative style, and union activity within the district. With the assistance of principals and union building representatives, I selected a sample of seven to fifteen teachers in each of those schools, once again seeking diversity in a number of variables: grade, subject, gender, union views, support of or opposition to the principal, extent of involvement in school activities. I also asked respondents to review the balance and representativeness of the sample. I interviewed teachers about their attitudes toward unionism and their union, about the specific labor practices in their school, and about the role of their principal in labor relations. I spent one or two full days in each of twenty schools, with the length of visit depending on a school's size. The 294 interviews of this study were semi-structured, and varied in length from thirty minutes to two hours. Interviews with administrators were generally longer than those with teachers, whose time was usually restricted by the instructional schedule. With very few exceptions, interviews were conducted in private, and respondents were assured that their responses would not be discussed with others in the district and that neither they nor their districts would be identified in the study report.

I took extensive, detailed notes during the course of the interviews. Very soon after, these were dictated onto tape and transcribed, yielding 2,500 pages of field notes. Included in Appendix B is an explanation of how I sorted, coded, and analyzed the interview data. In addition to talking and listening while in the schools, I spent a considerable amount of time watching. I informally observed classrooms, corridors, cafeterias, main offices, faculty meetings, teachers' rooms and after-school activities, looking for the effects of collective bargaining agreements. Did teachers assume supervisory responsibilities beyond the contractual requirements? Were teacher-administrator relations apparently cooperative or hostile? Was the school orderly and secure? Were parents present and active? Did teachers work beyond the time for which they were contractually obligated? Did students remain after school for extra help or activities? These informal observations, which were recorded in field notes, were useful both in confirming and disconfirming interview responses and in suggesting new areas of inquiry.

The basic documents of this study were, of course, the six collective bargaining agreements that I studied and compared intently. (A systematic comparison of contract provisions is included in Appendix C.) In keeping with the scavenger tradition of field researchers, I collected copies of statutes, memoranda, handbooks, bargaining demands, union publications, district publications, arbitration findings, and board policies from the six districts. These, along with six months of news clippings from the local newspapers, provided the written accounts of many of the issues and events I followed.

Throughout the field work, I made a concerted effort to gain a fair, accurate, and detailed understanding of labor relations in the schools. My experience conducting field work in other studies had taught me the hazards of inaccurate responses, provocative rumors, and partial explanations. I guarded against bias and error in a number of ways. First, by selecting diverse samples of respondents at all levels, I could solicit many sides of any story. Second, by interviewing a number of people at every level of the school organization, I could probe prevailing opinions and cross-check information about events, policies, and practices. Third, I used documents collected throughout the study to verify or refute data. Finally, I relied on my own skepticism and compulsiveness to learn how things really worked and why they worked as they did.

I had anticipated complexity and I found it. Even so, I underestimated the richness and ambiguity of the data. There was rarely a single, unequivocal answer to any question, even to one so simple as how many strikes there had been in a district. By being present in the district and the schools, it was possible to seek out the people with the answers, to solicit alternative views and to elicit the stories and anecdotes that explained various practices and outcomes.

Though complex, the data are by no means chaotic or meaningless. Overall, the views and explanations of respondents were remarkably consistent, and when they differed, the reasons for their differences were apparent. While I knew that my analysis would inevitably simplify the complexity I found, I also knew that a qualitative approach to this subject had allowed me to appreciate the variation and intricacies of an exceedingly complex process.

I have been quite conservative in reporting the data throughout the chapters that follow. The method by which I sorted, coded, and analyzed the data forced me to repeatedly review the range and distribution of responses, and to review emerging conclusions and generalizations. Although I have avoided statistics in discussing the data because of the purposive manner by which sites and respondents were selected, I do report prevailing opinions and predominant views. When I say that "most" of any group of respondents shared a common opinion, I am referring to at least 80 percent of that group. When respondents' views or opinions were divided or contradictory in any significant way, I have reported those differences.

Caveat Lector

In considering the conclusions of this study, I urge the reader to keep three things in mind. First, the research reported here does not address all aspects of collective bargaining in the sample districts, but focuses on the ongoing processes of contract compliance, contract enforcement, and contract administration. A final assessment of collective bargaining would necessarily rest on a consideration of all outcomes of the process—salary settlements, strikes, district resource allocation—not only the organizational ones.[24]

Second, the effects of collective bargaining are often inextricable from the effects of many other forces that have reshaped public education during the past two decades—declining enrollments, inflation, federal aid to education, desegregation, reduced school revenues, and urban fiscal crises. Dramatic changes have occurred as labor relations have become established in American schools,[25] and many of these changes have also interacted with collective bargaining. For example, the declines in student numbers have led to teacher layoffs and teacher transfers, which are typically regulated by contract in districts that bargain collectively. Sudden declines in school revenues have made it difficult for some districts to honor current teacher contracts. Court orders to desegregate staff have had to be reconciled with contractual provisions regulating staff assignments. It is impossible, therefore, to know what schools might have been like if it had not been for collective bargaining, and it is unwarranted to compare today with yesterday or to offer one explanation for why everything is so different. Robert E. Doherty observes:

> One cannot avoid a certain amount of untidiness when talking about the effect of collective bargaining on educational outcomes. We sometimes attribute to bargaining certain changes in educational performance on the sole ground that one preceded the other. As Samuel Johnson once observed of physicians, they tended to mistake subsequence for consequence. Opponents of bargaining see the baleful influence of the union in every aspect of declining achievement and increasing costs.[26]

Throughout the text, I will try to place the findings in a context that accurately reflects the complexity of life and work in and around schools today.

Finally, qualitative research of this sort necessarily sacrifices breadth of investigation for depth.[27] This study will tell a great deal about a small number of districts. Because these districts are few and have been selected to assure a balance of important variables, they cannot be regarded as statistically representative of school districts in America, but they can be viewed as a range of those districts that bargain collectively. It must be left to the reader rather than to tests of statistical significance to determine whether these findings are plausible, generalizable, and instructive.

The Findings

The experiences of the six sample districts are consistent with those reported by other researchers. Collective bargaining has augmented the rights and protections of teachers, limited the prerogatives of principals, and promoted the centralization and standardization of district personnel practices. Yet, the research revealed that the negative effects are not as far-reaching as critics of collective bargaining might suggest. While principals' formal authority had been restricted and teachers' formal authority had been increased, school site administrators in even the strongest union districts could manage their schools well. Principals were neither figureheads deferring to union representatives nor functionaries complying slavishly with the contract. While there was an increase in the regulation of school site labor practices by the district offices, schools were remarkably autonomous in interpreting and administering the contract. Collective bargaining agreements defined the obligations of teachers, but those obligations were often extensive, and most staff did more than the required minimum. Teachers had gained procedural job protections through collective bargaining, but administrators could still discipline and terminate teachers. In these sample districts, schooling had been altered, but not transformed, by collective bargaining.

Not only were the effects of collective bargaining on schools less extensive than is popularly believed, they were less uniform than one might expect. Teachers in the six districts had neither pursued nor won the same rights and protections, and differences in contract language produced differences in teacher work patterns and school practices from district to district. Some local unions were aggressive in representing teacher interests, while others were cautious and unassertive. Some district office administrators preferred centralized management of labor relations, while others maintained a more decentralized organization.

But more surprising than this variation in district level outcomes was the variation in labor practices among schools within the same district. Contracts, once negotiated, were implemented differently in different schools. Teachers and principals established their own labor relationships independent of the prevailing relationship at the district level.

The following chapters explore and elaborate these findings. Chapter 1 sets the stage for the analysis by describing the sample districts, their unions, contracts, and schools. Each of the succeeding four chapters examines a major concern generated by one of the effects of collective bargaining. Chapter 2 looks at the reallocation of formal authority and assesses whether, as a result of that reallocation, principals have lost the power to manage their schools. Chapter 3 examines the centralization and stand- ardization of personnel practices that have come about in response to collective bargaining, and it considers whether schools are becoming overly bureaucratic as a result. Chapter 4 examines the ways in which teachers' work obligations have been reduced and defined and assesses whether those changes have seriously reduced the services schools can provide. Chapter 5 examines the impact of procedural job protections won by teachers and assesses the complaint that these protections are responsible for the maintenance of incompetent teachers in the schools. In each of these four chapters addressing one of the prominent concerns about the effects of collective bargaining, there is evidence of wide variation in collective bargaining outcomes both among districts and among schools within the same district. Chapter 6 focuses on the variation that was found among school sites. It explores the reasons for the diverse outcomes by examining how principals and teachers mutually define the role of the union and the prominence of the contract in their schools. The chapter offers an explanation from within the schools of why collective bargaining effects are neither as far reaching nor as uniform as they are popularly believed to be.

Chapter 1

The Districts and Their Schools

Each of the districts included in this study has a unique character and history. The simplicity and informality of rural Northwood stand in stark contrast to the complexity and bureaucracy of urban Metropolis. Declining enrollments in Plantville present problems unfamiliar to Vista school officials, who contend with rapid growth. Economic decline dramatically affects negotiations in Mill City, and a history of cooperative labor relations in Shady Heights influences labor practices there.

As one who has talked with staff, walked the corridors, and eaten the school lunches in the various districts, I find the sites and the people both memorable and distinct. In thinking about how to report these findings, I was inclined to describe each district in some detail, hoping not to overlook or misrepresent anyone or anything. Full, rich case studies might adequately capture the complexity of places, circumstances, events, and people. However, a series of detailed case studies might also obscure relevant cross-site similarities and differences, making it difficult for both the writer and the reader to compare the experiences of the districts and to generalize from the data.

Therefore, in introducing the districts, it seems wise to strike a balance between expansive portrayals and schematic accounts, between reporting only the peculiar circumstances and only the general conditions. The following presentations of district information are intended to provide both introductions to the sites and comparisons of important variables.

The Sites

The settings of the sample districts vary widely, from the industry and activity of the urban Northeast to the farms and serenity of the rural Northwest. One district is immense, four are of moderate size, and one is quite small. During the course of data collection, enrollments were growing in two districts and declining in four (see Table II).

Metropolis,[1] the largest site in the study, is a major Eastern industrial city contending with unemployment, poverty, racial tension, and fiscal crises. In 1980 the Metropolis school district had a rapidly declining student enrollment of 240,000. Sixty-two percent of the students were black, 6 percent were Hispanic, and 32 percent were white or Asian. The racial segregation of neighborhoods in the district was apparent in the schools—some were all black, some all white.

The 279 schools of the district were divided into seven subdistricts, each administered by a district superintendent. In addition to the 191 elementary, forty-one junior/middle, and twenty-four senior high schools, there were four vocational schools and nineteen special schools. The district administered seventy-two categorically funded programs such as Title I and Right to Read. The professional teaching staff of 13,100 included regular classroom teachers, special class teachers, counselors, and home and school visitors.

Mill City,[2] a second urban district, sits next to a large, winding and now-polluted river. It once flourished as a midwestern industrial center and continues to be a strong labor town. Its population of 139, 000, residing at the center of a large metropolitan area, changed within two decades from predominantly white to predominantly black as many of the middle class moved to the suburbs. Recently, severe cutbacks in the city's major industry have compounded the problems of a community already contending with poverty and unemployment.

In 1979, there were 17,600 students enrolled in the Mill City schools. Enrollments were down from a peak of 33,000 in 1925 and were projected to decline by 3,500 more within four years. The district included twenty-three elementary schools, seven junior high schools, six senior high schools, and two vocational centers. Four schools had been closed because of declining enrollments, and more closings were projected.

Plantville,[3] the third and smallest urban district of the sample, was once a thriving northeastern manufacturing center, but now confronts serious economic decline. Its population of 45,000, which is white, multiethnic, and predominantly blue collar, is inbred and stable. Plantville residents have strong allegiances to the city and its labor traditions. Both partisan and patronage politics are lively in Plantville and command a great deal of local attention.

When I visited Plantville in 1980, there were ten elementary schools, two junior high schools, one vocational high school, and one senior high school. Two parochial schools competed actively and successfully for students and resources, with the school board paying transportation costs for parochial school students. The public school population of Plantville, then at 9,800, was declining rapidly, and the district projected an enrollment drop of one-third in six years.

Shady Heights,[4] the one truly suburban district in the study, is a sprawling northeastern bedroom community twenty miles from a large city. The district has traditionally been known for the quality of its schools. The community of Shady Heights is economically diverse; some homes are large estates, and others have dirt floors and lack indoor plumbing. While located in a strong labor state, the town is neither particularly prounion nor antiunion.

In 1979, there were 18,000 students in the Shady Heights schools, enrollment having declined from a peak of over 20,000 in 1973. The district had closed eight schools in four years and anticipated additional closings. There were twenty-one elementary schools, three junior high schools, three senior high schools, and one special education school. The district employed 1,200 professional staff.

Vista,[5] one of the two sample districts with expanding enrollments, provides an example of startling growth. In 1953, the Vista Consolidated School District employed four teachers and enrolled 125 students who rode horses to their four-room

Table II *Labor Characteristics of Sample School Districts*

Variables	*Metropolis* northeast urban	*Mill City* midwest urban	*Plantville* northeast urban
District Size	240,000 students 13,000 staff 279 schools	17,600 students 1,000 staff 23 schools	9,800 students 600 staff 14 schools
Growth	Decreasing	Decreasing	Decreasing
Bargaining History	15 yrs. 4 strikes	14 yrs. 3 strikes	7 yrs. No strikes
State Law	Defines broad bargaining scope Strikes permitted Principals may bargain	No enabling legislation Strikes prohibited Contracts are legally binding	Defines broad bargaining scope Strikes prohibited Principals may bargain Agency shop
Contract	Binding arbitration Seniority-based layoffs and transfers Class size limits Extracurricular participation	Binding arbitration Seniority-based layoffs, no seniority-based transfers No class size limits	Binding arbitration Seniority-based layoffs and transfers Class size limits Voluntary extracurricular participation
Union	AFT 95% membership Strength: very high	NEA 65% membership Strength: low/moderate	AFT 99% membership Strength: moderate
Labor Relationship	Adversarial	Cooperative	Cooperative

Table II — *Continued*

Variables	*Shady Heights* *northeast* *suburban*	*Vista* *southwest* *suburban-rural*	*Northwood* *northwest* *rural*
District Size	18,000 students 1,200 staff 28 schools	17,600 students 1,200 staff 19 schools	850 students 75 staff 2 schools
Growth	Decreasing	Increasing	Increasing
Bargaining History	14 yrs. 4 strikes	12 yrs. No strikes	10 yrs. No strikes
State Law	Broad bargaining scope Strikes prohibited Principals may not bargain	No legislation	Broad bargaining scope Strikes permitted Principals may not bargain
Contract	Agency shop Binding arbitration Seniority-based layoffs and transfers Voluntary extracurricular participation No class size limits	Does not include binding arbitration Required extracurricular participation Class size limits	Binding arbitration Seniority-based and per- formance-based layoffs Required extracurricular participation No class size limits
Union	AFT	NEA	NEA
Labor Relationship	81% membership Strength: high Cooperative	80% membership Strength: low/moderate Adversarial	80% membership Strength: moderate/high Conciliatory

school. During data collection in 1980, the 18,000 students were driving pickup trucks or riding buses and bikes to their nineteen schools (fourteen elementary, three junior high, and two senior high schools).

The population and economy of this southwestern community are expanding rapidly, and the school district opens two or three new schools each year to meet the demands of this growth. The community is predominantly white, middle class, and young, with the majority of households having students in school. There is, therefore, broad local support for the schools, but this support is moderated by a conservative concern about educational spending.

Northwood,[6] the sixth sample district, is geographically quite large (189 square miles), but small in student numbers (850 in 1980). It is an unincorporated northwestern community that includes both dairy farms and timberlands within its boundaries. Operating funds for the schools are provided largely by a tax offset from the timber taxes. Northwood residents have traditionally provided strong support for the schools but have also been fiscally quite conservative. The community has grown recently as commuters from a nearby city have moved to Northwood for the space, peace, and beauty it offers.

In 1980, the district's classes were housed in two buildings, a grade school and a junior-senior high school. Across the street from the secondary school building was the office of the superintendent, the sole district office administrator. Teachers once were all local residents, but as student enrollments increased gradually but substantially, it became necessary to recruit teachers from outside Northwood. Staff turnover is a problem for the district because nonresident teachers often leave to teach closer to their urban homes when jobs become available. In 1980 the entire staff numbered seventy-five.

Bargaining Histories

Each of the sample districts has been negotiating for a number of years. Metropolis, having the most experience, bargained its first teachers' contract in 1965. Plantville, having bargained the least number of years, signed its initial agreement in 1973. All have well-established bargaining practices. During data collection, the National Education Association (NEA) represented teachers in three of the districts (Mill City, Northwood, and Vista), while teachers in the remaining three districts (Metropolis, Shady Heights, and Plantville) were represented by the American Federation of Teachers (AFT).

Only Shady Heights had changed bargaining agents since the advent of negotiations. The NEA affiliate there won the initial representation election, but in 1966 teachers were dissatisfied with their first salary settlement and provisions calling for a longer work day and a longer school year. Under the leadership of a highly regarded president, the AFT affiliate won a challenge election in 1968. Since then the AFT has maintained unchallenged control of the teacher membership.

While negotiations were difficult and intense in all of the six districts through the years, only three had encountered strikes. There had been four strikes in Metropolis, where the local union was generally recognized as an aggressive and extraordinarily effective advocate of teacher interests. The first, lasting only three days, occurred in 1970. A second strike began with a three-week walkout in September 1972 and concluded with eight additional weeks of strike in January and February 1973. That was a bitter and violent confrontation in which the school department tried unsuccessfully to keep the schools operating and union officers were tried for contempt, assessed fines of $280,000, and jailed. There was a four-day walkout in 1978 and a twenty-one-day strike in 1980. Recurring strike issues included salaries, job security, the length of the work day, preparation time, and class size.

The three strikes in Mill City involved a range of issues. The first was a one-day strike in 1967 over the superintendent's refusal to hold a *representation* election. The second, in 1970, was a two-day walkout over salary. The third, which occurred in 1973, lasted sixteen school days and involved a range of issues, including salary, transfer procedures, and the hiring of specialists in the elementary schools.

The assistant superintendent in Shady Heights proudly notes that none of the four teacher strikes there resulted from a failure of the parties to reach a negotiated settlement. The first, a sympathy strike, was called in 1972 when the clerks' union could not settle its contract. The second, in 1974, occurred when budget cuts by the mayor led the school board to renege on its negotiated agreement. There was a one-day strike in 1978 after an agreement reached between the school department and the AFT over layoff language was not approved by the school board. The mayor called both parties to meet through the night and ultimately settled the agreement in favor of the teachers. The fourth work stoppage was a one-day sympathy strike on behalf of the bus drivers in 1979.

State Laws

Teachers negotiate under state collective bargaining laws in all districts but Mill City and Vista. The statutes each define a broad scope of mandatory bargaining issues—typically wages, hours, and conditions of employment (for example, class size, grievance procedures, and evaluation). In addition, laws permit strikes in Metropolis and Northwood after impasse procedures have been exhausted. By law, principals are excluded from collective bargaining in Northwood and Shady Heights.

Collective bargaining proceeds in the absence of enabling legislation in Mill City and Vista. Court cases have established that the negotiated contracts in Mill City and other districts of the state are legally binding; Vista teachers do not negotiate under such legal protections, and their agreements are incorporated as board policy rather than being signed as independent contracts. Vista teachers and administrators are well aware that their agreement has no legal force in the state and could be set aside by the school board at any time.

The Contracts

The sample contracts that were in force in 1979 and 1980 varied in length, detail, and formality. Northwood's, the simplest, was fifteen mimeographed pages. While it regulated such things as reductions in force and grievance procedures, it did not address such standard contract items as class size, teacher meetings, instructional load, or school advisory committees. By contrast, the Metropolis contract was a seventy-five-page bound book that specified many things about day-to-day school operations. It stated, for example, that the principal should not read aloud printed materials distributed at faculty meetings and that each teaching period should be shortened when there was a long assembly. The contracts of the other four districts were roughly similar in length and complexity and fell between these two extremes.

An analysis of the contracts reveals that a collective agreement is not necessarily strong because it is long or complex. For example, the Vista contract, while broad in scope, is weakened from the union's perspective by the absence of binding arbitration. Similarly, language in the Mill City contract stating that teachers "may not refuse administrative transfers" discourages teachers from challenging administrative violations of the contract. An analysis of the noncompensation provisions in the sample contracts suggests that they might be rank ordered according to strength as follows:

1. Metropolis
2. Plantville
3. Shady Heights
4. Mill City
5. Northwood
6. Vista

A detailed comparison of the contracts' noncompensation provisions affecting school site practices is included in Appendix C.

The Local Unions

The Metropolis Federation of Teachers, with its AFL-CIO affiliation, was the strongest and most active of the teachers' organizations in this study. This union negotiated on behalf of many diverse employee groups—nonteaching assistants, secretaries, psychologists, and dentists—and it employed twelve full-time professional staff members. From 1965 to 1980, the leadership of the Federation remained virtually unchanged. In 1980, however, a challenge election unseated the incumbent president while reelecting his administrative council. The court, in an effort to define the rights of the new and former presidents, ordered that they should conegotiate the teachers' contract. For the first time in fifteen years there was intense dissension within the union.

The strength and leadership of the Shady Heights Federation of Teachers had remained constant over the years. The president of the organization was the second in its history, having replaced the original president, who left to become an officer in the statewide union. In his new role, the original president continued to participate in local contract negotiations and to maintain a long-term working relationship with the assistant superintendent. With an agency shop provision,[7] union membership stood at 1,000 in 1980, but even prior to that requirement 800 teachers voluntarily paid their dues. Wide teacher participation in periodic picketing and strikes regularly demonstrated the teachers' support for their organization.

The Plantville Federation of Teachers, which also had won an agency shop provision, included among its members all but three teachers and principals in the district. Most principals had themselves been leaders in the teachers' union at one time and were reportedly strong supporters of teacher interests. There was, however, growing tension between the teachers' Unit A of the Federation and the principals' Unit B, and some principals had begun talking with representatives of the Teamsters Union as a potential bargaining agent.[8]

There had been several changes in union leadership since the beginning of bargaining in Plantville. The current president, who pursued a more conciliatory course with the district administration than his predecessor, was described by teachers as" very decent, fair, and honest." The president he replaced was variously characterized as "unprofessional," "rowdy," and "dogmatic."

The president of the Mill City Education Association had been in office since 1973. While he was generally regarded as "good" and "competent," teachers there often reported that, over time, he had become less forceful than was necessary to represent their interests. He was reported by all sides to pursue a cooperative labor relationship with the school administration, and some teachers complained that that relationship was less confrontational than it should have been. Yet there was no apparent effort to replace him with a more aggressive leader. Teacher support for the Mill City Education Association was only moderate, with 650 of the 1,000 teachers in the district belonging. There was no agency shop provision that would require bargaining fees from nonmembers. Some teachers who did not join sought to differentiate themselves from the laborers in the city's mills, while others considered the organization too moderate to deserve their support.

Leaders of the Northwood Education Association were long-time residents and teachers in the community, regarded by both teachers and administrators as outstanding educators, committed both to the future of the district and to their organization. Union membership included about 80 percent of the teaching staff. Some teachers refused to join because they could not belong to the local unless they joined the state organization. There was little pressure exerted on nonmembers to join—the president's spouse was not a member—and some nonmembers attended local meetings. The union was low-key and moderate in its approach, seeking an intentionally cooperative relationship with the school administration.

Approximately 80 percent of Vista teachers belonged to the local union, whose leaders were highly regarded as both teachers and officers. While those leaders preferred moderate approaches for resolving differences with the administration, several incidents in the preceding several years indicated that they would act more aggressively in defending teachers' interests if they believed it necessary. For example, 600 teachers picketed school board meetings during difficult negotiations in 1979.

Union strength in these districts was not directly correlated with contract strength. For example, the Northwood contract was simple and key items were unaddressed, but the union leaders there played more active and influential roles in defining district policies than did their counterparts in Mill City. The strength of a union was apparent in the actions of its leaders, the success of its ventures, and the regard accorded it by its membership, the school department, and school administration. That strength was influenced, but not determined, by contract strength. An analysis of these factors suggests the following ordering of districts according to union strength:

1. Metropolis
2. Shady Heights
3. Northwood
4. Plantville
5. Mill City
6. Vista

The Labor Relationships

The labor relationships between leaders of the teachers' unions and district office administrators were intentionally cooperative in four of the six districts. The most notable of these was Northwood, where the original district superintendent had nurtured a close working relationship with the teachers' union and was said by teachers to have had a "true open door policy." He was subsequently fired by the school board and replaced by an officer in the state National Guard who ran the schools in regimented style and rapidly formalized the relationship between the administration and teachers. One year later, this interim administrator was replaced by the current superintendent, who restored an informal, cooperative labor relationship with the teachers and actively worked to maintain what he called "open communication." There had been but one formal grievance filed since the advent of collective bargaining in Northwood, with teachers typically relying on an informal "problem solving policy" that set out steps for resolving differences prior to formal action.

In Mill City, Shady Heights, and Plantville, union presidents met frequently and informally with the superintendents or assistant superintendents to resolve differences before they became major issues. Although the labor relationships were not as conciliatory as the one in Northwood, all sides sought to avoid adversarial encounters in day-to-day contract management. The numbers of grievances filed in Mill City and Plantville were low—approximately five and ten per year, respectively—and reflected these efforts to avoid formality. The number of grievances in Shady Heights was considerably higher—approximately 100 per year—but that number was more indicative of both sides' preferences for formally stated issues than it was evidence of strained relations.

The labor relationships in Metropolis and Vista were notably more adversarial. The Metropolis Federation of Teachers had long taken a very combative approach to enforcing its contract. While this adversarial labor relationship may once have been defined by the personalities involved, it seemed over time to have become institutionalized. Challenges and accusations were routine. Metropolis teachers could rely on seven full-time union staff members to assist them in filing grievances, and the school department had counterpart staff in each subdistrict to help principals respond to those grievances. Well over 250 grievances were filed by the teachers annually, and approximately thirty-four moved on to arbitration.

By contrast, the adversarial labor relationship in Vista was obviously influenced by a change in personnel. The previous superintendent had nurtured a close working relationship with the union leadership, and teachers had made notable contractual gains on the basis of that relationship. However, the current superintendent was considerably more aggressive and management oriented. He believed in the productivity of "creative tension" and adversarial encounters. He knew the teachers' contract well and used it to the administration's advantage. Many teachers and administrators respectfully agreed with one respondent who said that the superintendent had "changed a folksy, loose, slack organization into one with discipline." Others thought that he had unwisely formalized the district. The superintendent served as the hearing officer in the grievance process, and because arbitration was advisory rather than binding, he had the final say in all grievances. Early on, he took an aggressive stance with the union by refusing to honor an arbitrator's decision in favor of the teachers and responding simply, "Guilty. Your move." The Vista union president rarely met with the superintendent for informal discussions but did talk regularly with each member of the school board, seeking to influence their views on district policies. The majority of the school board members were strong supporters of the superintendent; one member, elected with union backing, was regularly responsive to teacher concerns.

The Schools

The schools included in this study varied widely. Rarely could any be identified as belonging to a particular district, and, in fact, there were usually more differences than similarities among schools within the same district. Often there were two very similar schools in two very different districts. Therefore, no effort will be made here to generalize about district characteristics observable at the school site. However, it is important to review the wide range of schools on which the subsequent discussion is based.

The schools I visited included elementary, middle, junior high, and senior high schools, as well as one that housed kindergarten through twelfth grade. There were small (250 students), medium, and large (4,200 students) schools. Some student populations were all white or all black; many were mixed. One school was 145 years old, while another was but five months old when I was there. Several buildings were contemporary, modular structures, while most were of the brick center-entrance variety or the single-level winged construction of the 1950s.

Most of these schools featured traditional, graded instruction and offered special programs for the gifted, disadvantaged, or handicapped; one included a 100-acre farm. These schools sat in the midst of stable, changing, and changed neighborhoods. There were cows grazing across the street from one and abandoned, vandalized housing across from another. Most of the students from one high school went to college; from another they went to work; and from another, where the illiteracy rate was estimated at 30 percent, they went on to unemployment. The principals were young and old, male and female, black and white, progressive and conservative. Teachers were exuberant in one school, dispirited in another.

These differences, while dramatic, were but variations on the predictable pattern of schooling.[9] Each school had a principal who administered the building, a staff of classroom teachers and specialists who provided instruction, and students who were grouped into classes. The school day of each was segmented into periods of instruction and included some time for recess and lunch. All schools had common, public areas (library, cafeteria, playground) where students congregated informally. All schools had a curriculum that structured, either generally or precisely, the teaching and learning intended to take place there. The schools offered extracurricular activities, including sports, music, and interest clubs. Principals of all schools called staff meetings, evaluated teacher performance, disciplined recalcitrant students, and supervised fire drills. All schools carried out procedures for budgeting funds, ordering supplies, and requesting repairs, as well as for maintaining student attendance and grade records. In all the schools of this study there were collective bargaining agreements that were intended to regulate at least part of what went on there. The impact of those agreements and the unions that bargained them will be the subjects of the following chapters.

Chapter 2

Reallocated Authority

There was a time when principals held virtually unchallenged authority over their teachers. Howard S. Becker, reporting teachers' views in 1953, wrote:

> The principal is accepted as the supreme authority in the school: "After all, he's the principal, he is the boss, what he says should go, you know what I mean. . . . He's the principal and he's the authority, and you have to follow his orders. That's all there is to it." This is true no matter how poorly he fills the position. The office contains the authority. . . .[1]

Having no forum in which to pursue their interests, voice their concerns, or seek redress against administrative abuse, teachers were expected to submit to the principal's better judgment or greater power. But collective bargaining has changed that official relationship by giving teachers and their unions more rights and by restricting the powers of principals.

The teachers' contract sets forth new rules about school management that carry the force of law and demand the principal's attention. Through collective bargaining, the union has won the right to call meetings, defend individual members, and represent teacher interests with the principal. Grievance procedures now enable teachers to challenge administrative actions. Union liaison committees allow teachers to circumvent their principals and raise complaints about school practices directly with district administrators. Principals are thus subject to new constraints from both above them and below them as collective bargaining has centralized authority at the district level and decentralized authority in the schools.

Some school officials and commentators believe that this reallocation of formal authority has jeopardized the order

necessary for effective school management, that it has incapac-
itated the principal, undermined teacher loyalties, and precipitated union control of the schools. Some of those who
comment on these changes do so with concern. For example, R.
Theodore Clark, Jr., observes:

> Prior to the advent of collective bargaining in public education, the
> building principal was, in a very real sense, the final authority with
> respect to the day-to-day operation of his or her building. With
> collective bargaining, however, there has been a very real loss of
> authority of building principals. . . . To suggest that this has
> made the job of being a principal less attractive merely states the
> obvious.[2]

Others regard the changes with alarm. For example, Robert
P. Moser argues that this redistribution of authority may lead to
the "demise of the principalship."[3] This chapter examines how
contract provisions reallocate formal authority among teachers
and principals, and it explores the effects of those provisions on
the principal's capacity to manage. It concludes that, while
contractual changes in formal authority are extensive, teachers
often do not exercise the authority they have gained, and many
principals willingly share policymaking responsibilities with
staff. Principals in even the strongest union districts retained
sufficient formal and informal authority to manage their staffs
effectively.

Negotiation and the Contract

The process of collective bargaining was not the focus of
this study, yet a discussion of redistributed authority cannot
ignore the fact that principals are rarely active participants in
negotiation, even though much of what is bargained affects how
they can administer their schools.[4]

There were no principals participating in the teachers'
negotiations in four of the sample districts. Of these, Plantville
principals, who were represented in their own bargaining by the
local teachers' union, were not even consulted about the potential effects of contract provisions on their work. In Mill City,

where a lawyer negotiated on behalf of the school board, principals had no active roles. Northwood and Vista principals were not present at negotiations, but reportedly did discuss their concerns with their superintendents prior to bargaining.

Only in Shady Heights and Metropolis, the strongest union districts, were principals involved in negotiations. In Shady Heights, where representative principals observed and consulted during bargaining, the personnel director believed: "Principals should be involved in some manner in negotiations. They should go over proposals and explain how they would affect the buildings. In Shady Heights we use representatives of the elementary and secondary principals as observers during negotiations. They meet with us during caucuses. We run proposals by them."[5] Shady Heights principals reportedly exerted more influence in negotiations than did principals in Metropolis, where representatives from each school level sat silently on the management team. There had been public criticisms that these Metropolis principals, whose salaries were based on the teachers' wage scale, even attended negotiations, but a representative of the principals' association contended that neither the principals nor even the district administrators had much control over the final agreement, which was often a political settlement with the mayor's office. "The final giveaway," he said, "is not decided with middle management."[6]

Therefore, at the crucial point where the new contractual rules, restrictions, and obligations were being determined, principals seldom were present and active. Interestingly, most principals in this study approved of the overall results of negotiations. Many agreed with the Metropolis principal who said: "My own impression of the contract is that it puts into writing what principals have been expounding for many years— that is, the involvement of teachers in decision-making."[7] A few principals in all districts were displeased, however, that certain provisions had been negotiated without sufficient attention to their potential effects on schools. For example, in Mill City, there were principals who objected that teachers had been granted a duty-free lunch without the provision of cafeteria aides to supervise students.[8] In Metropolis, some principals were angry that contract language supposedly enabling them to supervise teachers' use of preparation periods was too vague to stand up in arbitration.[9] In Northwood, the secondary principal objected that the teachers had negotiated extra pay for certain extra-curricular duties.[10]

Notably, principals did not report that they had been refused a larger role in negotiations, nor did they suggest that they wanted one. Reluctant to participate in formal adversarial bargaining sessions with "their" teachers, they asked instead that principals' interests be more fully represented and forcefully defended by the school board and district office. Sometimes, they believed, changes in school practice had been traded for dollars during the heat of negotiations; concessions had been made that might have seemed cheap to the negotiators, but were considered costly by the principals. As one Metropolis principal observed: "The biggest problem with collective bargaining in Metropolis is that during the eleventh hour of negotiations, the board only concentrates on items that have a financial consequence. The others are often given away with horrendous consequences."[11]

While principals did not negotiate the sections of the contract that regulated school site practices, they were expected to administer their schools in compliance with them.[12] Not surprisingly, when respondents assessed the impact of various contract provisions on their work, they usually discussed the problematic ones; but further inquiry often revealed that principals believed some contract language clarified their authority and enhanced their positions. A Mill City principal observed:

> From the management side, probably anything that is negotiated is a liability, and yet there are some things that have been included in the contract to strengthen the administrative position. For example, regarding sick leaves or leaves of absence, it is now in print that the absent teacher must complete a form specifying the reason for absence. In addition, we have the right to ask for a doctor's statement verifying illness. It's also clear that falsification of this is grounds for termination. I like that; it's clear. It's in print.[13]

The Union Presence

As a newly authorized presence within the school, the union serves as a public reminder of the limits of administrative power and as the designated agent to guard against abuse of that power. Moreover, the union may rival school administrators for teachers' loyalties. Mitchell et al. comment on this change: "With the advent of strong teacher organizations, principals have found themselves confronted with an environment in which teachers can *choose* between loyalty to the school principal and loyalty to the organization as the legitimate interpreter of educational policy and practice."[14]

It is important when assessing the impact of teacher unions on school organizations to determine whether, in fact, teachers have transferred their loyalties to the union. The data of this study indicate that only in extreme situations did teachers do so. In part, this was because most local unions were run from inside the schools; local teacher unions were composed of local teachers, and in four of the six sample districts all union members and officers were teaching at least part time in district classrooms. In Shady Heights the union president was on leave from teaching, but all other officers had classroom assignments. Only in Metropolis was there a group of union leaders who were not daily involved in their own schools and did not, therefore, have ongoing commitments to students and administrators as well as to fellow teachers.

The introduction of the union into the schools had changed schools gradually from within. The union had not marched through the front door, staked out territory in the main office, and taken control of the daily bulletin. Instead, teachers' attitudes and expectations had been challenged and gradually changed by their colleagues. In most districts, there were no clear distinctions between "our teachers" and "the union," for at the school site our teachers had become the union. For example, one Vista principal recently returned to an elementary school where he had previously served as an administrator; he found a faculty more militant than when he had left five years before. The composition of the staff had changed little, but he found the same individuals "more willing to take a stand and to demand their rights. In the past, they were like sheep waiting to be led. The mood of the group has changed."[15] While union activity was widely reported to have changed teachers' expectations about their rights, it was rarely said to have altered their loyalties. One Shady Heights principal considered whether her influence with teachers had been undermined by the presence of the union in her school. She said, "No, no. Certainly not. If we had a problem, I would ask the teachers 'What's the best way to solve it?' and we would work on it together."[16]

The teachers' union emerged organizationally at the school site in several ways. First, union members within the school asserted their collective rights to call and hold membership meetings, to make announcements, to distribute information, or to post bulletins about union activities. Second, the presence of the union became apparent when teachers approached the principal in their roles as appointed or elected union representatives. Third, the union made itself known when contractually established committees represented teacher interests, raised teacher concerns, advised on policy, or embarked on sharing the responsibilities of school management. Each of these will be discussed in some detail.

Union Announcements and Meetings / The sample districts' contracts included very similar language establishing the right of the union to inform its membership and hold meetings within the schools. In each district, the union was guaranteed separate bulletin board space and access to teachers' mailboxes, and the membership was entitled to schedule meetings in school facilities before or after school hours. In Northwood, Metropolis, and Shady Heights, teachers were given time for announcements in faculty meetings, and in Mill City the union could meet with new teachers prior to the school year.

One might expect these newly gained union rights to have changed the perceived balance of power within the school, but they were of virtually no noted consequence in any of the districts and schools included in this study. Principals reported being untroubled by organized union actions, which usually focused on district issues such as the progress of negotiations, union elections, contract changes, or recent arbitration decisions. In fact, some principals who were dissatisfied with the school department's failure to keep them regularly informed about district labor issues reported relying on notices posted on the union bulletin board for current information.

Building Representatives / Of the six contracts included in this study, only those of Plantville and Vista specified the role of the building representative:

> The Principal shall recognize the Federation building representative as the official representative of the Federation in the school.[17]

> The Board recognizes the responsibility of the building representatives at the individual buildings . . . to represent their members of the Bargaining Unit.[18]

Other contracts referred to the building representative in related contexts. For example, the Metropolis contract stated that "coverage shall be provided during time when a Federation representative is absent because he has been selected to attend a meeting scheduled by the Administration."[19] In general, these contracts, which otherwise specified union roles and responsibilities in great detail, notably left the relationship between the building representative and the principal undefined.

Despite this lack of definition, there were union building representatives serving in the schools of each sample district. The number of representatives in each school varied from one to five, depending primarily on the size and complexity of the school. Their roles and functions varied widely. In each district there were a few who acted as industrial shop stewards, overseeing the enforcement of the contract and speaking to management on behalf of teachers, while others did little more than distribute union literature and collect dues; most fell between these extremes. There were building representatives who resented the job and accepted it only on a rotating basis, while others campaigned for the position. There were building representatives who intervened in a very narrow range of issues, such as class size or teacher transfers, and others who assumed major administrative responsibilities in the schools (e.g., scheduling courses or assigning supervisory duties).

Building representatives in the stronger union districts— Metropolis and Shady Heights—were generally more active and assertive than those in weaker union districts—Mill City and Vista. This seemed to result in part from the fact that they were agents of more aggressive unions, but it was also a consequence of the job protections teachers enjoyed under stronger contracts. For example, the building representatives in Mill City and Vista were often said to be inactive, reluctant recruits who served almost exclusively as informational liaisons between the union and teachers in the school. In Mill City, where all teachers were subject to administrative transfers without procedural protections, building representatives were very cautious about challenging their principals. One new building representative in Mill City took the job when no one else would volunteer. However, before agreeing to do so, she met with the principal and asked whether her accepting the position would be held against her. Although the principal assured her that it would not, the representative continued to believe that she was "sticking her neck out." She explained, "I want to stay here. I like this building and I like my job but the principal can make or break you."[20] Mill City teachers in other schools sensed the building representatives' vulnerability and seldom relied on them as advocates in disputes. One principal explained: "People don't go to the reps. They're not the typical shop stewards that will go up and stick their fingers in the boss's face. Ultimately, they're subject to the authority of the principal."[21]

In Metropolis, Plantville, Shady Heights, and Northwood the positions of building representatives were considerably more secure. Teachers in the first three of these districts were contractually protected against punitive transfers. Some building representatives in Metropolis said that the aggressive reputation of their union actually increased their job security. In Northwood, the representatives' security resulted more from the size and rural location of the district; there were no other schools to which teachers might be transferred, and teacher shortages increased job security. Representatives in these four districts tended to be more active and assertive than their counterparts in Mill City and Vista. They intervened more actively as advocates of other teachers; they assumed more policy-making and administrative responsibilities; and they were recognized more regularly as legitimate spokespersons for a school's faculty. Such patterns, however, were not consistent across all schools in the districts. Some Metropolis building representatives only posted notices; others in Vista initiated group grievances against the principal.

The position of building representative is often said to be an adversarial one, but the building representatives considered in this study were rarely characterized that way. Far more often they were described by both teachers and principals as cooperative, constructive, and, as one teacher said, "not tightly reined by the union party line."[22] One was described by the principal as "very bright, outgoing, honest."[23] Another was said to be "very anxious and eager. He thinks of things in terms of children."[24] The representative's commitment to the union was often viewed by principals as compatible with school interests: "She's super strong union, but always has the interest of the school in mind."[25] "He's staunch union but reasonable."[26] There were three building representatives, all in Metropolis schools, who were said to pursue consistently adversarial tacks with the administration. They were perceived by their principals to be antagonistic and disruptive. As one administrator said, "She's the noisiest wheel."[27] Interestingly, support for each of these more aggressive representatives was reported by teachers to be moderate at best. Teachers preferred that, whenever possible, their representatives maintain collegial relationships with the principals.

Most principals said that they had negotiated and nurtured cooperative, informal relationships with their building representatives, thus enabling them to hear about teacher concerns informally and to solicit teacher opinions about anticipated changes or problems. The role of personalities in this relationship was repeatedly said to be very important, as the following comments by a Metropolis principal illustrate:

> The building rep keeps the relationship wholesome here. Eight or nine years ago, that was not so. Then the building rep and I didn't get along. This one can say, "I think you ought to do X," and I'll say, "Yes, okay, I'll do X." That other rep might say, "I think you ought to do X," and I would say, "I will do Y."[28]

A number of principals reported seeking the representative's advice about an approaching problem, enlisting his or her support in dealing with an incompetent teacher, or urging the representative to grieve a maintenance problem for which the principal could get no action. Schools in which the building representative and principal were regularly at odds were very unusual, despite the fact that I intentionally sought out schools where such adversarial relationships existed.

While the role of the building representative was typically described by principals to be constructive and to make contract management easier rather than more difficult, some administrators expressed concern about these positions. Several principals thought that because building representatives were present in the schools, teachers inappropriately diverted their complaints away from the administration. One said, "We don't seem to get the same kind of concerns from the faculty that we once did. And frankly, I'd rather that we would have those concerns."[29] Interestingly, however, when teachers were asked whom they would go to about a problem in the school, very few said that they would go to the building representative rather than the principal.

Some principals were dissatisfied when representatives acted as advocates for individual teachers. One Shady Heights principal was adamant that building representatives who brought complaints on behalf of teachers were acting inappropriately. He explained that the position of building representative should be "between the union and its membership, not between the membership and the principal." He argued that in order to maintain productive relationships among the principals, department heads, and teachers, school administrators had to resist a representative's effort to speak on behalf of another teacher.[30]

Some principals, particularly those who lacked confidence about their own standing, were wary of building representatives who might become self-designated problem finders. However, such anticipated problems rarely materialized outside of Metropolis, where one story illustrates both the problem and a principal's strategic response. A new building representative examined the assignment roster and noted that two teachers remained beyond the instructional day for bus duty. Unaware that the entire school was being dismissed ten minutes early each day, the representative filed a grievance on behalf of the staff. The principal responded by posting a notice requiring all teachers to remain for the full day, thus ensuring that bus duty would fall within the instructional day. The grievance was quickly withdrawn by the building representative, who was reportedly "livid and embarrassed."[31]

The concerns voiced by principals about building representatives were often based on single events or on hearsay, or were speculations about potential problems rather than accounts of actual ones. Most did not regard the presence or activities of building representatives in their own schools as problematic, although those who did were far more likely to be in Metropolis than in any other district.

There were teachers, however, who criticized building representatives who assumed administrative duties, for example, scheduling courses or assigning rooms to teachers. One teacher who believed his representative was making decisions that rightfully belonged to the principal said that there was confusion in his school about "which boss to see."[32] However, representatives who assumed administrative responsibilities always seemed to do so with the principal's implicit or explicit approval; no principal reported unwillingly relinquishing such authority. For example, one Metropolis principal, whose building representative had reorganized classroom assignments in order to satisfy class size limits, emphasized somewhat defensively that, as principal, he retained the authority to make such changes official.[33] Nevertheless, it was clear that the building representative had gained considerable power in the school by arranging the changes. This representative's influence over school management was greater than his counterparts' in other schools, but his cooperative strategy resembled that of representatives in all districts who gained influence with school administrators by assuming advisory rather than adversarial roles.

Teachers approved of building representatives who served as sources of information and support rather than acted as antagonists. Such a representative could be relied on in case serious difficulties arose, but was not expected to provoke those difficulties. Teachers widely reported that they expected their principals, rather than their building representatives, to run the schools. When they did not, the problem was usually attributed to the inefficacy of the principal rather than to the aggressiveness of the representative.

Building Committees / Faculty advisory committees that met periodically with principals were provided for by contract in all sample districts but Northwood and Mill City. In Mill City such committees were mandated by the superintendent. In all districts where committees functioned, at least half of the members were elected by the teachers; other members might be appointed by the principal. In Metropolis and Plantville, the building committee and all participants were union members. In other districts, any teacher could serve. The committees met biweekly or monthly at the request of the teachers or principal.

Only the Metropolis contract defined the appropriate issues of committee discussion:

> School operations and questions relating to the implementation of the agreement.
>
> Proposed changes in existing policies and procedures.
>
> New policies and procedures.[34]

In addition, the Metropolis principal was required to consult with the committee before scheduling evening meetings or setting the criteria for distributing extracurricular funds and awarding extracurricular jobs. The role of the Metropolis building committee was advisory in all cases but one. In allotting extra-curricular funds in elementary and junior high schools, the building committee and the principal had, by contract, to agree; neither could make a unilateral decision.

Within each of the five districts where building committees were authorized, their strength and activity varied widely from school to school. In many schools, such committees did not function at all; in some they served as advisory councils; in others they set school policies.[35] For example, in one Vista elementary school, the faculty committee advised the principal on a wide range of issues—duty assignments, textbooks, assemblies, space and enrollment, parent and senior citizen volunteers, the use of the media room, and the parent conference schedule.[36] In a second, quite comparable school, the principal reported that the committee "never meets" unless required by the district office to address a particular issue.[37] In a third Vista school, the committee made budgetary decisions about the allotment of resources within the school, [38] while in a fourth, where no committee functioned, the full faculty addressed budget policies.[39]

There was similar variation in Metropolis, where the contract granted faculty committees the greatest formal powers. In one school the committee convened only to discuss the distribution of extracurricular funds, as it was contractually obliged to do.[40] In a second, the committee was central in determining the curriculum for the school.[41] In a third school, the committee acted mostly as a watchdog over the practices of the principal, who characterized his committee as "not a war board in toto; it's probably about fifty-fifty."[42]

Because the contracts virtually always limited the building committees to advisory roles, their levels of activity were largely a function of the principals' attitudes toward teacher participation. Where principals believed that shared policymaking was in their interests, the committees usually were active. For example, the principal of one Metropolis school where the building committee was perceived to function well explained his philosophy:

> I think some principals go into the meetings as if they're in some kind of arena where they have to come out winning. I see the

members of the committee differently. These people have to work six to seven hours a day with kids, and if they come in with a problem, then I know it's a problem and we seek a correction. I consider the committee a resource for me. I need the teachers' point of view in order to administer the school. It's important for me to know how teachers see things. I am not in their classes. They are the ones doing the work. If I don't get on to their concerns, then I know there will be problems for me as a principal. We may see an increase in absences or an increase in lethargy and that's not good for the school.[43]

The agendas of committee meetings in schools where the group was active typically included both broad policy issues—for example, discipline, curriculum, and testing—and specific complaints—for example, maintenance, scheduling and class size.

If a principal opposed teacher participation in school policymaking, he or she could easily discourage teacher activity. There were reports of stagnant, inactive committees in all districts. Occasionally, the principal had directly opposed a committee's activity. For example, one Mill City principal was said to have informed the committee that it "would not be making policy because he was the policymaker in the school."[44] A teacher in that school described the progress of the committee: "The going was rough. He [the principal] didn't agree with anything. He made it clear from the beginning that he didn't approve of the committee, that he was simply going along with the downtown order. How can anything be done with that kind of attitude?"[45]

More often, however, ineffective committees were said to encounter administrative disregard rather than direct opposition. One member spoke of her principal: "He would come into the faculty advisory committee meetings like a used car salesman—smiling and pretending to hear everything, pretending to listen. But he didn't do anything in response. By the second semester the committee was not even active."[46]

The agendas of building committees whose principals opposed them were dominated by narrow issues and complaints—the regularity with which bells rang, class size, or violations in the use of the public address system. The principal of one such school characterized his committee as playing "search for the issue," while the teachers characterized him as being hostile to teacher participation.[47] Levels of teacher participation in building committees were low when their advisory roles were strictly limited. The following teacher's account is typical of those from several such schools:

> It's in the contract; that's why we have [a committee] in this building. We're supposed to have ten members, but this year we have only nine. No election has been held in three years, and we will probably have the same people this year as we had last. The committee has no power, and that's why it doesn't function better.[48]

Teachers who found the committee to be ineffective often sought other channels of influence: "We gave up because the principal wasn't listening to the proposals that we made. Now it seems that he listens to the department heads, and so the teachers express their input through their departments."[49]

In all districts but Metropolis, the building committees seemed to affect school practices substantially only where the principal was sympathetic and supportive. Therefore, control over policy within the school was not effectively assumed by teachers without the implicit or explicit approval of the principal. Like the building representatives, building committees in all districts but Metropolis had virtually no contractual authority beyond advising the principal.

Metropolis was a unique and important exception. Advisory committees there had certain contractual rights that enabled teachers to exert control over school management even when the principal opposed them. If a committee was intent on impeding a principal, the contract language made that possible. It could restrict or delay the principal's actions by requiring a meeting to discuss all policy changes. The principal of one Metropolis school explained that in order to make policy changes, he had to provide the building committee with an agenda and then wait until they scheduled a meeting to discuss those changes. He said that, because of delays, it often took three weeks to fill a vacant extracurricular position. He objected to the formality of these deliberations: "I agree that it is important to consult with teachers, because these teachers on the building committee are the elected representatives. But, I believe that there are many ways to consult."[50] In a Metropolis elementary school, the Federation committee had refused to approve the principal's plan for an extracurricular program, and there was no program for a year because neither side would compromise.[51]

Sometimes Metropolis principals construed the committees' contractual authority to be greater than it actually was; a small number of Metropolis principals were uncertain about how far to go in satisfying the "meet and discuss" requirements. One had even asked a colleague whether he should convene the committee to discuss turning the heat on early in the building.[52] Such principals, who were uncertain of their formal authority or who were intimidated by the union, could empower the committees well beyond what the contract required.

Instances in which Metropolis building committees controlled rather than advised a principal were rare, and in some cases, such as the one where the committee refused to approve their principal's extracurricular plan, the teachers' uncompromising stance was judged by other adminstrators to have been warranted. In most Metropolis schools, as in the schools of other districts, building committees were characterized by principals as allies rather than as obstructionists.

Grievances and Arbitrations

There are many subtle and indirect ways to police a contract. Casual comments, complaints, reminders, warnings, and threats were all used by teachers in this study to ensure or provoke adminstrative compliance with the contract. While such actions were not contractually defined procedures, they all carried with them the implicit threat of a grievance. The grievance and arbitration procedures negotiated in all sample contracts provided teachers with the right to challenge administrative actions and to seek redress from district administrators, the school board, or an independent arbitrator. Through collective bargaining, teachers had been empowered to mobilize the district office against the principal.

The grievance procedures, which were similar in all sample

districts, specified a series of steps and deadlines by which a grievant could initiate a complaint, receive a response, and pursue it, if necessary, to a higher level. The first step, specified by each of the contracts, was to meet with the building principal. If the matter remained unresolved, the grievant could move on to a designated district office administrator—the assistant superintendent in Shady Heights and Plantville; the superintendent in Northwood, Mill City, and Vista; an administrative hearing officer in Metropolis. The Shady Heights and Plantville contracts included two additional steps prior to arbitration—the superintendent and school board. If the grievance remained unresolved after all these steps, the union could submit it to a third-party arbitrator. In Vista, the arbitrator's decision was advisory; in the other districts, it was binding.

The range of issues that might be grieved varied by contract. In Plantville and Northwood, the grievance had to be tied to a particular provision of the contract. For example, Plantville teachers might grieve classes that exceeded the contractual size limits, but they could not grieve inequitable distribution of supplies because the issue was not covered in the contract. Vista teachers could grieve any violation of board policy. In Shady Heights, Metropolis, and Mill City, a wide range of complaints about teachers' employment constituted acceptable grievances. For example, the Mill City contract included the broadest definition of a grievance: "A grievance is a claim based upon an event or condition which adversely affects the rights of a teacher and for which a solution lies within the province of the Board of Education."[53] Teachers in these four districts were entitled to, and did on occasion, challenge building principals on a broad range of issues—classroom assignment in Mill City, harassment in Shady Heights, student discipline in Vista, and the allotment of space for the teachers' lounge in Metropolis.

Interestingly, while the range of permissible grievances was quite broad, the number formally filed in the schools of this study was surprisingly small. Some schools, even in the strongest union districts, had experienced no grievances within anyone's memory. Many schools experienced fewer than three grievances per year. A small number of schools encountered seven or eight grievances in a year.

Teachers filed grievances with many and varied purposes. Some were initiated to resolve particular problems and were not intended to change the policies and practices of other schools. Other grievances were designed to set precedents for the entire district. Several examples will illustrate the range of issues grieved and the impact of the decisions on school policy and practice.

Many grievances were intended simply to remedy one individual's problem: In Shady Heights, a junior high school teacher grieved her teaching schedule, claiming that she was being required to carry an excessive number of difficult classes. The grievance was denied by the principal but upheld by the assistant superintendent for personnel, who required that her schedule be changed.[54]

Some grievances were filed to clarify teachers' work obligations:

> In one Mill City school, the principal required the counselor to dismiss ill children because no nurse was regularly on duty. The counselor objected that this function was not included in her job description and would erode her counseling time. When the grievance was resolved at the superintendent's level in favor of the teacher, all counselors in the district were relieved of such responsibilities.[55]

Grievances were filed to force district funds or services to a particular school:

> Special education teachers in one Vista elementary school filed a grievance because their classes exceeded the limits specified in the contract. One principal characterized the grievance as "a political move to influence staffing decisions." The grievance was dealt with at a school board meeting in the broad context of special education staffing. Ultimately, extra funds to provide additional teachers were provided by the school department. The grievance was never formally resolved.[56]

A grievance might be collectively filed by teachers in a public flexing of union muscle:

> Approximately fifty members of a Shady Heights high school faculty filed a grievance when their principal reprinted a parent's letter attacking teacher unions. In response to "the storm" of controversy, he included a copy of the First Amendment in the

next day's bulletin. The grievance was ultimately denied by the assistant superintendent for personnel.[57]

Staff filed grievances to hold principals to their contractual obligations:

> An elementary school building committee in Metropolis grieved the principal's scheduling an evening meeting with parents on the grounds that he had failed to consult about the date with the committee, as he was contractually required to do. The faculty, who were very apprehensive about returning to an unsafe neighborhood after dark, used the grievance procedure to register their dissatisfaction that the meeting was being held at all; since their attendance was required by contract, the principal's failure to confer provided the only basis for complaint. The principal agreed to discuss the date with his building committee.[58]

Grievances were jointly initiated by several teachers in a effort to force administrative compliance with the contract:

> A Metropolis high school union representative filed a grievance when the classes of several teachers in the school exceeded the negotiated limit of thirty-three students. The principal had delayed adjusting the class assignments and requesting an additional teacher. The union representative used the grievance to force him to do so. The grievance was not carried beyond step one.[59]

School-wide problems were sometimes grieved even when teachers doubted that formal action would resolve them:

> Virtually the entire staff of one junior high school in Shady Heights filed a grievance against the vice-principal for his poor handling of student discipline. The grievance was denied at the district level. Teachers explained that the grievance had failed because the staff had not provided enough supporting information.[60]

> A very similar grievance in a Vista middle school was compromised at level two when the principal agreed to establish a discipline committee within the school to review the problem.[61]

On occasion, so-called nuisance grievances were filed by individual teachers. One Shady Heights principal recounted the situation in his school when a special education teacher "filed a bible full of grievances. They were complaints of a personal nature. For example, one was that I took her sponges away. She wrote down every little thing and then she filed them all at once. I never really found out what happened to it. I think it was probably squelched by the union."[62]

Similar grievances in other schools were usually dismissed by fellow teachers as idiosyncratic, bothersome gestures. They seldom went beyond the first step of the grievance process. Teacher support was greater, though, when the staff of a school joined in a concerted effort to discredit a principal. There were two such cases reported in this study:

> In one Vista high school, the teachers filed ten grievances in one year against their principal. Among other things, they alleged that he had unilaterally extended the school day by thirty minutes, fired a department chairman without cause, scheduled faculty meetings on the day reserved by contract for union meetings, failed to administer a school-wide attendance register, rank-ordered teachers in violation of current evaluation procedures, assigned teachers to inappropriate coverage responsibilities during their preparation periods, and failed to assure that the air conditioning system worked. One teacher explained that the principal refused to reconsider any of these actions, telling staff that if they were dissatisfied, they could file grievances. "He said, 'Let 'em roll' and we did." The principal resigned before the grievances were settled, and the union claimed credit for his premature departure.[63]

> A Metropolis junior high school principal encountered twenty-six grievances in one year filed by a building committee that rejected his interpretations of ambiguous contract language. For example, the principal was contractually obliged to discuss changes in policy with the building committee, but he narrowly restricted the issues that he agreed were "changes in policy." The principal reported that the grievances alleged "anything and everything." However, the union's effort did not win broad faculty support and the principal fiercely protected what he believed were essential management prerogatives. For example, he retained the right to continue assigning teachers to cafeteria duty. However, four of the grievances were resolved with the principal's agreeing to provide information and share documents with the building committee. The principal explained that over time it became clear to the union leaders in the school that he "wouldn't back down." In 1979–80 no grievances were filed against him.[64]

As these two examples illustrate, the union's tactical use of the grievance procedures was not necessarily successful. Notably, in Metropolis, where the union reputedly used the grievance process to advance its interests, the junior high school principal in the second example successfully defended his position. It was not, however, without the investment of considerable time and energy.

Grievances that were not resolved at the school level were usually appealed. In such cases, principals might become defendants in hearings with district administrators who variously upheld their actions, told them to retrace their tracks and proceed with procedural correctness, or reversed their decisions. Where the grievance was found to have merit, the hearing officer might require that a disciplinary report be destroyed, that seniority be restored, that back pay be awarded, or that a teacher be reinstated. Often the merits of a grievance were not clear-cut: for example, in issues of evaluations, lack of disciplinary support, or inadequate supplies. In such cases, the grievance procedures provided the means to clarify contract language, define appropriate standards, and mediate disputes.

There were principals who regarded the grievance process as an orderly and productive way to resolve differences. One Mill City principal said: "I basically think the grievance [procedure] is a good thing. I don't look upon it as a negative process; I think it's healthy. It's not bad to have your positions and your decisions tested once in a while—to go head to head."[65] Other principals disliked the disruption and inconvenience that the grievance procedures might cause but believed that teachers deserved some means of redress. A few principals—particularly those in strong union districts—regarded grievance and arbitration procedures as time-consuming, destructively adversarial, and emotionally draining experiences that placed teachers and principals, supposed allies in the schooling process, into the seats of labor and management on opposite sides of the table.

Whatever principals' views of the appropriateness of the grievance process, virtually all agreed that grievance hearings consumed administrative time and spirit. Considerable effort, therefore, was made at all levels to resolve complaints informally, thus reducing the numbers of grievances that were actually filed in the schools. One might mistakenly conclude from the small number of grievances filed that the grievance procedures had little effect on school practice. However, principals' responses indicated that while the effects of the grievance procedures might have been indirect and difficult to observe, they were nonetheless extensive. When principals were faced with the possibility of formal, public challenges, many abided by the contract who otherwise might not have. Sometimes such compliance was good for the school, as with the principal who systematically evaluated staff because of his contractual obligations. However, in an effort to avoid grievances, some principals proceeded with unwarranted caution. For example, a Shady Heights principal explained, "I don't do things that would violate the contract. I avoid doing things that would give them reason to question me."[66] A Plantville principal assigned teachers to homerooms and accelerated classes on the basis of seniority, although the contract did not require him to do so. He was uncertain about what the contract said and explained that teachers might file grievances if he failed to do so. He said, "Years ago, you just wouldn't have done that. You would assign whoever you wanted."[67]

Interestingly, principals sometimes used the grievance procedures to resolve problems they could not. At their principal's request, Plantville junior high school teachers filed a grievance about the poor condition of a portable classroom. The grievance was ignored by the district office, and the problem was not remedied.[68] A Shady Heights elementary principal, who had been unable to resolve inequities in the science teachers' schedules, agreed to have them grieve the staffing shortage. In response, the district administration assigned another teacher to the school.[69] One Metropolis principal processed three grievances about building heat and cleanliness during his ten years on the job. He had himself initiated each of them through the building committee and reported having had moderate success in provoking district administrators to respond.[70]

However, principals who tacitly endorsed the filing of grievances might also find that those procedures undermined their authority. One Metropolis principal explained:

> We have a leaky roof in the school. We've had a leaky roof for years. I follow the procedure for getting it repaired year after year, but no action is taken. I know that if that becomes a Federation issue, they're much more likely to fix that building. Now isn't that sad? When my teachers come to me and say, "We know you've tried. Now let us try," then I know that they have more authority than I.[71]

It must be emphasized that respondents in this study often reported that the constraints imposed by grievance procedures on the principal's discretion were warranted and necessary. Teachers, principals, and district office administrators agreed that instances of administrative abuse had been far too prevalent in the schools prior to collective bargaining. As one Shady Heights principal said, "You know, there must have been some pretty arbitrary things going on that were done in the name of position power."[72] Teachers' access to grievance procedures has increased their potential power and reduced the impunity of principals. Principals, who once were accountable for their performance only to their superiors in the district office and on the school board, have since collective bargaining also become accountable to the teachers they supervise. And just as administrative powers have been abused, there are instances today where teachers' powers are being abused. But the data of this study indicate that those instances are few and that, overall, grievance procedures have not been bad for schools; they probably have made things better.

Liaison Committees

While the grievance procedures of all sample districts entitled teachers to challenge administrative actions, five districts further strengthened the teachers' position by permitting them to circumvent principals and raise complaints about school practices directly with district administrators. Only Vista provided no opportunity for such meetings. In two districts, Plantville and Shady Heights, liaison meetings were not formally convened, largely because the union presidents and assistant superintendents met frequently and informally to discuss issues that might have been raised there.[73] By contrast, the Northwood liaison committee met regularly with the superintendent and was described by one teacher as providing "a way to get around the rigidity of the principal."[74] The Mill City superintendent, who met monthly with union officers, characterized the content of their meetings:

> The kinds of things we do at those meetings are the nickel-and-dime stuff where they say, "What about this?" "I hear this about that," and I try to answer them. I want them to know that I'm involved that I'll listen. It's important that they see that we're amenable, and I think it's worked.[75]

Principals in these four districts very rarely said that such meetings compromised their authority in the schools. However, there were instances in both Mill City and Northwood where individuals complained about the teachers' allying with the superintendent against them. For example, a Mill City principal who had been reprimanded by the district office for monitoring teachers' arrivals and departures said that the central office "gave in to things on the basis of poor information, the result of feedback from the schools—informal and uninformed feedback."[76]

Again the case of Metropolis was unique. While most principals in the other districts were only mildly concerned about the roles of the liaison committees, some Metropolis principals were considerably more apprehensive. The Metropolis contract specified that the district superintendent and each area superintendent should meet monthly with union representatives "to discuss matters of educational policy and development, matters and problems affecting employees generally, as well as matters relating to the implementation of this Agreement."[77] Furthermore, the superintendent notified members of his administrative cabinet in October 1979 that they should accept direct calls from Federation staff members. One union leader explained that this was instituted in response to a backlog of unresolved grievances and was intended to provide a speedier resolution to problems.[78]

Several Metropolis principals complained that formal grievance procedures were being undermined as the union and district administration made deals that compromised principals' authority in the schools. One complained about union efforts to discredit him in meetings with the superintendent each month. He said, "The line principal is constantly excluded from this process."[79] A subdistrict superintendent who had observed the changes in labor relations since the advent of collective bargaining described the problem as he saw it:

> For any dispute, the union has four avenues of approach. One is at the school in the building committee; one is with the district superintendent; a third is in the monthly meeting with [the] superintendent; and a fourth, where it seems that the union is quite vigorous and successful, is in badgering Labor Relations or the assistant superintendent. I find that the union will often bypass the difficult routes in order to get to the superintendent. I would say that unfortunately there is too much caving in at the superintendent's level. I believe they should use the grievance and arbitration procedures that are provided in the contract, but the union will do everything to avoid that, and that's a good strategy, because they can get what they want at the superintendent level.[80]

It was clear that the union's successful negotiation of these liaison committees did not lead inevitably to the reduction of the principal's power. That occurred only when district administrators intervened in school site affairs, either to settle problems quickly or to maintain cooperative relationships with union leaders.

Conclusion

It is generally believed that as a result of collective bargaining there have been big changes in the relative authority of principals and teachers. In fact, an analysis of contract language confirms that teachers have indeed won access to more formal powers. Their contract specifies and regulates many school practices; the building representatives and building committees are entitled to oversee the administration of that contract; teachers may grieve contract violations; and liaison committees may take problems directly to the district administration. But it would be misleading to assume that the gains in formal authority won by teachers at the bargaining table have been translated directly into powers that are exercised in the schools. Nor is it accurate to conclude that the formal constraints on principals inevitably reduce their capacity to manage staff.

Unquestionably, the existence of the contract and the presence of the union have made it very unlikely that a principal in a unionized district could administer a school without attention to teacher interests. Those principals who in the past had relied primarily on their formal authority over teachers to ensure compliance reported that their positions had been compromised and that their effectiveness had been diminished by collective bargaining. However, most principals argued that effective school management could not be based on such formal authority. Many said that they relied instead on their informal authority, on the respect that they had earned for administering the school well. Often they worked cooperatively with building committees and enlisted the support of building representatives, while teachers supported their right to make final decisions and acknowledged their responsibility to manage the school.

Chapter 3

Bargaining and Bureaucratization

Since the early part of the century, school districts have been bureaucratically structured, with pyramidal organization charts, rules, procedures, and district office specialists assigned to oversee practices in the schools. But in many districts these bureaucratic features did not produce standardized school practices. For a variety of organizational reasons, school sites remained quite autonomous, many district policies were not enforced, instruction was seldom regulated, and supervision of teaching practice was rare. There was semblance of order, but little effective control.[1]

Collective bargaining has introduced new demands on district officials who negotiate and sign the teachers' contract and who are, therefore, legally obliged to ensure that its terms are met by all administrators in all schools of the district. Some educational commentators believe that the demands for standardization presented by collective bargaining will excessively rationalize school practice, reinforce the hierarchical structure of the district, promote the positions of specialists, and encourage school officials to reassert centralized control over school site practices. Such changes, it is said, would make schools less flexible, force roles to take precedence over personalities, discourage autonomy and initiative, and obscure holistic understandings of problems and remedies.

Arthur Wise, who has written extensively about this so-called bureaucratization, regards collective bargaining as one of the major forces transforming the schools: "The unionization of teachers and collective bargaining are likely to contribute to increasing rationalization. Unions will seek new rules and procedural safeguards, and management will counter with new rules and procedures of its own."[2] Wise predicts that these changes will have dire effects on the schools: "Major losers [in the struggle for power] will be teachers who will see their professional autonomy replaced by a bureaucratic conception of their role. The most tragic loss will be to the students who are cast as objects being prepared to assume their place in society."[3] Other school observers anticipate less severe outcomes, but agree that the character of schooling will be changed by the formalizing forces of collective bargaining.

This chapter explores both how and how much collective bargaining has promoted the bureaucratic character of the school district and bureaucratic control of the schools. It examines the growth of specialized labor relations offices, the standardization of school-site practices, the role of the administrative hierarchy in resolving disputes, and the prominence of negotiated rules and procedures in the day-to-day life of schools. The data presented here reveal a wide range of outcomes in the sample districts. The fact that the labor practices of some districts were found to be considerably more bureaucratic than those of other districts suggests that collective bargaining does not lead inevitably to bureaucratic control of the schools and that local actors exert considerable influence over its effects. The chapter concludes that personnel practices are somewhat more centralized and standardized as a result of teacher unionism, but that overall teachers and administrators have resisted changes that would transform their schools into rigid, rule-bound, hierarchically controlled institutions.

The Bureaus

The labor relations offices of the sample districts differed in size and complexity. In Shady Heights and Plantville, an assistant superintendent handled all personnel matters. The Northwood superintendent, as the sole district office administrator, managed all labor relations concerns there. Three Mill City administrators shared personnel responsibilities; and in Vista, where the position of personnel director stood vacant, two administrators, including the superintendent, managed the contract. In none of these five districts was a single district administrator assigned full-time responsibility for managing the teachers' contract. Only in Metropolis was a separate Personnel and Labor Relations Office established to administer the various contracts negotiated by the school board. Prior to 1964 in Metropolis, the only centralized personnel offices were those responsible for payroll and examinations.[4] After the advent of collective bargaining, the Labor Relations Office grew rapidly to its current size of 115 employees; ten professional staff oversee the teachers' contract, with one staff member being assigned to each of seven subdistricts. These administrative staffers, as they are called, have no line authority over principals, yet their experience in dealing with labor relations affords them considerable influence with building principals. One department administrator explained their roles: "Our major function is for contract maintenance. We are the consultants to the administration and our position is indeed advisory. Sometimes they don't listen to us; sometimes they do. I would say that it is less and less likely that they don't listen to us."[5]

It would be impossible to determine how much of this extensive Metropolis enterprise was the necessary response to union aggressiveness in policing the contract and how much of it was simply bureaucratic growth. Each was probably a factor.[6] One administrator emphasized that the structure and complexity of the office were consistent with the rest of the central administration. He said, "We are very bureaucratic here; we are a very bureaucratic and structured operation. I have even been accused of being the biggest bureaucrat, but I think it's a good thing. We have procedures to do things and we have structured ways of going about things."[7] Within this sample, then, only Metropolis had a separate labor relations office that warranted the label "bureau."

The Standardization of Practice

Standardization of work practice is generally assumed to be an intended outcome of collective bargaining.[8] The structure of teacher contracts and the implicit expectation of their uniform application throughout all schools in a district place new demands on the district office administrators who negotiate those contracts and are legally bound to uphold them. District officials have new incentives to centralize contract administration and to impose sanctions on particularistic school practices. The time, expense, and public embarrassment involved in processing, and potentially losing, grievances and arbitrations have spurred some district offices to inspect school site labor practices closely. The threat of district-wide precedents being set by careless school site administration has, in some cases, increased the monitoring of principals' school management. Union contentions that the school department is not keeping its side of the bargain have sometimes been translated into pressure upon school administrators to honor the contract, comply with district directives, and not make mistakes.

District administrators having labor relations responsibilities in the six sample districts sought to influence and regulate the labor practices of building principals in a variety of ways. They provide them with group training and individual assistance about such contractual matters as evaluating teachers and responding to grievances. They established themselves as the inhouse labor experts who should—or must—be consulted before principals took action. They regulated the release of relevant information, such as arbitration rulings, that principals would need in making their own administrative decisions. And in some cases they directly controlled the practices of principals who did not respond to less directive approaches.[9]

These practices were not evident in all districts, nor even in all schools in any one district. The examples provided here illustrate the kinds of centralized influence and control that were apparent at some times in some districts, but it is important to emphasize that district approaches varied dramatically and that throughout the sample many principals remained quite independent in managing labor relations in their schools.

Training / In Metropolis, there were ongoing, formal efforts to instruct principals about their contractual responsibilities and to train them in contract administration. Labor staffers met regularly with principals at their monthly subdistrict meetings and provided additional training workshops. One Labor Relations administrator remarked, "The training is so frequent, that the Federation sometimes says this office is running the system."[10]

In the other sample districts, training efforts were intermittent, if they occurred at all. Often they were scheduled in response to particular requests or problems. For example, the Shady Heights principals asked the personnel director there to meet with them annually to discuss new contract provisions.[11] The Mill City superindendent held a joint meeting with the principals and building representatives there to explain the responsibilities of each under the newly negotiated discipline policy.[12] The Northwood superintendent, who said that he did not formally train his two principals, dealt with problems as they arose: "I have never had to bring the contract out to tell one of the principals that 'you can't do that,' but I do have to remind them that there are limitations on what they can do."[13] Plantville principals reported no district office training efforts. In fact, the personnel director there was said to refer principals' contract questions to one of their better-informed colleagues.[14]

Assistance / There were many instances reported in this study where principals sought district administrators' specialized expertise and advice in responding to personnel problems. Frequently, they requested help when confronted with a grievance. One such Shady Heights principal described how he cautiously waits for assistance:

> I use delaying tactics. I say to the teacher, "What is the problem?" and then I answer, "I'll take it under advisement." That's all I really have to do. I simply have to give an answer back within five days, and so then I'll call [the district office] and I'll say, "Say, I don't know what to do about this. What do you think?" And that's a good way to handle it because you don't back off and you give them an answer, but you don't get yourself in trouble.[15]

Mill City principals had been instructed by the district office to notify the personnel director when a grievance was initiated so that they could be advised before responding.[16] Many Metropolis principals also reported that they would not act on a grievance without advice from their district staffers, who could help them weave their way through what they perceived to be a "maze" of procedural requirements. One characterized her staffer as a "sounding board";[17] another, who consulted her staffer regularly, explained, "I want to follow the correct procedure so that what I do won't boomerang on me";[18] a third called his staffer "my right arm."[19] Some Metropolis principals proceeded confidently and correctly without such consultations.

Training and assistance efforts were ostensibly intended to enable principals to manage labor matters on their own, and, for the most part, principals welcomed them. Shady Heights principals emphasized that while the personnel director was available for advice, he did not make them overly cautious in administering their schools. One said:

> Central administration does as good a job as is possible. They'll back us up. Whenever we question something, we go to them and we say, "We don't know whether this is possible under the contract. Shall we do it?" They will respond, "If it's good for the kids and it's good for the school, you do it and let them grieve it."[20]

However, some principals reported that they were unable to manage labor relations independently because their district office failed to distribute relevant labor information. This was repeatedly said to be a problem in Shady Heights and Metropolis, where principals reported having difficulty getting timely information about negotiation settlements, grievances, and arbitrations. For example, one Metropolis high school principal said that he and his colleagues had received no official explanation about a contract settlement a month after it had been signed and that consequently he had to rely on the union bulletin board for information about teachers' new rights and his new responsibilities.[21] A second Metropolis principal, who made a concerted effort to keep informed about labor matters, complained that principals only received grievance reports at six-month intervals and that they did not have access to the summary face sheets of arbitration findings as the union did. He noted that if the principals were not kept abreast of these decisions, it was possible for the union staffers to "come in bullying."[22]

While the complaints of Metropolis principals were largely

about delays in receiving important information, Shady Heights principals contended that such information was intentionally withheld from them. One elementary principal said, "We don't get any feedback at all about grievances from the central administration. The decisions are not disseminated. I don't know why."[23] Another elementary principal speculated that it was "probably a conscious policy" on the part of the personnel director: "Long ago, they agreed that we would be informed if it was some critical matter, and yet even that has not been followed through. I have to believe that they're trying to protect us from having these things interfere with our work in the schools."[24] A third principal said, "A grievance decision should be announced because it is the law and we must know the law." He explained that the personnel director had once said, "If we told you about all the grievances, we'd be spending all your time talking about them." While this principal reported that he understood such reasoning, he was not satisfied:

> On the other hand, the union—they know whenever their members file a grievance, and they know immediately what the decision of the grievance is. Well, often we have to get this information from the union members rather than from the central administration. This is even true regarding the contract. We don't see that thing for I don't know how long, and often we don't know what's in it and we have to learn from the union representative what has been negotiated.[25]

For whatever intentional or unintentional reasons information might have been withheld from principals, the effect was to leave some of them uncertain of their standing and dependent on the district office for information about what they could, should, and must not do. One Shady Heights principal said that upon hearing about grievance decisions from other principals, he often shrugged his shoulders and said, "Oh, so you can't do that any more?"[26]

The assistance and advice given to principals was often influenced by the cooperative working relationships that developed over time between union leaders and district administrators. Moreover, administrators with labor relations responsibilities in Shady Heights, Metropolis, and Plantville had themselves at one time been active in unions and were committed to making the contract work.[27] Sometimes when district administrators and their union counterparts allied to resolve problems, a principal, thought to be recalcitrant or inept, was the target of their efforts. One Metropolis subdistrict administrator said: "Within my district, when I hear from a Federation staffer that a principal is violating the contract, then I turn those situations around."[28] One union staff member said that he and the Labor Relations staff member

> resolve about 35 to 40 percent of what we talk about. I may call him or he may call me about an incident. We may be able to agree about what the contract says should be done. If it's clear, then he will inform the principal about how it ought to be resolved.[29]

He noted that the school department representative was supposed to support the administration. "Therefore, there's not a lot of deal-making to subvert the principal. Although sometimes we both have to do a little tap dance to get the principal to understand the contract and to be able to save face."[29]

While this kind of informal union-management collaboration was not pervasive—there were Metropolis subdistricts where the district representatives and union staffers barely spoke—the district office labor administrators in this study were, with the exception of those in Vista, at least as intent on ensuring that their principals complied with the contract as they were on protecting the prerogatives of management.

Control / There were instances where district administrators did restrict the autonomy of principals and exert more direct control over school site labor practices, but they were few. In Vista, where the superintendent was in frequent confrontation with the union, principals were required to carry out teacher-rating procedures that identified the top and bottom 6 percent of their staffs. Many believed that the requirement was in violation of the contract, damaging to teacher morale, and incompatible with constructive supervision. One secondary principal explained:

> As a principal, I feel free to observe teachers, to provide suggestions, and I do that because it's my desire to see that teachers do a better job. I don't observe because I want to see them be in the

> bottom 6 percent of the teaching staff. Overall, I think that ranking is detrimental to teacher supervision.[30]

Despite their objections, principals complied with these orders from the district office, in part because they were not legally protected by tenure and because the superintendent had instituted a system of merit pay for administrators.[31]

In Metropolis, where the Labor Relations office had no formal authority over building principals, staffers exerted pressure through the subdistrict superintendents, who did have such authority. One Labor Relations administrator explained:

> Our power base is in the persuasive power that we may have over the district superintendent who does have line authority over the principals. Some of our Labor Relations staffers have made themselves very important sources of help with the district superintendents, and through them they are able to exert influence over the building principals.[32]

At the recommendation of the Labor Relations staffers, some principals were required to rewrite negative teacher evaluations.[33] When one subdistrict superintendent who was a frequent visitor to the schools observed principals violating the contract, he reprimanded them verbally and followed up with written reminders.[34] Another subdistrict superintendent reported that he filed unsatisfactory performance ratings for two principals who had handled teacher ratings poorly.[35]

The Mill City superintendent instituted faculty advisory committees in the schools which were not required by contract. When he met resistance from three principals, he reportedly told them, "Either have them or you're finished,"[36] and the principals complied. The same superintendent standardized certain personnel practices in the schools. For example, one principal had required teachers to sign in and sign out, but the superintendent, who considered this monitoring inappropriate, insisted that it be stopped.[37] In these instances, the principals were required to grant more freedom and influence to teachers than they believed appropriate.

In each of the sample districts, then, there was some evidence of centralized efforts to train, assist, and occasionally control school site labor practices. However, in each district, there were also school administrators who ignored the training, refused the assistance, and avoided the control. Most principals viewed the increase in district office efforts to regulate their practice as modest, appropriate, and necessary. A few principals considered such changes as intrusive or excessive, but such responses seemed more indicative of how very divergent and unregulated school site practices had been than of how centralized they had become.

The Hierarchy of Dispute Resolution

School officials often speak respectfully about the "chain of command" in their districts and then offer many examples of how schools, in fact, are not administered hierarchically. Classroom instruction, taking place at the lowest level of the organization, provides legitimacy to the whole school enterprise, and while district administrators may believe that they are in charge of education in the district, teachers often regard themselves as the experts and administrators as their functionaries. While formal authority may move from the school board and superintendent on down to the teachers, many, including principals, believe that informal authority travels in the reverse direction.[38] While district administrators may always have had the right to supervise principals, it was often difficult for them to exercise that right in ways that would actually change principals' administrative practice. Short of firing them, district administrators had to rely on informal influence, intimidation, or charisma. Sometimes it worked; often it did not.[39]

The introduction of grievance and arbitration procedures into the teachers' contracts has provided district administrators with new mechanisms to reassert their formal authority. According to the contract, grievance appeals follow the hierarchical structure of the school organization, with district administrators having the authority either to reverse a principal's decision, negotiate a settlement with the union, or allow the grievance to be submitted to arbitration. One might expect that the pyramidal structure of the district would be reinforced by the grievance procedures. However, the findings of this research did not regularly bear that out. Some district administrators exercised their powers of review and drew disputes up the organization chart, but others avoided these powers and pushed decisions back into the schools. These different strategies and preferences of district administrators seemed to be as important as the aggressiveness of the local union in determining how frequently teachers and their unions filed formal grievances. A brief review of the districts' various approaches to grievances will illustrate these differences.

There had been but one formal grievance filed in Northwood since the advent of collective bargaining, reportedly due to the district's reliance on an informal "problem solving policy." The president of the teachers' union attributed the success of the policy to the superintendent, who originated it: "He's a pacifist."[40] It was clear, as well, that his success depended on the cooperation of the union.

Mill City teachers also filed few formal grievances, despite the broad contractual definition of issues that might be grieved. Five were formally filed in 1978–79, which the personnel director called "par for the course,"[41] although the union president reported dealing informally with approximately 200 complaints per year.[42] The union president favored conciliatory, non-agressive practices in resolving school problems; he personally mediated many potential grievances in the schools.[43] In addition, and perhaps in response to these attitudes, the district office had not geared up to respond in a centralized manner to more grievances. Responsibilities for personnel practices were divided among three people in the central administration, and there were no apparent efforts to consolidate them. The personnel director was not a step in the grievance procedures, though she was personally responsible for making staff assignments. An assistant superintendent advised principals about how to respond to grievances, but did so after conferring with the personnel director. The superintendent was also consulted in major personnel matters.[44]

Grievance practices in Plantville were shaped by a narrow grievance definition, a conciliatory union president, and an assistant superintendent who preferred negotiated settlements to adversarial encounters. The assistant superintendent spoke of his cooperation with the union president: "He and I handle the brush fires. . . . We try to resolve things together."[45] This cooperative approach, which led to few formal grievances, was endorsed by the union president.[46]

Grievance practices in Vista were largely determined by the attitudes of the superintendent, who served as hearing officer. He was an advocate of "creative tension," and he favored the grievance process for resolving disputes. He explained that he wrote "long and detailed findings . . . so that the readers will perceive me as an appellate judge, resolving the concerns of two disputants farther down the line."[47] One principal said that he and his colleagues were satisfied with the grievance process because they had "their inning" and because matters were being resolved more systemically than they had been before.[48]

While the superintendent had made use of the power available to him through the grievance procedures, he had not done so at the expense of the principals, whom he rarely ruled against. Rather, he had ignored the decisions of three arbitrators who had found in favor of the teachers.[49] Without binding arbitration, the stakes were not high for management, and it was possible for the district administration both to encourage grievances and to be uncompromising in settling them.

In Shady Heights, the administration also promoted the use of formal grievance procedures to resolve disputes. The personnel director estimated that 100 grievances had been filed formally the preceding year,[50] far more than in other districts of comparable size. Although he spoke of many efforts to resolve issues informally, he also expressed concern about unwise precedents being established through informal resolution. As we shall see below, he exercised careful control over whether particular grievances were settled within the district or in arbitration.

In Metropolis, the grievance and arbitration procedures

were resorted to regularly. Well over 250 grievances were filed by the teachers annually, and approximately thirty-five moved on to arbitration.[51] Several factors seemed to contribute to this outcome—the broad grievance definition, a complex contract, a very aggressive union, and the presence of a full-time hearing officer within the administration. While the grievance practices in smaller districts such as Vista seemed responsive to the current superintendent's attitudes, in Metropolis these practices appeared to have become institutionalized over time. Stakes were high in this large district, where a grievance or arbitration decision could potentially affect 279 schools. A full-time union officer had aggressively represented teachers in grievance hearings for a number of years,[52] and Metropolis teachers had the support of seven full-time union staff members in pursuing their grievances. The school department had counterpart staff members in each district to assist principals in responding to those grievances.

Therefore, the presence of formal grievance procedures in teacher contracts did not in itself lead to more hierarchical practices in the schools. In some cases, district administrators either were not forced to or did not choose to adjudicate disputes; they preferred that differences be settled within the schools, and there were consequently few formal grievances and many informal settlements. In other cases, the district administrators encouraged the use of the formal, adversarial procedures, thus increasing the number of grievances filed, centralizing the process of resolving them, and reducing the power of principals to control the outcomes.

In Shady Heights, Metropolis, and Vista, where there was frequent use of grievance procedures, district administrators regularly heard appeals of principals' decisions and decided whether to uphold them, to negotiate a settlement with the union, or to allow the issue to be resolved by an outside arbitrator. In these districts, the principal's subordinate position was emphasized when school officials ruled in favor of a teacher because the principal had violated the contract. One subdistrict administrator in Metropolis provided this explanation:

If a principal follows the contract and follows due process carefully and if the principal hasn't done anything that is obviously arbitrary or capricious, then he or she need not be concerned about grievances. For example, at the secondary level, principals are required to meet and discuss with the building committee of the Federation before developing criteria for extracurricular appointments. The contract is clear on this. If there is no agreement between the principal and the committee, then the principal's decision is final. However, in the elementary school, the contract is very clear that the principal and the committee must reach concurrence. Therefore, if the principal acts on his own without the support of the building committee, I would not be reticent in overruling the action of the principal.[53]

In some instances the merits of the cases were less clear than in others, but district administrators exercised their right to overrule principals. For example, in one Metropolis high school a teacher wore a T-shirt with a political slogan and posted a political sign on her classroom door. The principal removed the poster, told the teacher never to wear the T-shirt again, and filed a reprimand about her performance. In response to the teacher's grievance, the hearing officer found in favor of the teacher because there was no policy in the school department regarding the political activity of individual teachers and because the principal had never forewarned the teacher about this kind of activity.[54] The principal, however, regarded the teacher's behavior as "improper partisan politics among teachers during school" and considered his own response appropriate and the grievance decision unfounded.[55]

In deciding how to respond to grievances, district administrators reported weighing whether it was better to settle complaints within the school district than to risk having them move to arbitration, where an individual unfamiliar with the district would render a binding decision. Even though the grievance may have been filed against a principal, it was the district administrator who ultimately decided whether to compromise with the union. Often that decision depended on the potential long-term effects on district labor practices as much as on the merits of a particular case, for an unfavorable arbitration ruling might set a costly precedent for an entire district. For example, if teachers were freed of bus duty in one school as the result of an arbitration, they would probably be freed in all schools. Therefore, a district administrator might consider it to be in the interests of all schools to compromise with the union about the practice in one school. From the district-wide perspective, such a settlement might be well advised. However, from an individual principal's perspective, such a settlement might compromise the program and policies of the school and reduce his or her sense of autonomy or power.

The Shady Heights union president said of the district personnel director, "He's shrewd, he won't choose a case [to take to arbitration] unless it includes an important principle or unless the evidence is clearly on the administration's side."[56] This was confirmed by the personnel director.[57] Shady Heights principals were overall quite satisfied with the representation they received from their personnel director, but they did report having to submit to his judgment. One principal had received a grievance from a teacher who requested a transfer to a higher grade; the principal thought the teacher would not perform well there. However, he and the personnel director agreed not to "fight it because the contract language was vague about in-school transfers. We didn't want to set a precedent." He regretted the decision, but agreed that it was necessary: "I don't like the situation, but that's what unionism does."[58]

Metropolis, Shady Heights, and Vista provided evidence that the grievance procedures could reinforce the hierarchical structure of the school district. Principals in such districts were well aware that they were middle managers whose judgments were subject to review from above. However, such review occurred much less frequently than many suppose.

Reliance on Rules and Procedures

Anyone who has dealt even briefly with the Internal Revenue Service knows that rules and procedures are prominent in the day-to-day operations of public bureaucracies. Special needs or circumstances matter little when they collide with The Regulations. One might reasonably expect that teachers' contracts, being sets of rules and procedures that carry the force of law, would increase the prominence of regulations in the schools. Such rules might either promote more reasonable and orderly school practices or unwisely restrict the options of teachers and administrators. They might be applied selectively or enforced unconditionally. The data of this study reveal that while collectively bargained rules and procedures commanded administrative attention, compliance had not become a preoccupation. Most negotiated rules were seen to have improved personnel practices, while a few were said to be unduly restrictive.

Differential Enforcement of Contract Provisions / Although all contract provisions were theoretically of equal weight, an analysis of contract compliance in the schools revealed that some were enforced while others were not. Each provision typically fell into one of three categories:

1. *Fully implemented* provisions that were virtually always complied with at all schools.

2. *Partially implemented* provisions that were weakly complied with at all schools.

3. *Variably implemented* provisions that were enforced in some schools, ignored in others, and informally renegotiated in others.

Whether a provision was fully, partially, or variably implemented appeared to depend on two factors—its importance to teachers and its enforceability.

Fully implemented provisions were ones that were both highly valued by teachers and enforceable—strong provisions from the union's perspective. In these instances, contract language did determine practice. In this study, the contract provisions that fell into this first category dealt with seniority layoffs and transfers, class size limits, and duty-free lunch guarantees. Each will be considered briefly.

Job security was, not surprisingly, a central concern for teachers. When asked what issues they might personally grieve, more teachers responded that they would initiate formal complaints about job security than about any other issue; many said that it was the only issue they might grieve. One Mill City teacher expressed the views of many other teachers:

> It's not very fair if you have a job for a long time. You work and you work and you work and you expect that that kind of loyalty will provide some stability over time in your position. It's not fair if then you are taken out of that job and put in another school. . . . If [teachers] cannot work for the stability of their position, then they really have nothing to work for.[59]

Seniority-based layoff and transfer provisions were perceived to be teachers' protections against arbitrary job loss. Despite some teachers' beliefs that such provisions might compromise the educational program, there was no instance in this study where seniority rights were waived for the sake of the students.

Class size limits were also closely enforced in the schools of this study. They were believed to make teaching responsibilities more manageable, and they protected jobs. One Plantville teacher said,

> I would initiate a grievance about the issues that are closest to me. For example, if somebody tried to take advantage of the class size limitations. I realize that class size is tied to class assignments and unless we watch closely, some other teacher's job would eventually be on the line.[60]

Teachers insisted that class size limits be honored unless temporary adjustments would not jeopardize any staff jobs. These provisions were very closely monitored in the four districts experiencing declining enrollments. In Vista, where enrollments were growing, large classes were occasionally tolerated. Within particular schools in Metropolis, Shady Heights, and Plantville, teachers had agreed to have large and small classes within the school, but the overall class size average for the school was maintained.

The third provision that was regularly implemented and closely monitored at the school site was the guarantee of a duty-free lunch, provided for in all the sample contracts. Teachers were adamant that this negotiated right be honored, and they often contended that the assurance of a duty-free lunch implied that they should not be required to supervise the cafeteria at any time. No teachers reportedly volunteered for cafeteria duty in Mill City, where the contract freed them of this responsibility; and in other districts, where teachers might still be called for cafeteria duty as long as they also recieved a duty-free lunch, there was often union pressure on principals to relieve all teachers of this supervisory responsibility.

Partially implemented provisions were important to teachers, but were not easily enforced via grievance procedures. Such provisions included assurances of equitable treatment, standards for student discipline, and guarantees of adequate building security or maintenance. For example, the malfunctions of heating systems in old buildings aggravated many teachers but were not considered to be contract violations that could be remedied through formal procedures. One union staff member in Metropolis estimated that for each school in his district he could write up thirty-five grievances about violations of facilities provisions in the contract. He did not do so, though, because he believed that the administration would not respond to them.[61] Outdated texts and worn or damaged equipment were often similarly tolerated. One Shady Heights teacher complained that he had but one set of books for three classes. While the contract could have been cited to remedy the problem, this teacher had not done so because he doubted it would make any difference.[62] Teachers also reported having little hope of enforcing general contract language on student discipline. For example, in one Mill City school where teachers repeatedly complained about lax discipline by the principal, no teacher suggested relying on the newly negotiated discipline policy to improve the situation.[63] Teachers were, for the most part, resigned to pursuing their concerns about discipline informally, outside the contract.

However, in the extreme, the contract would be invoked as a last resort—occasionally with success, but often not. Many broken windows in a school, roofs that leaked repeatedly into classrooms, chemistry classes without experimental equipment, and a vice-principal who was widely perceived to give no disciplinary support to teachers all precipitated grievances in the schools of this study. But these were the exceptions; this second type of provision, typically unenforceable and weak from the union's perspective, had consistently little effect on school practices.

Variably implemented provisions were enforced in some schools, ignored in others, and informally renegotiated in others. There were many such provisions, including those that regulated the assignment of teachers to supervisory duties, defined the length and frequency of meetings, specified the appropriate use of preparation periods, and designated the role of the building committee. In many cases, school practices deviated from the negotiated contract language. Several examples will illustrate how variably such contract language was interpreted.

Five contracts set limits on the frequency and length of staff meetings. However, the actual meeting schedules varied considerably from school to school within any district. In most schools, principals reportedly called fewer meetings than the one per week contracts generally permitted. However, in one Vista school, a newly appointed principal had routinely called two or three meetings a week and had never met opposition from his staff.[64] A Shady Heights principal reported that he sometimes called an extra meeting: "Occasionally things come up—something that I have to get to them fast, something about a new program that is coming. And so I call a meeting at that time and there is no problem."[65] One Plantville principal reportedly had been forced by the union to reschedule two meetings because he had not provided the required forty-eight hours' notice;[66] but in another Plantville school the principal reported that he occasionally called a faculty meeting without the advance warning, with this explanation to his staff: "I know this is not according to the contract, but it would be mutually beneficial if we all met." The teachers, he said, accepted this because he did not "call meetings for the sake of calling them."[67]

Teachers in several districts were contractually entitled to repayment in time or money for lost preparation time. However, there were teachers in Plantville schools who refused repayment for covering extra classes.[68] Principals in two Metropolis schools reported that repayment was only occasionally required by teachers, although in many other schools payback was expected by most teachers.[69]

The supervision of erratically late buses was reported to be an ongoing problem in Shady Heights, where buses sometimes did not arrive until after the end of the teachers' contractual workday. When this happened in one secondary school, the teachers cited the length-of-day provisions of their contract and told the principal that they would not supervise students.[70] However, in another Shady Heights school, where teachers accepted these responsibilities, the building representative himself remained on bus duty one day until 5:00 P.M., when the bus finally arrived.[71]

Only a very few contract provisions were actually enforced throughout the schools and districts where they had been negotiated. These included seniority layoff and transfer procedures, class size limits, and duty-free lunch guarantees. Virtually all other noncompensation provisions were variously enforced, amended, or ignored. This variation in levels of contract implementation is largely the result of school site factors that will be discussed more fully in Chapter 6. However, it is important to emphasize here that there were exceedingly few instances in this study where the teachers' contract might be said to have been running the school.

One set of procedures—those that regulated teacher layoffs and transfers—calls for further discussion. Being fully implemented provisions, they were applied district-wide and had a major impact on the schools of four districts. They provided the one example in this study where negotiated procedures seemed to have become self-propelled and where their evenhanded application had, in some instances, produced irrational results. These provisions warrant close consideration here not because they are typical of negotiated rules, but because they show the ways in which detailed procedures that are rigorously enforced can affect school practices.

The Unique Case of Seniority Procedures / Collective bargaining for teachers has developed while student enrollments have been declining rapidly in many of the nation's public schools.[72] During the 1950s, when enrollments in many districts were rapidly expanding, principals often had not only the right, but also the responsibility, to staff their schools.[73] Principals in all districts reported that during periods of growth they had recruited teachers for their schools, sometimes raiding them from other schools in the district. Then, Mill City principals could interview prospective candidates and reject any whom they considered unsatisfactory.[74] Metropolis principals could select particular individuals from district-wide eligibility lists, and Metropolis teachers could request voluntary transfers after having been informally recruited by principals in other schools.[75] Today, principals in these districts retain the authority to interview teachers new to their districts, but they cannot exercise the same control over staff assignments when, because of teacher layoffs, vacancies must be filled by transfers.[76]

Reduction-in-force provisions had been negotiated or were prescribed by law in five of the six sample districts. Only Vista, with its burgeoning enrollments, had not addressed the issue contractually. The Northwood contract set forth multiple criteria for teacher layoffs (overall instructional program, experience and qualifications of staff, and seniority), but the district had never used them because enrollments continued to grow and staff attrition was high. The four remaining districts used seniority as the sole criterion to determine teacher layoffs.

Layoff decisions proceeded from the district offices rather than from the school offices, for they were based on district-wide staff seniority lists. For example, all secondary English teachers were placed on the same list in the order of their initial employment dates. When a position in English was eliminated by the district office, the least senior English teacher in the district was laid off. Therefore, whether or not a school was itself experiencing enrollment declines, it might lose a junior teacher, however outstanding or central to the school's program that teacher might have been.

After layoff decisions had been made, a transfer process followed in which teachers whose positions had been cut were reassigned to the openings created by layoffs. This became necessary when the positions that had been eliminated (e.g., one in the South School, two in the East School) did not correspond to the positions of teachers who had lost their jobs (one in the North School, two in the West School). Principals' power to screen transferred teachers had been reduced, and in some cases eliminated, by the negotiation of the seniority procedures that regulated transfers.

The transfer language of the four contracts was similar. In Plantville, vacancies were to be filled strictly according to the seniority of the applicants. In Mill City, various factors, including seniority, were to be weighed by the school department in placing a surplus teacher. The Shady Heights contract specified that if all teachers' qualifications were equal (and these were minimal paper qualifications), the most senior teacher filled the vacancy. The transfer provisions in the Metropolis contract permitted displaced teachers to make five choices, from which the school department selected the final placement; the principal had no contractual authority to intervene in this process. Transfers in Metropolis were further complicated by federal requirements to balance school staffs by race and experience. The contract specified elaborate rules by which this was to be carried out. Each teacher carried both a building and a district seniority standing that influenced the outcome of transfers. Again, the principal had no authority to intervene in the process.

The actual transfer practices of the districts conformed closely to those prescribed by contract. In Plantville and Shady Heights, district-wide seniority lists and the teachers' requests alone determined placements.[77] In Mill City, the district office did permit principals to interview teachers from the transfer list and informally influence district office decisions about final placements. They could not, however, recruit teachers from other schools to fill their vacancies.[78] The Metropolis principal was reported to have virtually no formal or informal influence on the placement of transfers, those decisions being made by district office administrators on the basis of teachers' requests.[79]

Principals in each of these districts expressed concern about the effects of seniority-based transfer practices. Some principals regretted the loss of particularly talented or committed junior teachers, but there was little mention of substituting performance for seniority criteria. Principals expressed less concern that overall staff quality in the district was being undermined because of seniority-based layoffs than that they had lost control over who would teach in their schools as a result of seniority-based transfers.

Of the four sample districts that were reducing staff, Mill City principals could exert the most influence over the process and Metropolis principals could exert the least. Because these procedures were closely enforced, the differences among districts were largely a consequence of differences in contract language. In Mill City, where involuntary transfers were a major issue at the bargaining table, principals were apprehensive about losing what influence they retained over these decisions. One school principal said:

> I'm very concerned over this thing of seniority transfers, and I see somewhere down the road that seniority is coming into full blossom. I can anticipate the time when I'm not able to interview teachers if I have a vacancy in the building. Instead, the seniority list will determine who goes here and who leaves my building.[80]

Another Mill City principal emphasized the importance of retaining what discretion principals had over transfers:

> If it is a noncertified occupation, such as in industry, I can see seniority as a good thing because in those jobs you're task oriented rather than people oriented. However, normally with a vacancy in the building, the principal has had the opportunity to interview and provide recommendations to the personnel director about the candidate of his choice. I think that that's important. There may be something very critical about the position. For example, if I had three males in the special ed program, it might be essential for me to find a strong female for the position.[81]

Metropolis principals repeatedly expressed dissatisfaction that they had too little power to review the qualifications of teachers to be transferred involuntarily. One explained:

> If I could have one wish, it would be to be able to conduct a thorough interview and to observe potential teachers in my school. I believe that the selection of the staff should be the number one most important responsibility of the principal. If a principal is able to get good teachers in the building, then 99

percent of the other problems will dissolve, and the principal can spend time on improving the program rather than solving one teacher's problems.[82]

In Metropolis, seniority-based layoffs and transfers presented particular problems for courses requiring particular teaching competencies. One principal told of an advanced mathematics program that would end when the current teacher retired because routine transfer procedures could not provide an appropriately qualified teacher for the course and the principal was not permitted to recruit from another school in the district.[83]

In addition to complaining about losing good teachers and inheriting less effective or unqualified teachers as a result of seniority layoff and transfer provisions, principals objected to domio sequences of teacher transfers that disrupted their schools after teacher assignments had been made. Such difficulties were reported occasionally in Plantville, Mill City, and Shady Heights and often in Metropolis.

For example, one Shady Heights elementary principal told of a particularly outstanding second-grade teacher who, as a result of two other transfers in the district, was bumped from her position two days before the beginning of school. She was replaced by a fourth-grade teacher from another building. After three weeks of school, the grievance of yet another teacher gave her rights to the second-grade position, and so the recently assigned teacher was sent off to another school and replaced by a third.[84] A Mill City principal who recounted a similar situation in her school observed, "From the standpoint of the person who seeks a transfer, I can understand. However, from the standpoint of the class that's settled and ready to go, I wonder how that helps kids."[85]

The problems principals encountered with sequential transfers seemed to have been more the result of the negotiated procedures themselves than of decisions made about those procedures by district office administrators. There was evidence, however, that district administrators could and did exert some control over them. For example, in Shady Heights, the union leaders and district administrators had agreed to modify the administration of transfer procedures so that all transfer disputes would be resolved before the beginning of school; involuntary transfers would regularly be resolved prior to voluntary transfers. The union president explained that to have allowed bumping "would have been a disaster. The industrial model just doesn't fit here."[86] While this adjustment did not empower principals to control staff assignments to their schools, it did moderate the disruptive effects of the procedure.

Some of the blame attributed to collective bargaining for these apparently impersonal transfer procedures is unquestionably misplaced. The changes were precipitated by such things as declining student enrollments and years of racial imbalance. In the past, staff changes would probably have been resolved by administrative judgment, often influenced by favoritism or patronage politics. Virtually all teachers and administrators agreed that seniority-based procedures had introduced a large measure of equity into very difficult decisions that were being made in very difficult times. However, the fact remains that while such procedures might have been evenhanded, they were not without consequence for the school and its programs. When administrators could exert no control over the procedures to temper their impact on children and programs—for example, when sequential transfers continued throughout the year—students were bearing more than their share of the costs of decline.

Conclusion

While the trend toward centralized administration of the contract was apparent in all six districts of the study, no district had achieved anything resembling lockstep conformity in labor practices. Labor relations in the schools continued to be quite particularistic. Central office specialists in Shady Heights and Metropolis had gained power and status with their expertise in labor relations, but principals and teachers continued to make the routine decisions that mattered in the schools. Grievance procedures had reinforced the hierarchical structure of some districts, but school districts frequently resolved disputes less formally. Teacher contracts had joined school board policies and school handbooks in defining routine procedures and standards, but the schools had not become rule-bound. Personalities continued to be more important than roles.

Most teachers and principals in all districts but Metropolis agreed that the organizational changes that had taken place were, for the most part, modest, appropriate, and constructive. Even in Metropolis, where the evidence for bureaucratization was strongest and where certain centralized practices presented problems for the schools, principals had not been hamstrung by the requirements for standardized practices. Many administrators agreed that the changes had introduced needed order and equity.

The experiences of these six districts suggest that there are strong orgainzational forces within the schools restricting and moderating the centralization that might be expected to accompany collective bargaining. Professional norms that support inclusiveness, value flexibility, and commend responsiveness are not readily replaced by respect for organization charts, procedures, and uniformity. The teachers on whose behalf the contracts of this study had been negotiated recognized the educational need for autonomy, and they widely supported principals' efforts to maintain some independence from control. Consequently, district office efforts to standardize school practice were, at best, moderately successful. District administrators regularly contended with teachers' and principals' vigorous defense of their autonomy and confronted the difficulties of imposing centralized control on a decentralized organization. Collective bargaining had not provided the occasion for the wholesale bureaucratization of the schools.

Chapter 4

Defining the Teacher's Job

The Teacher as Public Servant—devoted, selfless, tireless, obedient, and respectful—is a central figure in nostalgic recollections of The Good Old Days. But today's teachers are popularly regarded as being different from those of the past—more concerned with themselves, less concerned with their students and the public good.

Central to this changed perception is the fact that unionized teachers have negotiated working conditions that limit the powers of management and increase teachers' control over their hours and responsibilities. Such contract provisions, designed to reduce administrative abuse, to make the job of teaching more manageable, and to preserve more time for instructional preparation, are said by some to compromise school services. Where once principals could require teachers to arrive early, leave late, attend Parent Teacher Organization (PTO) meetings, sponsor several extracurricular activities, and chaperone Saturday night dances, most contracts now specify the limits of a teacher's obligations.[1] In-school work hours are defined, after-school commitments are limited in number or eliminated altogether, and the number and length of staff meetings are fixed by contract. Where once principals could assign teachers to courses and students to classes without regard to size or balance, such assignments must now be equitable and not exceed the contractually defined class size or teaching load limits. Where once principals could require teachers to supervise the halls or attend meetings and parent conferences during nonteaching time, the contracts of many districts have now established the teachers' right to use this time as they, not their principals, see fit. As one

Vista principal said, "I can't say 'be there' or 'do this' anymore."[2]

Many district contracts have not only defined, but have also reduced, teachers' work obligations. R. Theodore Clark, Jr., believes that there develops along with these changes a "trade union mind-set" that discourages teachers from doing more than the required minimum:

> In years past the teacher who put forth extra effort, stayed late to tutor students, sponsored extracurricular activities, attended open houses, and so on, was respected for his or her extra effort. With the establishment of a union mind-set in some districts, pressure is increasingly brought to bear on the teacher who gives such extra effort.[3]

According to this view, reduced work obligations have lowered professional standards as well.

This chapter examines the negotiated changes in teachers' work obligations and the effects of those changes on school services and operations. It shows that bargaining about teachers' responsibilities has led to a variety of results in the sample districts. In some cases, contracts specified extensive obligations for teachers, and the resulting level of school services was high. In a few cases, districts had negotiated low work requirements for teachers that jeopardized the effectiveness of the schools. While collective bargaining in itself did not lead to problematic reductions in teachers' work, some districts had agreed to changes that did. Many teachers throughout the districts did far more work than their contracts required, but such extra efforts were understood to be voluntary. In general, contract language did not determine what most teachers actually did, but it did influence their collective sense of what they could be expected to do.

Length of the Workday

In industry, the length of a work shift defines the maximum time workers, who are paid at an hourly rate, spend on their jobs. By contrast, salaried workers in the private sector often are expected to work well beyond the eight-hour day and the five-day week. Teachers stand somewhere in between. While they are salaried, their workday is usually defined, either by board policy or by contract.

In this study, the length of the students' instructional days varied considerably from district to district (see Table III), the shortest being at the elementary level in Plantville (five hours and forty minutes) and the longest being at the elementary level in Northwood (seven hours). Included were periods for lunch that ranged from thirty to forty-five minutes. The instructional day had been altered little by collective bargaining; school hours in most districts had been in effect for many years, having been changed in some cases during the 1950s when some schools were on double sessions. Therefore, it is the length of the teachers' workday rather than of the students' instructional day that will be discussed here.[4]

Five of the six contracts in this study specified the hours of the teachers' workday. The longest was in Northwood, where teachers were committed to work eight hours (one hour beyond the instructional day), and the shortest was in Metropolis, where the teachers were only obligated to be present in school while students were in classes. The Vista collective agreement was unique in calling for a "professional workday," the length of which was based upon the teacher's "professional responsibilities and duties." It gave the principal the right to require teachers to report before and after school "to attend to those matters which properly require attention at that time." It also permitted teachers to determine when their work was done.[5]

In practice, the in-school work patterns of teachers varied greatly among districts, within districts, and within schools. The contract language obviously determined the workdays of some teachers. As a group, the teachers in Metropolis and Plantville spent fewer hours in their schools than did the teachers in Northwood or Mill City, but they frequently stayed longer than their contracts required.

In every district there were some teachers who arrived an hour or more before the start of the instructional day; most were present fifteen to thirty minutes early. They used this time to prepare for their classes, to meet with parents, to attend faculty

Table III *Negotiated Length of Teachers' Workdays*

School District	Instructional day		Teacher workday		Teacher workday beyond instructional day	
	Elementary	Secondary	Elementary	Secondary	Elementary	Secondary
Northwood	7 hrs.	7 hrs.	8 hrs.	8 hrs.	1 hr.	1 hr.
Mill City	7 hrs.	6 hrs., 45 min.	7 hrs., 30 min.	7 hrs., 30 min.	30 min.	45 min.
Plantville	5 hrs., 40min.	6 hrs., 15 min.	6 hrs., 10 min.	6 hrs., 45 min.	30 min.	30 min.
Shady Heights	6 hrs.	6 hrs., 15 min.	6 hrs., 30 min.	6 hrs., 45 min.	30 min.	30 min.
Metropolis	6 hrs., 45 min.	6 hrs., 15 min.	6 hrs., 45 min.	6 hrs. 15 min.	None	None
Vista	6 hrs.	6 hrs. 30 min.	Professional workday		Determined by professional responsibilities	

meetings, or to talk informally with other staff. There were a few teachers who regularly arrived at the latest time that was acceptable. In Metropolis, where the contract permitted teachers to report to school with the students, there were a few teachers who signed in at the main office at the time that classroom instruction was to begin. One secondary principal estimated that 6 percent of his teachers arrived at the last moment "and don't move fast enough to their classes."[6]

The arrival patterns of teachers differed greatly within a school and seemed to depend mostly on personal preferences. There were, however, discernible school site patterns in teachers' after-school departures: in some buildings teachers left the school at the contractually specified time; in others they worked later. These patterns reportedly had developed over many years. Teachers usually reported working well beyond the required in-school hours. A small number, usually including those with many years of teaching experience, reported that they completed all their work in school, but the majority said that they usually took work home and spent from three to thirty hours of uncompensated time per week on instructional preparation or school-related activities. Teachers recounted in considerable detail the many responsibilities they could not complete during the workday: shopping for classroom materials, making instructional games, grading papers, preparing worksheets, writing tests, doing library research, and reviewing and ordering textbooks. Principals regularly corroborated these reports of extra work, but noted that while these efforts were essential to effective instruction, the use of additional time remained within the control of teachers rather than administrators.

Although many teachers in all districts did remain in school beyond the instructional day, few were seen providing academic help to students. Secondary teachers often designated one afternoon per week for tutoring or make-up work (this was required by contract in Shady Heights), and some students did remain for these sessions. However, elementary teachers rarely worked with students after school for more than ten minutes. This was found to be as true in schools where teachers were available an hour after the instructional day as it was in schools where they remained but a few minutes.

There was no single explanation for the fact that students seldom worked with their teachers after school. Most teachers and administrators attributed it to various social conditions rather than to collective bargaining. For example, sometimes parents refused to let their children stay after school. A Vista principal said, "We have had fights with parents who wanted them to be home right away."[7] He, like others, cited parental concerns about safety, music lessons, religious instruction, and responsibilities for siblings as the sources of the problem. Older students were said to resist staying after school because of jobs.

Bus schedules presented further obstacles to after-school tutoring. In some schools, virtually all students were bused and therefore left promptly at the end of the day. Some districts provided late buses for students who remained after school, but such buses were often unreliable. In one Plantville secondary school, late buses were scheduled three days per week. However, if no administrator was present at the close of the day, the bus was cancelled. Since this occurred often and unpredictably, teachers and students did not count on after-school time for make-up work.[8]

School board policies in three districts further restricted after-school help. In Mill City and Vista, teachers were required to notify parents in advance before detaining students. Shortly before my visit to a Mill City school, a new teacher had been reprimanded for permitting a student to stay and talk longer than fifteen minutes.[9] In Plantville, the school board notified teachers that they might be held liable for student safety if they detained students more than fifteen minutes, when crossing guards left their posts.[10] In some schools, principals, teachers, and parents were apprehensive about the threat of assaults in nearly empty schools during the late afternoon. This was a prominent concern in Metropolis, where most teachers left promptly after the close of school, often at the urging of principals concerned about their safety. In several schools, it was the custodian rather than the principal or teachers who decided when the staff and students would leave. In one Plantville secondary school the custodian routinely cleared the building for lockup at 2:30 P.M.[11]

Many teachers reported having various demands on their

after-school time. Some attended graduate courses, often in response to administrative urging or to a negotiated pay scale that rewarded additional training. One Plantville principal noted proudly that all teachers in his school had attained or were working toward master's degrees,[12] and a teacher in that school observed that, for the principal, graduate courses took priority over after-school work with children.[13] Teachers also were assigned to various district-wide committees (e.g., instruction for the gifted, curriculum evaluation, and textbook selection) that took them out of their schools immediately at the end of classes.[14] Finally, current economic and social conditions often required teachers to leave school promptly for second jobs or to assume child-care responsibilities.

These altered conditions and priorities had introduced variation into teachers' work patterns that reportedly was not common twenty years ago. The combined effects of many uncertainties—Will the students be allowed to stay? Is it safe to remain in the school? Will the late bus run? Is this the teacher's college day? Does the teacher have a meeting?—seem to have reduced the expectation, the possibility, and therefore the probability that teachers and students would remain after school to work together. While part of this change might have been due to contract language that specified working hours, more seemed attributable to the expanding scope of teacher responsibilities, changes in student behavior and community expectations, and current economic exigencies.

While many principals noted that they could no longer require teachers to remain in school after the contractual workday, few reported that it presented more than occasional problems for them as administrators. In Northwood, where teachers remained in school for eight hours, and in Mill City, where teachers were required to stay seven and one-half hours, principals were satisfied with the amount of time teachers worked in school. There was, as well, no dissatisfaction reported by Vista principals, who could require teachers to be present in school to fulfill particular responsibilities. There were, however, principals in Plantville and Shady Heights who expressed some concern about the impact of defining the teachers' workday on the availability of their staff. The ambivalence of this Shady Heights principal's response was typical of others: "Of course, there are always the ones who close up for the day and that's it. But even those—some of them are quite good, and they may be quite efficient. But I would like to see more staying."[15]

Metropolis principals were more critical of their teachers' contractual workday, which began and ended with the students' instructional day and included no time for emergency conferences or after-school help. One junior high school principal, who complained that he could not require teachers to remain after school for conferences, said, "I try to work out everything within the schedule of the day, but that isn't always convenient for the parents, who would prefer to come after school."[16] Other Metropolis principals reported that such limitations on teacher hours occasionally compromised the quality of school services, but said that teachers often agreed to meet with parents or colleagues after school hours.

These data provide no clear answer about the optimal length of the teachers' workday. The Metropolis experience suggests that a workday ensuring no time beyond instructional hours presents problems for both students and principals. But it was not apparent that an eight-hour workday ensured higher levels of teacher service than one including an extra half hour of unscheduled time, particularly since few students remained after school for extra help and most teachers said that they worked additional hours at home.

Extracurricular and Volunteer Activities

The practice of paying teachers to participate in extracurricular activities predates collective bargaining. The six sample districts had long compensated teachers with pay or release time for selected extracurricular work—for example, coaching football, directing the band, and advising the newspaper. There was an additional group of activities for which teachers were expected to volunteer their time—for example, coaching cheerleaders and advising the chess club or literary magazine staff.

Generally, in the past, paid positions required substantially more time than unpaid positions and often were related to boys' interscholastic sports. While some teachers were compensated and others were expected to volunteer, staff participation in the extracurricular program was regarded as both a professional and an employment obligation.

Collective bargaining has not introduced the practice of paying teachers for extracurricular work, but it has, in many districts, increased the number of activities that carry stipends. District administrators and union negotiators often reported that while the increase in paid sponsorships was occasionally the result of concerted union efforts at the negotiating table, more often the school department was acknowledging a teacher's previous contribution to the schools.[17]

Among the sample districts, there were three that required extracurricular participation by teachers, two that made such participation voluntary, and one that both made it voluntary and compensated virtually all faculty participants. It is useful to review the kinds of extracurricular programs and the levels of teacher participation that resulted in each case.

Required Participation / The contracts of Northwood and Vista required each teacher to assume one activity sponsorship. The Mill City contract did not address extracurricular responsibilities, but school handbooks included similar obligations. Some of the sponsors—such as yearbook advisor, pep squad coach, dramatics advisor, forensics coach, and most major atheletics coaches—received annual stipends for their work. Advisors of such activities as the chess club, Y Teens, Latin club, and intramural sports either were not paid or were given token pay (e.g., $100 per year to advise the student council). In practice, teachers who were paid for one activity were usually not required to volunteer for another.

The extracurricular programs in these districts were varied and reflected the initiatives of individual faculty members—for example, a photography club in Vista, a model car building contest in Mill City, and Students for Christ in Northwood. Because teachers considered this part of their job, administrators reported having little trouble finding activity sponsors. Shortcomings in the extracurricular program were usually attributed to student apathy. One Mill City principal said, "Teachers would be more active if the students wanted it."[18]

Voluntary Participation / By contrast, the contracts of Shady Heights and Plantville included no requirement for teacher participation in the extracurricular program. In fact, the Shady Heights agreement specified that participation in noninstructional activities was "strictly voluntary."[19] Again, coaches and advisors of major activities were paid, and there were small stipends for those who advised selected clubs. The range of extracurricular activities in these districts' schools appeared somewhat less extensive than in those where teachers were obliged to participate, but there were many impressive examples of volunteer efforts. For example, in one Shady Heights high school, faculty members sponsored chess, computer, and math clubs without compensation.[20]

The differences between these districts and those with required participation were more apparent in teacher attitudes toward such responsibilities than in the range of extracurricular offerings. For examples, Shady Heights and Plantville teachers reported being well aware that they, rather than the administration, would decide whether and when they would sponsor activities. Principals in these districts attested to wide faculty participation in after-school activities, but reported that it was difficult to find volunteers for evening activities, especially to chaperone dances.

The range of extracurricular activities in each school seemed sufficient to meet the needs of the students, but the number of teachers participating was said to be smaller in these two districts than in Mill City, Vista, and Northwood. The success of the programs typically rested on a few very active teachers. While the principal's enthusiasm and participation in extracurricular programs was an important factor in their success in all districts, that commitment seemed more critical in Shady Heights and Plantville than in Mill City, Vista, or Northwood.

Paid Voluntary Participation / The provision for extracurricular activities in the Metropolis contract was unique. Like the others, it set out a pay scale for coaches. Beyond that, each school was allotted a number of paid extracurricular hours (at $17 per hour), the use of which was determined within the school by the principal and building committee. The Metropolis school department also permitted secondary schools to trade two instructional positions per year for additional extracurricular hours.[21]

The extracurricular programs in Metropolis schools were varied, including many of the activities offered by schools in other districts. In addition to the standard fare, many Metropolis schools earmarked extracurricular funds for student tutoring programs, particularly at the elementary level.

The difference between Metropolis and the other districts was less in the range of offerings than in the fact that virtually all teachers were paid for participating. When Metropolis teachers were asked to give examples of unpaid participation in extracurricular activities, they could name only a few, often one-time special events—for example, a Saturday workshop with parents to make instructional games and a senior citizen's banquet. There were a small number of teachers who volunteered often. For example, one Metropolis teacher drove students to sports events, worked for the United Way through the school, sold refreshments at football games along with members of the senior class, and served on the school's human relations committee. She was, by all accounts, exceptional.[22] There were, however, many reports of teachers who worked well beyond the hours for which they were compensated in their extracurricular assignments and who thus volunteered many hours of their time.

In general, however, the expectation prevailed among Metropolis teachers, and some principals as well, that teachers should not be expected to volunteer their time. In many schools there was no norm supporting teacher involvement outside the classroom; such participation was not regarded as a professional obligation, although extra instructional preparation often was. There was subtle and sometimes explicit pressure on teachers not to volunteer. One principal called it "the union party line: Don't do more than the contract says. If you do, you're making it bad for everyone."[23] Most teachers said that while they had never experienced such direct pressure not to volunteer, they believed that their peers would frown upon extensive uncompensated efforts.

Changed Teacher Attitudes / The experiences of the sample districts indicate that while collective bargaining had apparently not affected the range of extracurricular offerings available to students, in some districts it had affected the mix of paid and unpaid sponsorships. As more activities were paid and fewer were supported by volunteer efforts, a larger proportion of the school budget was allocated for noninstructional programs. In a district such as Metropolis those costs were substantial. Moreover, teachers' attitudes were said to have changed. In those districts where participation was not required by contract or board policy, principals had to rely on friendly persuasion or veiled threats to ensure sufficient coverage. It was not so much that teachers sought pay for their work. Rather, the widespread introduction of stipends reinforced the notion that teachers' professional obligations were defined rather than diffuse and that they, rather than their principals, had the right to determine whether they would participate outside their classrooms.[24]

A few teachers and administrators expressed concern that teachers might seek compensated positions out of greed rather than genuine interest in the students or the activity. Generally, this fear was unsubstantiated. In five districts, the compensation in all activities but athletics was so modest that it seemed unlikely to attract teachers who were not genuinely interested in the program. In Metropolis, the pay was sufficient to lend credence to this concern, but teachers and administrators there did not consider it to be a problem. In fact, in Metropolis as elsewhere, principals frequently said that many teachers were reluctant to participate in any extracurricular programs whether compensated or not. Teachers were regularly said to seek control over their noninstructional time and to limit their obligations to those related to classroom instruction.

Meetings

When asked to recall employment conditions prior to collective bargaining, veteran teachers typically recounted instances when they were required to attend precipitously scheduled, long, seemingly irrelevant meetings. Once such teacher recalled being obliged to watch hair-styling demonstrations at an evening PTO meeting.[25] Such tales have become lore and are not offered here as hard retrospective data. They do, however, illustrate why most teachers believe their contracts must include some limitations on the frequency and length of staff meetings.

All of the sample districts but Northwood specified the maximum number and length of meetings that teachers could be required to attend beyond the instructional day. As Table IV shows, contract provisions in four of those districts were similar.

Metropolis board policy, which had been in effect long before collective bargaining, called for early student dismissals to permit staff meetings. In keeping with that policy, the Metropolis agreement stated that all staff meetings had to be held during the instructional day; however, twice a month principals, having obtained the district superintendent's prior approval, could require teachers to remain thirty minutes after school.

In practice, fewer meetings were called in all districts than the contracts allowed. Only at the elementary level did principals schedule meetings each week, and then they were usually only

Table IV   *Contractual Frequency and Length of Meetings*

School District	Permitted frequency of meetings	Permitted length of meetings
Mill City	1 per week	1 hr.
Vista	1 per week	1 hr.
Shady Heights	3 per month	1 hr.
Plantville	1 building meeting per month;	1½ hrs.
	1 curriculum meeting per month	1 hr.

thirty minutes long. Overall, principals reported that they believed the allotted time was sufficient, and many noted that they cancelled meetings for lack of agenda items. One Northwood principal who believed that regular meetings were important acknowledged that he "scratched for items to include."[26]

There were a small number of principals who were dissatisfied with the restrictions on meetings. They contended that one hour per week provided enough time to convey information about administrative routines, but was insufficient for staff development. "There is enough time to deal with trivia," one principal explained. "However, there are some things that I would like to have an afternoon to deal with. I don't have enough time for staff development."[27] Undoubtedly, there were principals who could have used longer periods of time productively, but few suggested that they could. In addressing the need for staff development, some full-staff meetings were designated for inservice training, and many groups of teachers met about instruction during preparation periods and lunch or after school. While contractual limits on meeting times are sometimes said seriously to restrict the principal's discretion, the respondents in this study rarely said that this was the case.

Class Size

Teachers and administrators who were asked to list the positive effects of collective bargaining often began by mentioning reductions in class size. Experienced teachers would typically recall the large classes they confronted as novices. One district administrator in Plantville told of an elementary class he taught with fifty-three students: "There were one-way aisles."[28]

All districts except Mill City and Northwood included some contractual restrictions on class size. These ranged from a class size goal of twenty-five in Shady Heights to a fixed maximum of thirty-eight in the Vista secondary schools (see Appendix C for more detailed information). Distinctions in the class size limits were made for various levels and subjects: for example, elementary classes were to be smaller than secondary classes; and

English classes were to be smaller than social studies classes. Only in Metropolis was the class size maximum of thirty-three to be constant for all levels and subjects.

Teachers and principals generally agreed that there were educational advantages to having classes restricted to about twenty-five or thirty students. A few administrators were skeptical about the value of small classes, citing the failure of research to demonstrate any positive correlation between class size and student performance and arguing that such provisions reduced the productivity of schools. While the educational worth of class size limits was debated, interviewees agreed that changes in class size would not have been made without collective bargaining. For those who contend that reduced class size permits better instruction, this union achievement is an instance where student and teacher interests coincide.

Teacher unions are interested in class size provisions not only because they believe that such limits improve instruction or teacher morale, but also because they protect jobs. Job security was a central concern for teachers in Plantville and Metropolis, where enrollments were declining rapidly, and teachers there knew that an additional student in each district classroom would eliminate many teachers' jobs. Consequently, class size limits in Metropolis and Plantville were closely enforced; but class sizes varied in Mill City and Shady Heights, where the contract did not establish a maximum or provide teachers with any authority to control student assignments. In Vista, where enrollments were growing, larger classes were occasionally tolerated by teachers who knew that accepting additional students did not jeopardize any current teaching positions.

Principals argued that some class size limits were necessary given the history of large classes and the current economic pressures to maximize teacher productivity. However, they did question whether it was educationally sound to place absolute limits on class size or to police those limits closely. One secondary principal in Vista observed, "While class size works to my advantage many times, it can become a problem, particularly when the teachers and administration disagree about allocation decisions."[29]

The Metropolis limits on class size were more restrictively

enforced than those in any other district. They permitted no adjustments for subject or level—typing and chemistry classes were both limited to thirty-three students. No contractual allowance was made for ability groupings within a school that would permit smaller classes for children with remedial needs. Furthermore, the official class size count in Metropolis included all students who were listed on the teacher's roll, whether or not they had ever entered the class. One principal said: "We have students we call 'ghosts' who haven't even dropped into school, let alone dropped out, and yet their names haven't been officially removed from the school rolls. Until they are, these students must be counted into class size."[30] In areas of the city where attendance was low, this meant that some classes were unnecessarily small while others were large. In high schools, the restrictive application of this provision sometimes kept students from courses that were technically full but actually had space. Many Metropolis teachers said that they would not insist that class size be measured by the number of students on the roll, but some were apprehensive that such a compromise might affect another teacher's job security.

Metropolis, however, represents the extreme in this study. In other districts, the class size limits varied by level and subject, and students were not included in the count if they were not attending the class. The Plantville contract specified both a district-wide elementary class size average of twenty-three and a classroom maximum of twenty-eight, thus permitting within-school ability groupings of students. Such class size provisions that set grade-level or school-wide averages provided broad protection against abuse while allowing the principal and teachers to decide how best to allocate teaching resources within the school.

Preparation Time

Neither teachers nor administrators disputed the need for designated noninstructional time when teachers could meet with other teachers, grade papers, or prepare lessons. High school teachers in these districts had long had one unscheduled period each day because of departmental scheduling. However, elementary teachers had only recently gained preparation time through collective bargaining.

All sample contracts assured elementary teachers twenty-five to forty-five minutes of unscheduled time each day in addition to their duty-free lunch. During this time subject specialists usually taught their classes. Secondary teachers were guaranteed one unscheduled period per day, which was usually forty-five minutes to one hour long.

The dispute about preparation time was never about its need, but about its use. Should the principal supervise the teacher's use of preparation time, or is this rightfully left to the teacher's professional discretion? Should teachers be permitted to leave the school during this time? What constitutes appropriate use of preparation time? Can teachers be required to cover the classes of absent staff members during preparation periods? If so, should they be compensated in either time or money? These questions were raised and debated by teachers and administrators throughout the study.

The Northwood and Mill City contracts included no restrictions on the use of preparation time. The Shady Heights agreement said that teachers could leave the building with the principal's permission;[31] the Plantville contract permitted them to leave only "for valid educational reasons."[32] The Vista contract stated that during preparation time, teachers were expected to "normally devote themselves to preparation and similar professional pursuits."[33] The Metropolis contract said only that "the time is to be used for preparation."[34]

The language of these provisions was vague; "preparation" was never defined. This ambiguity presented no apparent problems in five of the districts, where principals generally reported that they were satisfied that time was used productively—sometimes for grade-level meetings, usually for grading papers, and occasionally for a break either inside or outside the school. Only in Metropolis was the use of preparation time a prominent concern.

Metropolis administrators reported that when preparation time was negotiated for elementary teachers, they had expected that the building principals would have the right to supervise its use. However, subsequently an arbitrator ruled that in the absence of more explicit contractual language, "preparation" could be broadly interpreted and teachers could determine how best to use the time.[35] As the union president explained, "Teachers can go to the bank, bowling or ballroom dancing."[36] This issue became a public one when a newspaper photograph showed a teacher washing his car on school grounds during preparation time.

While the issue of preparation time was more prominent in Metropolis than anywhere else, teachers there appeared to use the time much like their counterparts in other districts. Some Metropolis principals believed that preparation periods were being abused in other schools, but few believed that this was a problem in their own. One teacher explained how the time was used in her school: "The people I know work during these periods. I suppose there are some who go to the bank, but if they do that, then they have to do their work at home."[37]

There were principals in various districts who were dissatisfied that they could not assign teachers to supervise the building or to attend conferences during preparation time. As one Shady Heights principal explained: "You have to ask, 'Are you willing to come to a meeting during your nonteaching time?' They seem to guard that time jealously. But if I ask them, 'Are you willing to attend?' they will."[38] Some principals reported, however, that teachers did not acquiesce to such requests.

Class coverage was the one use of preparation time addressed contractually. The Shady Heights, Plantville, Metropolis, and Northwood agreements permitted teachers to be assigned to coverage when substitutes were unavailable and specified a variety of payment rates. Shady Heights teachers were paid $5.00 per class after ten uncompensated coverage assignments; elementary teachers were not paid when specialists failed to relieve them in their own classes. Metropolis compensated teachers in time or money for each secondary coverage assignment beyond four per year and paid back elementary teachers for any lost preparation time. Northwood teachers were paid $10 per hour for each class coverage; elementary teachers were compensated by one-sixth their daily rate when specialist teachers were absent. Plantville teachers earned $8.00 for each coverage assignment or lost preparation period. Vista teachers could be assigned to cover classes in emergencies without pay, and Mill City secondary teachers would be assigned coverage assignments on a rotating basis. Teachers said they were displeased when they were asked to cover classes; no one suggested that he or she would do it for the money, and some teachers in all districts reportedly accepted the assignments but refused compensation.

Once again, the most problematic situation occurred in Metropolis, where teachers were contractually entitled to be repaid in time or money for any administrative use of their preparation periods. Teachers who were asked to attend in-service training, participate in grade-level meetings, or be interviewed by curious researchers usually expected to be compensated, much as they expected to be paid for extracurricular supervision. Some Metropolis administrators opposed preparation payback both on principle and because of its administrative inconvenience. One subdistrict administrator argued that teachers should not be paid twice for the time they worked.[39] An elementary principal called it "the worst, stupidest idea that ever came down the pike."[40]

In Metropolis, principals were under school department pressure to compensate teachers in time rather than money for lost preparation periods. They might hire a substitute teacher to repay administrative debts to one teacher after another throughout the day. However, this required skillful scheduling to avoid disrupting classroom instruction. One principal explained the problem:

> If Miss Jones lost her prep period last week and today I have a *per diem* substitute, I will assign her to Miss Jones's class at a particular time. However, I might discover that Miss Jones had a reading lesson planned for that particular time. The substitute takes the class to pay back Miss Jones and the students miss their reading lesson.[41]

Some principals had devised ways to avoid disruptions. For example, one elementary principal supervised her own weekly assemblies and freed teachers during that time, thus compensating them for lost prepartion time.[42] However, such inventive solutions were reported infrequently.

Supervisory Duties

In the past, teachers in the sample districts were said to have been responsible for students wherever they might have been during the school day. Schooling, like parenting, was assumed to be a full-time responsibility, and the teacher was accountable *in loco parentis* for safety and social instruction. Before and after school, on the playground, in the corridors and cafeteria—even in the bathrooms—teachers supervised their students.

Gradually, through successive changes in board policies and collective negotiations, the teacher's instructional and supervisory responsibilities were differentiated. Throughout the sample districts, teachers characterized classroom instruction as professional work and supervision as custodial work. One Shady Heights principal provided this illustration:

> There's one gentleman in the building who will stay until five o'clock to help kids if they want help. But, if I ask him, he'll refuse to stay and supervise the buses. They seem to believe that the supervisory responsibilities can be worked out—that they *should* be worked out. But about their teaching, they seem to believe that if they don't do it, nobody can or will do it.[43]

Teachers also objected to supervisory assignments because they were typically tedious duties in unpleasant locations where unfamiliar students might challenge their authority. Some teachers were displeased with the policing function of these jobs. In their classrooms, they might have flexible rules, but as monitors they were expected to enforce school-wide regulations. For these reasons, teachers in all districts sought to reduce the number of supervisory duties.

Despite the reported importance of building supervision, the six sample contracts were not very explicit about either expectations for or limitations on supervisory duties. The Mill

City contract freed teachers only from lunch duty.[44] The Metropolis agreement said that teachers should be relieved of nonteaching duties "to the extent possible."[45] The Vista contract says that the "Board will continue to make an effort to reduce all non-teaching duties within the confines of District resources and capabilities."[46] Neither the Shady Heights nor Plantville contracts directly addressed the issues. However, related contract provisions regulating such things as duty-free lunch, preparation time, or the length of the workday were interpreted by teachers and principals to mean that teachers would be unavailable for such responsibilities as cafeteria or bus supervision.

In practice, teachers in all districts assumed some supervisory duties, although there were wide variations among districts as well as among schools within the same district. Generally, elementary teachers were assigned more such duties than secondary teachers. In Northwood, Mill City, Plantville, and Vista, elementary teachers in some schools supervised the schoolyard and the buses both before and after school; they monitored the playground during recess and the lavatories when classes were dismissed for a break. In most cases, lunchroom aides or the principal supervised the cafeteria. Secondary teachers in some schools in each of these districts assumed hallway and bus duties. In most cases, it was the building principal who saw the need for coverage and who organized teachers to provide it.

Overall, teacher supervision was less extensive in Shady Heights and Metropolis than in the other districts. Shady Heights elementary teachers were not on duty before or after school or in the cafeteria. However, high school teachers continued to assume lunch duty and, in at least one high school, were assigned to hall duty before and after school.[47] In Metropolis, teachers generally did not supervise students outside their classrooms except to walk them to specialists' classes, recess, or lunch. The contract permitted but one teacher at a time to be assigned to recess. With a few exceptions, nonteaching assistants rather than teachers monitored the cafeteria and the halls.

The principals of these schools expressed varying degrees of interest and concern about the order and security of their buildings. Many were quite satisfied with the coverage provided by teachers and aides; a few were distressed that they could not assign more teachers to supervision. One elementary principal in Metropolis, like many principals interviewed throughout the study, said that she could think of no instance where her school lacked proper supervision.[48] Yet, another Metropolis principal said, "Taking teachers off duties in the school is the worst thing that has happened since collective bargaining."[49] A Plantville principal who was very concerned about student safety and staff liability assigned extra teachers to playground and after-school duty, saying that he would never permit his students to be supervised by aides, because it simply was not safe.[50]

One Metropolis district administrator charged that the "unofficial position" of the Metropolis Federation of Teachers was that teachers had "no more responsibility for the safety and welfare of students than a passing stranger."[51] Yet no principal reported such instances of disregard by teachers. Instead, principals said that staff could virtually always be asked to supervise the building on a one-time or emergency basis. As one Metropolis principal said, "If a problem developed in the building that required teacher supervision, I would doubt if the teachers would not already be doing something about it."[52] Yet school administrators expressed concern that the union "promoted the feeling that it's the principal's role to assume supervisory responsibilities."[53] It was ongoing demands for supervision that were difficult for these principals to meet.

Cafeteria Supervision / The most prominent of these ongoing demands was cafeteria supervision. Large cafeteria spaces, filled with hungry, rambunctious students, and the ever-present threat of food fights presented difficult supervisory problems that recurred day after day. How these problems were resolved in the schools of this study depended on whether the contract permitted teacher supervision at lunch, whether aides were available to assume the assignments, and how resourceful the principal was in devising alternative solutions. In Vista, where teachers could be required to monitor the cafeteria as long as they also had a duty-free lunch, an elementary principal said cafeteria supervision was "only a coordination problem. Everyone here takes a turn."[54] In Plantville, most principals assumed that teachers could not be assigned to the cafeteria because they were entitled to a duty-free lunch. When aides were available, they were usually assigned to lunch duty; in one Plantville elementary school, aides in the bilingual program supervised the lunchroom.[55] Several principals said that the aides were ineffective in these roles without regular training and support, but one Shady Heights principal, who was satisfied with the aides' performance, explained his strategy:

> I think the principal is being paid an enormous salary to supervise students. I don't want to spend my time doing that. Some of these people will tell you that their teacher aides can't handle the job. I tell these aides, "You have to learn to run this building with or without me. I don't want you to be in here bothering me about lunch duty." Of course, I don't mind if they bother me, but I want them to understand that they're in charge, and they do a good job of it. They manage to supervise that building.[56]

A Mill City principal was inventive in ensuring that his aides would be effective:

> The reason it works is that the kids know that the aides are boss and that they'd better listen to them or else. I stay in my office during lunch and I don't go down there unless it's absolutely necessary. The kids can talk, but if they holler, they get a demerit. Three strikes and you're out. If you're out, you don't get to see the monthly movie. Also, the teacher who has the most students who cannot see the monthly movie must stay with those students, so it's a way of encouraging support from the teachers as well. Frankly, I wish all the kids would go home for lunch.[57]

There were a number of principals who were not assigned aides or who were unconvinced that the aides could manage alone. One Shady Heights principal who had no aides spent one and one-half hours in the cafeteria each day.[58] A Mill City principal who had aides nonetheless personally supervised lunch. He said: "I'm on lunch duty every day. . . . We have good lunchroom aides, but they don't have the authority to handle all the problems that might come up. There are days when I don't even get a lunch."[59] Such principals complained that cafeteria duty was a poor use of their administrative time. Both teachers and principals agreed that inadequate cafeteria supervision might lead to classroom problems. This Mill City principal blamed the teachers:

> Teachers have abdicated their responsibility for lunch hour. Kids come in from recess still very up and active, and it takes time to settle them down. Much of this activity comes into my office— settling fights and that sort of thing. But it also comes into the classroom. Now, I would not say that it's a great big, horrible disruption, but it's a problem.[60]

Teachers, on the other hand, usually regarded cafeteria supervision as an administrative problem. One Shady Heights teacher said:

> It's the principal's responsibility to see that the aides are trained. The teachers have suggested an adequate training program and we look on this as an administrative type of responsibility. . . . Frankly, I find it hard to justify lunchroom supervision as an educational process. This is not an educational issue; this is a convenience issue. The teachers need to eat lunch.[61]

There was rarely a case reported in this study where teachers had compromised the contractual gains they had made in cafeteria duty, even though they were aware that inadequate supervision might make their own work in the classroom more difficult.

The Schools' Reduced Supervisory Capacity / The growing distinction in districts such as Shady Heights and Metropolis between instruction and supervision, and the consequent division of labor between teachers and aides or principals, has changed the supervisory capacity of schools there. While society continues to heap responsibilities on the schools and to define the task of schooling quite broadly, teachers in this study sought to limit the scope of their responsibilities. By reducing their supervisory roles, teachers made it clear that they were not to be regarded as full-time caretakers, but as professionals with instructional expertise.

In one respect, these changes ensured more efficient use of professional time. Inadvertently, however, this separation between classrooms and corridors might suggest to students that public behavior is less important than classroom behavior. A Metropolis elementary principal said that as a result of releasing teachers from nonteaching duties, "the official presence of teachers is not there. Teachers are no longer seen by students to be responsible for the entire school. As a result, the students don't have the same respect for all teachers that they do for their classroom teachers."[62] Parents may expect the schools to socialize their children's public behavior, but the schools may be less and less organized to do so. This was not perceived to be a problem in four of the sample districts; but in Metropolis and Shady Heights, where the contract had been interpreted to restrict supervisory assignments closely, principals could only rely on their informal authority with teachers to ensure full coverage, and because teachers disliked these jobs, administrative persuasion was sometimes unsuccessful.

Conclusion

Union pressure to define teachers' work obligations was, by all accounts, either a response to real administrative abuse or a defense against potential administrative abuse. In Metropolis, where accounts of past abuses were widespread, one principal observed:

> The thickness, the scope, of this phone book of a contract is, in my view, an indictment of how administrators ran their schools in the past. There were many abuses, and consequently, there are many things in the contract that shouldn't be there. But they are there because they are the responses to abuse. I have been in schools where faculty meetings extended for an hour and a half on a Friday afternoon, and therefore, that is dealt with in the contract. I have been in faculty meetings where the principal read the agenda to the teachers, and consequently, that is in the contract. I was never an administrator before the advent of the Federation, but the principals at that time must have been very powerful people.[63]

Even in the small district of Northwood, teachers looked to their contract to protect them from unreasonable administrative demands. During the one-year tenure of a Northwood superintendent who was generally perceived to be hostile to teacher interests, the teachers' contract doubled in size. He had publicly informed the staff, "If it's not in the contract, you don't have it," and the union had responded with demands for more explicit language about working conditions. When he was replaced by a more conciliatory administrator, the union continued to insist that work obligations be contractually defined, despite the school board's assurances that the new superintendent "understands how this is done."[64] The union president explained that teachers were wary of relying on trust that might be violated by a subsequent superintendent.

It was generally reported that the definition of teachers' work obligations had reduced past abuses of their time, energy, and commitment and that, in this regard, the effects of collective bargaining had been constructive. But some contract provisions significantly reduced teachers' responsibilities and consequently introduced problems for school managers. For example, the Metropolis contract, which set short work hours and excluded virtually all noninstructional duties, had, it seemed, gone beyond what was necessary to protect teachers from abuse. The experiences of some schools there suggested that when there is more emphasis on limiting teachers' obligations than on limiting administrative abuse, the contract can work against, rather than for, effective schools.

Reducing teachers' contractual obligations also generally increased the difficulty of principals' work. Districts that defined teacher responsibilities quite narrowly increased the demands on their principals to be versatile, inventive, and inspiring with their staffs. As we shall see in Chapter 6, some principals succeeded in eliciting high levels of teacher service and performance even under the most restrictive contract, but success was never certain. One Metropolis administrator assessed the prospects for success this way: "A super principal can perform this. A good principal with a good staff can perform this. A mediocre principal with a good staff might perform this. But a good or poor principal faced with recalcitrants cannot have an effective school."[65] No school included in this study could be said to be staffed by "recalcitrants"; the large majority of teachers were repeatedly characterized as responsible, if not dedicated. But the varied experiences of the six districts indicate that while many teachers go well beyond the minimal requirements of their job, all are not equally guided by professional consciences. A contract that defines the minimum implicitly endorses that minimum, and this defined minimum shapes district-wide expectations of what all teachers must do and what dedicated teachers should do. For the principal who administers a contract requiring few noninstructional services from teachers, there is only the hope, not the assurance, that teachers will stay longer or do more when they are needed.

Chapter 5

Maintaining Staff Competence

Many factors are thought to contribute to successful schooling, but, as many parents will attest, it is finally the classroom teacher who matters most. Good teachers can be effective in the worst schools, and poor teachers can fail even in the best settings. Those who puzzle over the current problems of the public schools often express concern about the quality of teachers. Robert Benjamin notes:

> A wide variety of observers across the country believe that the single greatest problem afflicting the public schools is the quality of its teachers and their work. When asked, "In your opinion, what are the main things a school has to do before it can earn an A?" respondents to the 1980 Gallup Poll of public attitudes toward the public schools listed first, "improve the quality of teachers."[1]

Teacher incompetence is blamed on several factors. Some observers cite inadequate college preparation or school district failures to screen job applicants, and they turn to competency exams to remedy the problem.[2] Others argue that poor teachers are not those who would fail standardized tests, but those who fail to function effectively under routine school pressures, who can not get along with children, or who have given up trying to be good teachers. The problem, they say, is one of teacher performance rather than teacher preparation, and the remedy, they believe, is in cautious tenure awards and dismissal of incompetent teachers. They advocate more administrative control of the exit from the profession, but complain that such control is prevented by the procedural protections in teacher contracts and the successful defense unions provide to those teachers whose competence is challenged.

This chapter explores the impact of collective bargaining on administrators' capacity to maintain quality teaching staffs. The findings of this study reveal that within the schools there are different views about how much responsibility teacher unionism should bear for the persistence of poor teachers. Many respondents, including a surprising number of unionized teachers, agreed that strong contracts and strong unions play a large role in protecting incompetent teachers and reassuring lazy ones. They reported that the contractual procedures for teacher evaluations, transfers, and dismissals were excessively restrictive and that the union's formal defense of teachers unwisely interfered with legitimate administrative efforts to terminate them. They suggested that, if it were not for collective bargaining, poor teachers could be summarily removed from the schools.

There were others, however, including a substantial number of administrators, who believed that the problem of incompetence was more complex and that such singular blame of unionism was more convenient than accurate. While these respondents acknowledged that collective bargaining made teacher dismissals difficult, they argued that other local factors, including administrative incompetence, combined to explain the persistence of poor teachers. The evidence from the sample districts supports this second view, demonstrating that teacher unionism complicates, but does not prohibit, the discipline and dismissal of poor teachers. It suggests that the problem of incompetence, which predates collective bargaining, would probably not end if the procedural protections of the contract and the defense provided by the union were suddenly to disappear.

Demographic Background

During the 1950s and 1960s, when many school districts were opening new schools each year, teachers were in short supply and selection criteria were often relaxed to fit the available applicants. The immediate challenge was to find a teacher for every classroom. As one principal recalled, "During the sixties, we were chasing warm bodies."[3] Those teachers hired during periods of enrollment growth typically were granted tenure as readily as they had been granted employment. With administrative attention captured by the demands for more desks, books, and buildings, school officials rarely refused teachers permanent positions.

Many of those teachers hired since 1950 remain in the schools today, and in districts where enrollments are declining as rapidly as they once grew and where applicants for teaching positions far outnumber the available jobs, attention has turned to the performance of those with tenure—those who are widely believed to be invulnerable to dismissal efforts. In those districts where a large percentage of the teachers hold tenured positions, there is general discouragement about the prospects for upgrading staff.

There were marked differences among the sample districts in the extent to which teacher incompetence was perceived to be a problem, and those differences appeared to depend largely on enrollment trends. In Vista and Northwood, where enrollments were expanding and staff turnover was high, teachers and principals reported being quite satisfied with the quality of their teachers. By contrast, school officials in districts with declining enrollments (Plantville, Mill City, Metropolis, and Shady Heights) reported more problems with incompetent teachers. Administrators faced with demands for staff reductions in these districts confronted older, more settled teachers who believed their jobs to be safe. Moreover, because the districts with declining enrollments were also located in communities with declining economies, unsuccessful teachers could not easily take jobs outside of education, and the teaching force was consequently even more static. As the more junior, and sometimes more enthusiastic, teachers lost their jobs to declining enrollments, the inadequacies of the staff who remained and the difficulties of removing them became more apparent. While there is no way of knowing whether teacher incompetence is a greater problem in districts with declining enrollments than in districts with expanding enrollments, respondents in this study perceived it to be so.

Who the Poor Teachers Are

In discussing issues of competence, respondents typically placed teachers into one of three categories. The large majority of teachers were said to be dedicated and hard working. Teachers of the second group, who were variously characterized as "slouchers" or "corner cutters," were said to be marginally effective. Those in the third group, the "incompetents" or "dead wood," were described as totally ineffective.

Estimates varied about the percentage of teachers who made up each group, but there was general agreement that at least 80 percent of the teachers in the schools were dedicated, some 15 percent might be marginally effective, and no more than 5 percent were said to be incompetent. Despite respondents' emphasis that these were only guesses, there was surprising correspondence in the estimates within districts and schools. For example, a district office administrator and a union leader in Plantville estimated independently that 5 percent of the teaching staff could be called "dead wood."[4] The principal and eight teachers in one Mill City school all reported that there were no incompetent teachers in their school.[5] And the staff of a junior high school in the same district identified between two and four teachers who were not doing their jobs.[6]

There was also broad agreement about the characteristics of the three types of teachers. This Mill City principal talked of the dedicated teachers:

> The majority of teachers still do a lot. In fact, I would say they do a superhuman job. No, I don't think that they are affected in their service and performance by the negotiating. I have yet to ask someone to do something over and beyond the contract where the teacher said "no." The contract has affected only the lazy people.[7]

A Metropolis junior high school teacher characterized marginally competent teachers as those who "fail to keep up on educational changes. They are the kind who are content to have the kids come in and copy work off the board. Their performance wouldn't be improved unless they were monitored very closely and unless their jobs depended on it." She went on to contrast such teachers with three in the school who, in her view, were incompetent and

> should never be teaching anywhere in a classroom in the United States of America. One is mentally ill; the second is mentally unstable and beats the children. The third one comes in late and thinks he is doing an excellent job but is totally incapable of controlling the chaos in the classroom.[8]

A Shady Heights principal provided further descriptions of the incompetents: "The kind who sleep in class, who are absent without notifying us, who are late without calling in, who use abusive language toward children, or who come into the classroom under the influence of one thing or another—these are the people who are offensive to the whole staff.[9]

Respondents said that collective bargaining had affected the work of these three groups of teachers differently. Dedicated teachers were said to be internally motivated and thus uninfluenced by the protections of the contract. This Plantville principal's comment is typical of many: "Good teachers are good teachers regardless of the union."[10] One teacher explained, "I feel responsible for myself. I give it the best shot and if it doesn't work, then I go home and worry about it. I really do."[11]

Surprisingly, most respondents also contended that the work of incompetent teachers was unaffected by the contract. A Plantville teacher observed, "If they're going to be bum teachers, then they're going to be bum teachers."[12] A Vista union leader said, "They don't even see the need for the Association to defend them."[13] A Mill City teacher said, "They're just poor teachers. They have no relationships that are effective with students. They couldn't do better, no matter what the contract said or whether there was no contract at all."[14] Often incompetent teachers were reported to be nonunion members or to have minimal union involvement, yet as district employees they were entitled to be represented by the union in contesting any administrative action against them. One Plantville teacher summarized the problem: "I don't think they do less because of the union, but the union protects them in what they do."[15]

While the performance of both dedicated and incompetent teachers was reportedly unaffected by the contract, sometimes marginally competent teachers were said to use the contract as an excuse for cutting professional corners. For example, a Mill City principal described a teacher in her school:

> There is a teacher in the building who will do nothing except on school time. He leaves at the time the school day ends. I know that he has to be cheating on classroom time if he's able to complete all the things he has to turn in to me. I think that that has to be the result of the union.[16]

While many believed that such teachers felt protected by the union, few believed that they intentionally did a poor job. One Mill City teacher thought that marginally effective teachers used the contract to rationalize their own failures:

> I think that the contract becomes an excuse for those who are already in the profession and find that they can't do the quality of work that they expected. I don't think anyone comes into the profession with the view that they will do only what is required. They all expect to do more and then reality hits. All of us at one time or another give up on some of the things that we thought we might do, and you justify that giving up by pointing out that you don't do it because it's not in the contract.[17]

The "reality" of which this teacher spoke was often said to have changed in recent years as the social responsibilities of schools increased and their instructional failures became more obvious. Teachers whose work might have been satisfactory twenty years ago now confront different demands and standards. One veteran Mill City teacher expressed his frustration:

> In order to function and to maintain any kind of mental balance in school today, you have to be damned good. Twelve years ago, I would go home from my work, and I was ready to do other things. I had energy. Now I'm exhausted and it takes me two hours to recover from the work of my day. The conditions of work here

have changed dramatically. It's gotten to the point that if a kid doesn't have breakfast, then it's your fault.[18]

The Difficulties of Terminating Incompetent Teachers

Tenure laws and union contracts include not only protections for teachers but also procedures for their dismissal. District administrators in the sample districts were adamant that the means for terminating poor teachers were available, and they frequently blamed principals for the fact that those procedures were seldom used. A Mill City district administrator who estimated that 15 percent of the teachers were not doing their jobs rejected the explanation that collective bargaining was to blame: "No, there is no excuse for having that 15 percent around. If the principal would do the job, then those people would be terminated. It's difficult, but it's possible."[19]

Principals, however, were not so confident that inferior teachers could be fired for cause. Some argued that the evaluation procedures required by the contract were too complex and demanding. Others said that the skillful defense provided by the union made terminations unlikely even if principals could master the evaluation process. Yet others contended that district and school site administrators who favored concession over confrontation reduced the likelihood that poor teachers would ever be dismissed. Finally, some principals and district administrators observed that the involvement of other governmental authorities (e.g., the courts and state departments of education) in dismissal cases ensured that the worst teachers would have long tenure in their jobs. Each of these factors will be discussed in some detail.

The Evaluation Process / State laws specify permissible reasons for terminating a tenured teacher, the most straightforward of these being some very serious incident with children, for example, a sex offense. Administrators reported having no problem resolving these cases informally. A Mill City administrator explained, "The first teacher we terminated was the easiest. That was on a morals charge. You simply get the information and you present it to the person and you say you'll go public with it unless they resign."[20]

Other causes for dismissal were more difficult to document. For example, according to the state code regulating terminations in Mill City, a tenured teacher's contract "may not be terminated except for gross inefficiency or immorality; for willful and persistent violations of reasonable regulations of the board of education; or for other good and just cause." Administrators reported that they were uncertain about the practical meaning of "inefficiency" or "persistent" or what might constitute "just cause." Therefore, most principals did not begin by advocating the dismissal of tenured staff members unless there was incontrovertible evidence of incompetence. Instead, they usually began with the preliminary steps of filing a disciplinary report, assigning an unsatisfactory rating, or seeking a teacher's transfer to another school. If the teacher did not have tenure, they might recommend nonreappointment. In order to have any of these actions upheld, principals had to document the faults in a teacher's practice. The contracts of four of the sample districts included procedures for observing and evaluating teachers, and the remaining districts—Vista and Northwood—incorporated such evaluation procedures into board policies. There were similar requirements in all six districts. Staff members were to be observed and evaluated regularly by their principal or department chairperson. Typically, nontenured teachers received annual ratings and tenured teachers were evaluated every two or three years. The Shady Heights contract required evaluators to give teachers twenty-four hours' notice in advance of observations that were "for the purpose of evaluation of subject matter competence."[21] Teachers were to receive written copies of their evaluations or ratings and were to be informed of their shortcomings. If school officials intended to assign unsatisfactory ratings or to recommend a teacher's transfer or dismissal, it was necessary to offer that teacher recommendations for improvement and the opportunity for reassessment.

There were time limits imposed by the sample contracts and

board policies on the observation and evaluation process. For example, Vista principals were to complete their observations of probationary teachers by March 10. In Metropolis, principals could not assign unsatisfactory ratings unless teachers received written reports within five days of the observation. The Shady Heights contract required that any teacher receiving an unsatisfactory rating "must have been observed at least once a quarter for not less than twenty (20) minutes."[22] Teachers in all districts had the right to reply in writing to their evaluations and to have those responses included in their permanent files. Plantville teachers could, by contract, discuss their evaluations directly with the superintendent.

Teachers were evaluated on a variety of factors. For example, the Mill City evaluation form included twenty-four assessment items ranging from "teaching techniques" to "self-control and poise." Each teacher was rated on a four-point scale ("excellent" to "unsatisfactory") for each item. Evaluators assigned overall ratings for a teacher's performance, professional qualities, and personal qualities, then specified strengths, weaknesses, and suggestions for improvement for teachers with low ratings. Finally, they made recommendations for reemployment or tenure either "without reservation," "with reservation," or "would not recommend."

This Mill City evaluation instrument was considerably more structured than the open-ended form used by Vista evaluators, which included no fixed categories for assessment, although some were offered for reference in the evaluation handbook (e.g., "maintaining classroom control," "pupil behavior," and "program articulation"). The form simply provided blank space for the evaluator to present and discuss his or her "recommendations and commendations."

In order for principals to transfer or terminate teachers successfully, they had to comply with these procedures and write evaluations that would be defensible in the grievance and arbitration hearings that might follow. The standards for such evaluations were, for the most part, not prescribed by contract, but had been established over time by other principals' successes or failures in convincing a school board, arbitrator, or judge.

Such evaluations had to include specific evidence observed and recorded by the principal; they could not be based on hearsay.

There was disagreement among administrators about whether the evaluation procedures were unreasonably burdensome. The president of the Metropolis principals' association believed they were:

> Given the fireman nature of school administration and the thin administrative control that exists in schools because of the small number of administrators, the principal is not in a position to follow through effectively with all the procedural requirements of the contract. To do so would require full-time devotion to collective bargaining. This would mean avoiding other burdens that the principal has.[23]

A subdistrict superintendent disagreed:

> The due process is extremely simple if people will follow the steps. For unsatisfactory ratings, it is cut and dried. The first is that the teacher be observed and that there be a conference held without a write-up and without Federation representation. At that time, it's necessary to indicate clearly the steps that the teacher should take for improvement. No documentation is needed at that step. Once any documentation is introduced, then the teacher must be permitted to have representation. This must be done early, before Christmas. If it is clear that the teacher is failing, then there should be follow-up observations in January, February, March, and April, giving the teacher sufficient time between each one to improve. Following each observation, the teacher must be issued a written evaluation within five days of the observation. This five-day limit is the only contractual requirement that principals have. At the follow-up conferences, the principal must set out the needs of the teacher and enumerate the helps that are to be provided to remediate the problems.[24]

Some principals reported that they found the evaluation process so demanding that they avoided formal attempts to transfer or terminate staff. A Metropolis elementary principal expressed such a view: "You can get rid of the undesirables but it is a very difficult process. It is so difficult that it tends to make us not want to go through it as much as we might or should."[25]

There were many principals, though, who argued that the procedural protections were both warranted and workable. They had successfully transferred or terminated teachers for poor performance and were adamant that the procedures and standards, while time consuming and exacting, could be mastered. Some expressed disdain for their colleagues who failed to take action on problem teachers. A middle school principal in Metropolis observed that principals "frequently use the Federation contract as a cop-out for being responsible. For example, if there are teachers who are to be rated unsatisfactory, they may conclude that it's not worth the fighting and they may tell parents that they are powerless when they are not really powerless."[26]

Such differing responses from principals illustrate the obvious fact that administrators, like teachers, vary in style and competence. Some principals welcomed the right to assess teachers' work, while others preferred to confine their attention to the budget, curriculum development, or building maintenance. Some principals viewed the negotiated procedures as useful road maps; others considered them annoying red tape. Some principals readily mastered the deadlines and details for observing and evaluating staff, while others reported being overwhelmed by their complexity.

Discipline Hearings and the Union's Defense / If a principal writes a negative evaluation, assigns an unsatisfactory rating, or recommends a teacher's transfer or dismissal, that teacher may file a grievance. Such grievances may lead to a series of formal hearings with school department officials, school boards, and, ultimately, arbitrators. Termination cases may end with formal court proceedings. Typically, as the appeal moves up the steps of the grievance procedure, the hearings become more formal and more adversarial. Sessions with the school board or an arbitrator may resemble courtroom hearings with lawyers, witnesses, crossexamination, a transcribed record of the proceedings, legal briefs, and a delayed decision. Only Shady Heights and Metropolis reported holding such formal hearings to resolve disputes over evaluations and ratings, but principals in all sample districts who sought to dismiss teachers could expect to be crossexamined in legal, contentious proceedings. Recognizing this, some principals were more careful and thorough in documenting teachers' weaknesses, while others became wary, cynical, and resigned to endure teacher incompetence.

In disciplinary cases, the burden of proof rests with the administration. One Vista teacher characterized the union's attitude: "We'll support the teachers and you prove that they're weak."[27] The seriousness of dismissal deliberations was believed to warrant such protections, and it was generally agreed by both labor and management that substantial documentation was necessary before any dismissal efforts could be undertaken. Principals regularly reported that two years of groundwork were necessary to prepare a successful case. During this time, the teacher had been given the opportunity to succeed or fail with at least two groups of students, had been observed a number of times, and had received remedial attention from the administration or fellow teachers. If the teacher's performance had not improved and there was convincing evidence of failure or malpractice, the district might move for dismissal.

There was great uncertainty among the administrators of this study about how much evidence was necessary to make a good case for transfer or dismissal. Several principals reported instances where seemingly strong cases were not judged to be strong enough by the district officials. For example, this Shady Heights principal reported:

> I made a move to dismiss a teacher two years ago. I had compiled a record—a real book about one inch thick. It included anecdotes, letters of complaint from teachers, specific evaluations—all the kinds of information that were necessary, including a recommendation that the individual not be rehired. However, when I submitted that, the decision was made that we couldn't win with this kind of document, that there wasn't enough information to make a solid case. They made the judgment somewhere along the line we would lose. I found out later that the same recommendation had been made by a previous principal who compiled a similar document and had received a similar answer.[28]

Although a number of principals expressed concern that poorly substantiated cases would fail, district administrators and union officers reported that the union's most effective defense strategy was in challenging the procedural correctness of the administration's case. Unsatisfactory teacher ratings were regularly upheld by arbitrators and hearing officers on substantive grounds, but were often dismissed for procedural irregularities.[29] If a Shady Heights teacher was not given twenty-four hours' notice before being observed for competence in a subject area, if a Mill City principal did not confer with the teacher following the observation, if a Metropolis evaluator failed to produce a written report of the observation within five days, the rating might be discounted, however deserved it might have been.

The unions had been quite successful in defending their membership in most districts of this study. This was particularly true in Shady Heights and Metropolis, where respondents often said that an imbalance existed between the strength of the administration's prosecution and that of the union's defense. A few principals complained about the union's role in disciplinary hearings, but most acknowledged that it was necessary. A Mill City principal who had dismissed two nontenured teachers explained: "They had the right to go to the Association for support—sure they did. And also if I didn't do my homework, then I would have been in trouble. Eliminating poor teachers is possible and the vehicle necessary to do the job is there in the contract."[30] Most principals simply wished that the administration could be more successful in building and presenting its case. But, overall, the school administrators were untrained and unpracticed in documenting teachers' failures, and most did not regard that work as rewarding.[31] By contrast, union leaders saw the task of defending teachers in adversarial proceedings as central to their jobs. They were, for the most part, well prepared and determined, if not eager. One Metropolis principal observed, "The administration is always a step behind the Federation."[32]

Many teachers in this study argued that their union was too diligent in defending incompetent teachers. They believed that the union should decide who deserved support and who did not and that it should confront teachers with their responsibilities and shortcomings. A Shady Heights pricipal recalled that in earlier days the union could and did behave that way. At that time, he had taken steps to dismiss three teachers, one of whom was asked by a union leader if he considered himself to be a good teacher: "'Can you teach?' they said to him, and he said, 'No.' Well, then the union told him that he was not worthy of their support. But you can't rely on the union to do that anymore because, by law, they must represent the teachers."[33]

Teachers were widely unaware of the union's legal obligation to defend all members of the bargaining unit. For example, one teacher who served as a department head in Metropolis said, "I see incompetent teachers being protected. I believe that it's about time for the administration to move on these people. I think if the administration had documented information about a teacher's poor performance, then the union should push to terminate that person."[34] While many teachers argued that their union should accede when the administration had a strong case, union leaders recognized that they might be sued for failing to fairly represent their staff.

Recently, the union's duty of fair representation has gained recognition in education. The doctrine, which originated with U.S. Supreme Court decisions about railroad unions' discrimination against black workers,[35] requires that the union must "act for and not against those whom it represents." In a 1975 state court case having direct bearing on the practices of one sample district, the teachers' union was found at fault for failing to fairly represent the interests of all members of the bargaining unit in a promotional dispute. The court said that the union had a statutory duty as the exclusive bargaining agent "to fairly and adequately represent the interests of all of those for whom it negotiates and contracts." It further ruled that if a union "decides to pursue a grievance, it must not do so in a perfunctory manner."[36] This case dealt with an issue of promotion, but the principle of fair representation was interpreted by lawyers, union officers, and district administrators to apply with equal force to cases of performance. In all districts but Northwood and Mill City, union leaders spoke about their obligation to defend forcefully any teacher whose position was threatened, however weak that teacher's case might be.

There are as yet no clear standards for what constitutes fair representation. One Metropolis district administrator contended that the union there went far beyond what was necessary to protect itself from suit: "The Federation argues for an additional chance for the teacher whenever it's possible." He further argued that the union should be more actively concerned about the caliber of teachers it defended: "The Federation claims that they want to enhance the teaching profession. I believe that if they can identify a teacher who abuses the teaching profession, then there ought to be a kind of understanding between the administration and the Federation that the teacher deserves only minimal defense."[37] Most union leaders, however, were adamant that they should not "police their own." One Vista building representative expressed this view: "I can only ask the question, 'Did I hire that teacher?' And the answer is 'no.' I don't have the authority to hire someone and I can't tell them who to fire."[38]

Despite this stance, several instances were reported in even the strong union districts where union representatives and staff members quietly supported administrative efforts to discipline a teacher. For example, one Mill City principal asked a union leader to observe a teacher's problems with classroom management. When the principal subsequently recommended that the teacher be transferred, he met no resistance from the union.[39] In Metropolis, where the union had a reputation for vigorously defending even the most incompetent teacher, one principal reported, "Even the union doesn't want to have incompetent teachers. [The union staffer] makes that clear. He will represent a teacher who has been written up but he doesn't do a lot to defend them if be believes that they're doing wrong."[40] Another Metropolis principal reported holding a disciplinary conference with a teacher and a union staff member. The principal explained his expectations to the teacher, who turned to the union leader with complaints. The union leader responded, "He's simply asking you to do your job."[41]

It would be impossible to say how common such cooperation between the union and the administration was, but it seems likely that it occurred less frequently in districts such as Shady Heights and Metropolis, where union leaders were more apprehensive about their legal obligations. Probably union representatives in all districts were more inclined to cooperate with administrators at the school level, where meetings remained informal and there were hopes of improving a teacher's performance, than at the district level, where proceedings became more public and union leaders had to be intent both on persuading the membership of their effectiveness and on protecting themselves from court action.

Other Factors Affecting Outcomes of Discipline Cases / Due process and savvy union defense are the two most frequently cited factors interfering with administrative efforts to discipline teachers. Both, of course, are the result of collective bargaining. This study revealed that there are other, less publicized, factors not directly related to collective bargaining that substantially affect the outcomes. These include prior administrative decisions to grant tenure, the school department's historic preference for transfers over terminations, the difficulties of enlisting district office or school board support for dismissals, and the intervention of other governmental authorities in dismissal cases.

First, many principals reported that their efforts to eliminate staff where hindered by prior administrative decisions made by their colleagues or superiors. Some blamed other principals for initially granting tenure to teachers who never deserved it. One Mill City principal charged, "This simply results because someone didn't have enough guts to say no in the beginning, when the teacher was being considered for a continuing contract. Tenure was a problem before collective bargaining."[42] Another Mill City principal agreed, "It all goes back to the years when the teacher was being evaluated, when hard decisions were not being made, when, quite frankly, some administrator didn't have the guts to do what was right."[43]

District administrators were likewise blamed for preferring to transfer teachers rather than terminate them. While such transfers were supposedly intended to provide teachers with a fair chance at success, they were said by many simply to shuffle the problems through the district and to complicate subsequent discipline efforts. A novice teacher transferred to a school having a lazy or indulgent principal might be granted tenure by virtue of elapsed time rather than improved performance. Furthermore, repeated transfers of problem teachers potentially interfered with systematic dismissal efforts. For example, state laws regulating dismissals in Metropolis required that a teacher receive unsatisfactory ratings for two consecutive years before being terminated. A subdistrict superintendent there explained that teachers were usually reassigned after their first unsatisfactory rating to one of five schools they requested. Since such teachers were unlikely to choose any school with a principal who supervised performance closely, they would probably not receive a second unsatisfactory rating. This administrator concluded with discouragement: "Ninety-five percent of the problems fall through the cracks."[44]

Third, a number of principals charged that even when they prepared strong cases against incompetent teachers, there was no assurance that the district administrators and school board would agree to pursue them. Often school officials were said to sidestep terminations and choose less extreme actions. Some of those interviewed suggested that patronage politics plays a role in such decisions; others attributed the inaction to cowardice. The failure of district administrators to follow through on dismissals was reported in several sample districts, but Metropolis again provided the extreme example. Of some 13,000 Metropolis teachers, approximately thirty were rated unsatisfactory each year; six were recommended by the associate superintendent for dismissal, and two were actually terminated.[45] In several cases, dismissal efforts had reportedly been quashed or reversed "at high levels of the school district." Such reversals, which were said to be politically motivated, were never reviewed or fully explained.[46]

Finally, some teachers dismissed by the districts were reinstated by other governmental authorities. Several district administrators reported that the courts, to which teachers might appeal their terminations, were requiring ever-increasing proof of incompetence. A Shady Heights principal complained of the

> interpretations that are coming from the [State] Commissioner's office that are extremely rigid and require extensive documentation of personnel before a dismissal is possible. You know, we have

a saying around here that if you want to get rid of a teacher, you'd better catch that teacher raping the mayor's daughter on city hall steps at high noon.[47]

A Metropolis district administrator said that state courts "take a very jaundiced view of teacher terminations."[48] Moreover, teachers in Metropolis had access to three routes of appeal: arbitration, the courts, and the superintendent of education in the state. One such decision was appealed for six years before it was finally decided in favor of the school district.[49]

In each of these cases, it was neither the procedural demands of the contract nor the defense provided by the union that protected incompetent teachers. Instead, their continued employment was ensured by school and district administrators' reluctance to terminate staff and other institutions' unfavorable reviews of dismissal decisions. One Metropolis subdistrict superintendent was asked to consider how much collective bargaining was responsible for the persistence of incompetent teachers in the schools. She replied: "Was it ever any easier? Were there ever any more employees dismissed before collective bargaining? That's important. I think there weren't."[50]

The Varied Responses of Principals

Principals responded in different ways to the opportunities, obstacles, hazards, and uncertainties of dismissing staff. Many presevered according to the rules, conducting repeated observations, assigning unsatisfactory ratings, and recommending dismissals. One Metropolis principal who had assigned unsatisfactory ratings to five teachers reported, "None [of these ratings] fell through, but they were accompanied by tremendous aggravation and were enormously time consuming."[51] A Shady Heights principal who had documented the poor performance of a teacher but could not convince the district office to press for dismissal observed with satisfaction, "I'd like to tell you though, finally that teacher is no longer with us. He finally got tired of me being after him, and I continued to be critical of him in writing.

I'm convinced that this is the only way to get rid of incompetent teachers."[52]

Some principals who found the formal procedures too confining or who doubted that the school department would back them relied on informal tactics to remove poor teachers from their schools. Instead of moving systematically from observations to evaluations to grievance proceedings and ultimately to school board or court hearings, such principals would "lean on" poor teachers to leave. A Mill City principal confronted a novice teacher:

> It was her first year but it was going horribly and at the end of the first semester I called her in. I said that effective immediately I would ask that she be removed from the classroom. I had called supervisors in to try to help her with her work. I said that there were two ways she might respond to this—one would be to resign and consequently not leave a bad record behind her. Secondly, she could fight me on it. But I told her, "You must understand, I am not going to have you back in the building." The next morning she came in and said that she would resign.[53]

Similarly, a Plantville principal informally pressured a veteran teacher out of his school. Parents and colleagues had complained about this teacher's classroom behavior, claiming that he had emotional problems. The principal had written two letters to the school department about the teacher's performance, but thought that there was insufficient evidence to pursue dismissal. Therefore, he recommended "quite emphatically" that the teacher take a year of leave without pay to consider whether he should continue teaching. The teacher agreed not to challenge the principal's judgment.[54]

Such informal maneuvers were sometimes said to be the only ones that worked given the complexity of due process, the aggressiveness of the union, and district administrators' lack of follow-through. However, informal strategies were by no means surefire. Their effectiveness depended on the personal power of the principal, the degree to which a teacher could be persuaded or intimidated, and the reluctance of union representatives to become involved in cases of alleged harassment. Moreover, while informal approaches may have sometimes served the interests of students, they also may have abridged the due-process rights of teachers.

Some principals settled for teacher transfers. A principal who tries to dismiss a teacher does so on behalf of the entire district in the belief that no student in any school should be subjected to an incompetent teacher. Sometimes, however, when principals were convinced that dismissals were unattainable, they would confine their efforts to improving the quality of teaching in their own schools. One such Metropolis principal spoke of "trying to get rid of three a year."[55] Such principals were active and determined to eliminate poor teachers, but their sights were narrowed. As a consequence of their successes, incompetent teachers were said to collect in schools headed by principals with less resolve.

Finally, of course, there were a few principals whose response was to avoid, avoid. They observed few, if any, classes and routinely rated teachers as satisfactory. They rationalized their inability to eliminate poor teachers by blaming the contract, the union, the courts, or society.

Teachers' Attitudes toward the Tolerance of Incompetence

The unions' pursuit of strong job protections and their forceful defense of teachers whose competence is challenged might suggest that teachers as a group think jobs should be protected at all costs. However, teachers in this study carefully differentiated their views from what they believed were standard union positions. They stressed that the number of inferior teachers was small, and often exaggerated by those outside the schools, but insisted that the continued presence of even a few incompetent colleagues should not be tolerated. Because their work is quite interdependent, teachers found the presence of an incompetent colleague to be quite troublesome. This Plantville teacher echoed the concerns of others:

> This creates dissatisfaction if you're teaching next door to one of these people because they have undisciplined classes. Or if you're

at the second level of a course that they have taught at the first level and you continually meet children who are not prepared for your course, then that makes you angry.[56]

The presence of incompetent teachers was also said to be demoralizing. As one Shady Heights principal observed, "Teachers think, 'Why should I knock my head against the wall when he's not even doing his job?'"[57]

Teachers were not optimistic that incompetent teachers would be removed from their ranks, but they argued that principals should persist in evaluating staff and setting high standards for teacher performance in the schools. Not only was this believed to affect, however minimally, the work of poor teachers, it was also said to improve morale among those who were doing their jobs. Several schools provide interesting examples.

One Vista principal denied that there were incompetent teachers in his school, but said that the performance of two who had tenure concerned him: "One constantly sits on the fence, and the other can't see that the times are changing." He did not intend to initiate any formal action, but said, "I constantly have to be aware of what they're doing. I think I have been able to make them perform at least at an average level."[58] Teachers in the school, however, said that little was being done about the teachers' poor performance. One reported, "I haven't seen any efforts to do anything about it. The administration's hands may be tied." Another said, "The philosophy seems to be to live it out, to not make waves." A third said, "No one's leaned on in this building to improve performance. These teachers have been given good suggestions [by other staff] about what they might do, but they don't really believe that they're below the level of performance that is expected of them." Yet another teacher concluded, "Zero is being done about their performance administratively."[59]

There were six schools in this study where the pricipals reported being powerless to deal with incompetent teachers but where the staff contended that the administration could and should have been doing more. Teachers were mildly critical or even openly contemptuous of principals who acted helpless. A

Mill City teacher said, "There is a lack of leadership by the administration, a lack of commitment to confront people with their failures."[60] A Shady Heights teacher said, "They have been permitted to be relaxed about their work. Nobody says to them 'Hey look, it's time to get to work!'"[61]

But there were also schools where principals actively pursued incompetent teachers. In one large Shady Heights secondary school, teachers estimated that three to five teachers were incompetent. There was broad agreement among the teachers interviewed that the principal actively confronted the problem despite the constraints of due process, the union, and district office priorities. One said, "I would say that the principal is doing his damnedest to terminate two incompetent teachers' service, but I think he's being overruled at a high level in the school department. It's not clear why." Another said, "The principal is on some of the teachers' backs for better performance. You know, they'll talk in the office or he'll visit the classes regularly. He really does make an effort to get them to change, and other teachers appreciate this." A third teacher described the principal's effort to deal with "two notorious cases": "The heat is on them from Mr. ———. They were told, 'Report to the office with your plan book. Report with your grade book.' As a result, others who might slack off are more aware of their responsibilities."[62]

The teachers of this study did not sanction incompetence among their peers, but they often did not know how to do anything constructive about it. Strong norms of equity among teachers discouraged individuals from confronting poor peers. Instead, staff looked to their principals to set high standards for teachers' performance and to insist that they be met. The experiences of the sample schools show that principals can effectively exert pressure on poor teachers, whatever the strength of the contract or the union may be, and that if their administrative actions are deserved, the principals will receive at least the implicit support of their staff.

Conclusion

Reports from the sample districts indicate that many teachers and administrators accept the popular view that unions are responsible for the continued employment of poor teachers. However, investigations in each district revealed that the problem is complicated and has several sources. The data confirmed that due-process guarantees and union defenses make it more difficult for districts to dismiss teachers; success is unlikely without careful documentation, attention to procedural requirements, and perseverance. Yet there are other factors, stemming largely from the reluctance of district administrators to terminate employees, that contribute to teachers' very high rates of retention. The process of dismissal usually requires sustained commitment and coordination by several administrators in the district. If they falter, everyone may blame the contract for requiring too much or the union for defending too well, but that blame is probably only partially correct.

The reports from the schools also demonstrate that principals who are intent on improving staff performance are not powerless. If such principals have district office support, they may initiate actions to terminate teachers. If that support is not forthcoming, they can follow procedures to transfer poor teachers and upgrade the quality of staff within their own schools. If even transfers are unlikely, they can observe regularly and insist on high performance, thus prodding unsatisfactory teachers and encouraging others.

Chapter 6

Accommodation in the Schools

This research provided two views of collective bargaining—a view from above that enabled me to compare the labor practices of six districts, and a view from below that allowed me to compare the labor practices of schools within those districts.

Each of these perspectives made it apparent that collective bargaining does not come packaged with a standard set of outcomes. There are big differences from district to district in how union leaders and district administrators behave, in what they negotiate, and in how they translate contract language into practice. Labor relations in the Vista schools were overall more cooperative and less rule-bound than labor relations in the Metropolis schools, for the Vista contract placed fewer restrictions on school administrators and guaranteed fewer rights for teachers; its union was less aggressive and less successful in enforcing the contract.

The view from below revealed a different and notably less predictable sort of variation—the variation in labor relations practices among schools within the same district. There were sample schools where the contract was very prominent and there were schools within the same district where principals and teachers did not mention it. There were schools where the contract was rigorously enforced and schools where teachers knowingly bent it for the good of the school. There were schools with many grievances and schools with none. There were schools where a number of teachers did little more than the contract required and schools where most teachers went well beyond its minimal requirements. There were schools where labor relations were hostile and schools were labor relations were cordial.

It is reasonable to attribute district-wide differences in labor practices like those noted above in Vista and Metropolis to district-level variables such as union strength, union leadership, district office style, and contract language. It is much less apparent how to explain the variation in labor practices found among schools within the same district. That is the subject of this chapter.

Varied Outcomes in the Schools

In some cases, an examination of the labor relations practices of two schools within a district revealed dramatic differences in administrative style, union assertiveness, contract prominence, and the level of teacher services. The following brief descriptions of two Metropolis high schools highlight such differences.

Metropolis High School No. 1 / The labor relationship in this high school was adversarial, with the principal and the union building representative engaged in open, hostile conflict.[1] The principal reported that there was a union emphasis on being able to say, "I caught you"; the building representative called labor-management relations "abominable." Teachers said that the principal deliberately forced grievances; the union had filed five grievances about school site practices within a year. Although teachers did not fully support the building representative, they did insist that the contract be closely policed, and they very rarely bent its provisions to meet the needs of the school. For example, teachers assumed no supervisory responsibilities since their contract required none.

The principal, who characterized his administrative style as "democratic, with blends of dictatorial," reported that he found the meet-and-discuss requirements of the contract burdensome; teachers charged him with being "aloof, brusque, and arbitrary." One teacher stated, "He manages the building inefficiently and arbitrarily, making almost all decisions himself, from placing personnel to setting the bell schedule." Teachers reported that colleagues pressured them not to volunteer for extra duties or activities because of the principal's authoritarian stance toward them. One explained, "The idea is, 'don't give it to him.'" Teachers expressed strong dissatisfaction with the overall organization of the school and blamed the administration for problems of discipline and disorder. For example, when a teacher was stabbed by an intruder several staff members thought the principal might have done more to make the building secure. The principal responded that such problems should be "collective concerns." Relationships between teachers and the principal were typified by distance, distrust, and blame.

Metropolis High School No. 2 / The union organization in another Metropolis high school was quite strong, but the labor relationship in the school was exceptionally cooperative.[2] The principal, said to be "firm and decisive" and to "go by the book with the contract," actively pursued a close working relationship with the building representative and building committee. He said: "The building committee becomes a resource that I can call on for assistance in administering the school. . . . Their involvement in this committee leads to their acceptance of responsibility for the school. . . . The faculty here have a commitment to this school. We have an understanding that this is *our* school, and not *my* school, or *his* school." Teachers approved of this cooperative venture, the building representative explained: "The building committee serves as an advisory committee for Mr. ——— and he serves as a consultant for the advisory committee." One teacher reported, "Here the principal and faculty get along. I have seen schools were the relationship is hateful."

Teachers also reported being very satisfied with school discipline, order, and security. The principal was said to be visible: "He's in the hallways. He's checking the bathrooms. He's observing what's going on in the school. He's not sitting in his office, and the teachers know that he knows what's happening." One teacher said, "He's a strong principal and an extremely good disciplinarian. He is completely supportive of the faculty and staff, and he runs a very tight ship." Another said, "This guy means business."

The contract, while respected and adhered to by the administration, was occasionally bent for the good of the school. The principal said, "Teachers in this school don't make an issue of class size unless they're really choked." In order to maintain advanced math and language courses which had small enrollments, teachers agreed to teach combinations of small and large classes, thus complying with the class size averages but not with individual classroom limits. One teacher explained, "We have to give and take." No teachers reported pressure to refrain from volunteer activities and there were reports that such participation was common. As the building representative explained, "Teachers feel part of it here."

The role of the contract and the relationship between the principal and teachers differed in these two schools. Teachers in the Metropolis High No. 1 were considerably less flexible in responding to school needs, teacher-administrator relationships were more formalized, and practices were more rule-bound than in Metropolis High No. 2. These differences persisted even though the same local union represented these teachers and the same contract defined their working conditions.

Other intra-district differences were not always so extreme. Two elementary schools in Plantville illustrate less dramatic, but equally important variations.

Plantville Elementary School No. 1 / The principal of this elementary school was a strong advocate of teacher unionism but believed that the principal should set the standards for the school: "The teachers," he said, "will go along—contract or no contract."[3] One teacher described the principal: "He's not an anti-union principal. His father was a union man and he's proteacher, unless you mess things up. Then you'll have to answer to him. He's a strict principal. He likes a tight building." This principal had firm expectations about the performance of his staff. He required teachers to begin supervising the school at 8:20 A.M., fifteen minutes before the beginning of their contractually defined work day, and he assigned teachers to supervise the school at the end of the day. Neither was required by contract. He monitored the after-school help that teachers provided for students by requiring weekly reports of conferences held. He ran a system of staggered lunches that assured teacher supervision of the cafeteria and playground—an unusual arrangement in the district. Although the school-wide average on class size was enforced, students were grouped by ability so that classes varied considerably in size within the school, sometimes exceeding the contractual limits.

The teachers, all union members, reported being very satisfied with the school and its administration. One said, "He is extremely organized. He knows how to delegate authority. He has high expectations, but he's as supportive as he can be." There had been no transfer requests in four years, and one active union member said, "I would do anything in my power to stay in this building." However, teachers agreed that incompetent staff would not last in the school, "They wouldn't be working for Mr. —— if they didn't do the job. They'd be transferred out. He puts too much pressure on people he's dissatisfied with." Teachers expressed considerable regard for the principal's leadership and tolerant acceptance of his extra demands. One said: "The loyalty here is to him rather than to the union. If he told us to stay late, why everyone would. People help him out and he's good to others in response. I guess that's not quite kosher as far as the contract's concerned, but we do it." The contract had low prominence in the school, and the building representative reported having a good working relationship with the principal, against whom no grievances had ever been filed. A teacher explained, "Because there is this personal relationship between the principal and the teachers, things do not get grieved here that would be grieved in another building. Those kind of things would be considered nitpicking here."

Plantville Elementary School No. 2 / The principal of this elementary school was also a strong union supporter, but he assumed a laissez-faire stance toward the teachers, the school, and the union.[4] One teacher said, "He's extremely casual and unauthoritarian. He lets us do our own thing. He's totally permissive. He makes absolutely no demands on us." Another said, "He likes to kick issues under the rug and hopes that they'll go away." The principal was reluctant to monitor the arrival and departure times of teachers, commenting, "I don't like to be a police officer. They say I'm too easy on them." The staff expressed concern about two teachers who were not doing their jobs: "They're never made to toe the line by the principal."

The teachers, all union members, were not active in the union, and the building committee did not function. The issues that concerned teachers in the school—lack of administrative direction, late deliveries of supplies, lack of staff influence over school policies, and tolerance of incompetent teachers—were not preceived to be union issues. As one teacher said, "You simply can't file a grievance about not getting your crayons on time."

Teachers had organized lavatory and recess supervision on their own but believed that the building also should have been supervised before school. Some teachers initiated extracurricular activities, and the principal reportedly neither opposed nor supported such efforts. One staff member said, "The teachers in this building would like more consistent direction, but don't get me wrong, we don't want to manage the building. We want to be able to teach." As one teacher said, "There's no serious contention in this building. . . . It's more an issue of omission than one of commission."

Labor relations did not differ dramatically at these two Plantville schools as they did at the Metropolis schools described earlier. For instance, in these two Plantville schools, grievances were rare and the principal and building representative were said to cooperate. Yet there were important differences in administrative leadership, the role of the contract, and teacher services. Both Plantville principals respected the contract, but the first asked teachers to go beyond it for the good of the school; they complied. The second principal pursued a cautious course, asking no more of teachers than they were obliged to give. Teachers approved of the first principal's direction, but expressed dissatisfaction with the second principal's lack of leadership, however contractually correct it might be.

As these examples from Metropolis and Plantville suggest, differences in principals' administrative styles appeared to be central in determining the character of the school site labor relationship, the prominence of the contract, and the level of teacher services at the school site. One might legitimately question what other factors influence these outcomes—for example, the level and location of the school, history of building labor relations, style of the building representative, or prevailing union sentiments of staff. Overall, with the occasional exception of staff or building representative attitudes, these factors did not seem to carry great weight. For example, labor relations were generally more tranquil at the elementary than at the secondary level, but there were schools where that pattern was reversed. Teacher morale in schools serving middle-income students might have been expected to be higher than in schools serving very poor students, but there were schools of both kinds with satisfied and with dissatisfied staff.

Although such variables were not controlled in this study, two schools presented the opportunity to consider the variables' importance when the principalship changed, and other factors such as location, union strength of the staff, and the economic level of students remained constant. A brief account of what happened in each of these schools will illustrate the apparent importance of the principal.

Vista High School / Under a previous administrator, Vista High School had floundered; labor relations were strained.[5] One teacher described the problem:

> [The previous principal] was authoritarian, but he was never in control of the faculty or the students. We were afraid of him. He was shouting and slamming all the time. The association and the principal were in constant battle. Department meetings with him were very difficult. Nobody could really figure out what he wanted. . . . We didn't have control of anything. Students would leave the campus; they wouldn't be in classes. It was general confusion.

Ten grievances were filed in one year against this principal. One teacher describing the labor relationship said, "It was war."

By contrast, this principal's replacement was characterized as taking "a problem solving approach to things." One teacher said, "He's very innovative and doesn't come to the teachers with a decision but with a problem. And he gets things done." Another teacher said, "The principal makes decisions that have to be made. He's strong, and there's a good feeling about him." The principal was said to be very active and visible in the school. Student absenteeism, which had been the highest of any high school in the state, declined dramatically. Teaching performance was observed and evaluated. One staff member said that more teacher evaluations had been done by Christmas "than five administrators had done in five years." Morale among teachers was reportedly very high. Under the new administration, the building representative, who had initiated grievances the previous year, assumed broad administrative responsibilities for student attendance. A teacher said that the labor relationship changed from being "below average and poor" to "above average and good." No new grievances were filed, and teachers reported voluntarily accepting various supervisory responsibilities for the good of the school.

Shady Heights High School / A new principal, described by teachers as "very professional" and "authoritarian" replaced another who they agreed had been a failure.[6] One teacher characterized the former principal's shortcomings:

> The previous principal was an inconsistent disciplinarian. He was particularly concerned about what couldn't be done. He had a "hands tied" mentality. He had a buddy approach to dealing with the faculty. . . . He ruled by granting favors. He did things like eliminate the sign-in/sign-out sheet for teachers. He disciplined infrequently and indiscriminately both students and teachers. There were a lot of problems in the building; students were late in class; there was a lot of noise in the corridors; students would come to class unprepared to learn.

When the new principal arrived, teachers were impressed by his purposefulness and were inclined to support him. One teacher said, "People took him very seriously. He met minimal resistance from the faculty. They were dying to have someone come in and do what he did." He quickly reinstated checks on teachers' performance. Staff members were required to sign in and out and received letters of reprimand if they were late more than three times. Teachers were required to be in their homerooms when the bell sounded, to stand in the corridors between classes, and to formally supervise the halls before, during, and after school. The principal expected them to go beyond the requirements of the contract. His demands were not grieved even though this was a school with a strong union organization, and the principal was thought by some to be anti-union. As one teacher said, "He hates the union, but he knows how to work with people. He's very sharp and he's always prepared. . . . He doesn't break the contract, nor does he make the ridiculous demands that principals do in some other schools."

Teachers reported that the changes had restored order to the school; virtually everyone believed the reforms had been productive. One teacher said: "The morale and performance of teachers have gone up since he has been principal. People no longer take days off, just to take days off. People have accepted the new rules for the sake of the building." Another teacher summarized her satisfaction, "You have to do the classroom job because now the conditions are good and the school is running well."

These two examples underscore what the others have suggested—that the levels of teacher service, the enforcement of the contract, and the quality of labor relations are subject to considerable influence by the principal.[7] Teachers in some schools assumed extra supervisory responsibilities, used preparation periods for in-service training, attended extra meetings, reallocated student assignments within the school, and volunteered for extra activities. Teachers in other schools cut corners on the workday, refused noninstructional duties not included in the contract, and insisted on literal enforcement of teacher observation procedures. There was, of course, variation between these extremes.

The School Organization and Unionism

While the popular view may be that teacher unions closely monitor the implementation of their contracts and force principals to standardize practices in conformity with negotiated provisions, this study does not confirm that view. The principals' formal authority had been constrained by the collective bargaining agreements, but the power that principals exercised varied greatly from school to school. As we saw in Chapter 3, the contract provisions were found to be differentially implemented; some were closely enforced and some were not. The exact content of contract language was not a reliable indicator of school-level practices.

What, then, accounted for this variation? What enabled principals to exercise extensive powers despite their contractual restrictions? What permitted the contract to be variously enforced, ignored, abridged, bent, and violated? What is it about schools, teachers, and principals that produced these differerences? Three characteristics of the school as an organization seem particularly important in explaining these varied outcomes. These include the interdependence of teachers and administrators, the breadth of teacher concerns that extended well beyond the contract, and teacher ambivalence about unions. Each of these will be explored below.

Interdependence / Even before the advent of collective bargaining, the relationship between teachers and principals was highly interdependent.[8] The success of each depended, in part, on the cooperation of the other. Teachers could not be effective in their classrooms without fair and balanced class assignments, while principals could ensure order in the school only if teachers upheld administrative rules and policies. Principals could not supervise all the activities in the school and, instead, granted teachers considerable discretion in their work. In return, teachers often offered their allegiance.[9]

While it is probably true that principals once could wield considerably more power than they can now, that power was never really absolute, largely because of the decentralized character of schooling. Classrooms are cellular; teachers are the street-level bureaucrats; and principals simply cannot closely inspect the work of their staff.[10] Teachers have always successfully reserved certain important powers for themselves. The principals may have ordered the books, but the teachers taught the lessons—they decided how to use those books. The principals may have taken attendance at faculty meetings, but teachers decided whether to listen or participate. Covert insurrection was always a teacher's option in responding to the powers of the principal. Moreover, whatever the principal's powers, he or she could not run the school alone.[11] Even before collective bargaining, principals had to be attentive to teacher interests if they were to command teacher loyalty. The principal and teachers—like the family to which they are often compared—informally negotiated ways of working together that served their mutual interests. To be sure, some of those families were repressive, some of the principals dictatorial, and some of the teachers cowed. But in general, norms of teacher-administrator reciprocity took precedence over rules and definitions of responsibilities.[12]

Collective bargaining, teacher unions, and contracts have been introduced at the school site into the context of this interdependence. One Shady Heights principal explained how he relied on reciprocal relationships with teachers to manage his school:

> I want safety first. I don't want kids hurt and I don't want their clothes torn. Then secondly, I want teaching going on all the time. Teachers like that. They like to be able to use their time to teach. They like me to support them in that. And when they're teaching all the time and making me happy, then they know that if they need something I'll help them out. If they have to leave for a special medical appointment then I'll go in and take their class.[13]

Teachers in this study relied on their principals for many things that made successful teaching possible—a balanced roster, a manageable selection of students, adequate texts and supplies, and the maintenance of order in the school. And principals, who face expanded responsibilities with declining resources, were increasingly dependent on the professional commitment and good will of teachers to make their schools work.

What Teachers Want: / While it may be appropriate to speak of *union* priorities when considering district-level labor issues, it is necessary to speak of *teacher* priorities at the school site. In this setting, union affiliation is but one of the teacher's concerns. The relationship between teachers and principals extends well beyond the relationship of labor and management, and in order to comprehend the complexity of that relationship, it is necessary to consider the breadth of teacher concerns.

Teachers were asked through a variety of interview questions about what they needed and wanted in their work.[14] Eleven concerns emerged repeatedly. Because of the method by which the data were gathered, it is not possible to rank order these responses; however, there was remarkable consensus about the importance of each of these items to most teachers.

First, teachers sought *salaries* that enabled them to live comfortably. While some were satisfied with their wages, others bitterly compared themselves to unskilled laborers who earned more. Those with families to support often complained about the need to have a second job. One Vista teacher estimated that 20 percent of the teachers in his school held extra jobs during the school year. He said that this resulted from teachers being "mostly middle-class people who expect to live at that level." He reported that the maximum family income level necessary to qualify for a rent subsidy exceeded the beginning teacher's salary in Vista.[15] It is in the pursuit of higher wages that the large majority of teachers said they supported unions.

Second, teachers wanted the *job security* they believed that they were due for accepting positions of public service. They wished not only to retain jobs, but also to retain positions in particular schools, grades, and classrooms. Teachers who reported that they would file grievances only under extreme conditions often said that the threat of job loss would provide sufficient reason. For example, one Plantville teacher said, "I really can't think of anything, not even class size, that would make me initiate a grievance. I suppose if it meant my job, I'd do it. Yes, I'd definitely grieve that. I'd even go so far as to get myself a lawyer."[16] A Mill City teacher said that she would grieve a transfer "out of turn" into a situation she did not like. "I like it here. I like my room. I like my work."[17]

A third, and sometimes related, concern for teachers was that they be assigned a *reasonable number of students and a reasonable number of classes*. Many teachers believed that the size of their teaching load—in both number of students and number of classes—determined the possibility of success in their work. Teachers in this study overwhelmingly believed that they could be more effective teaching groups of twenty-five to thirty students than they could be with larger classes. Furthermore, because class size provisions protected jobs, they were considered doubly important in districts experiencing enrollment declines. One Mill City teacher said, "With the direction that Mill City is going, we are going to see larger class sizes and fewer teachers. And when that happens, I believe that educational goals go down the drain."[18]

A fourth priority of the teachers was the *reduction or elimination of nonteaching duties*—for example, clerical jobs, cafeteria supervision, or lavatory duty—which they regarded as a misuse of their professional time. A fifth and related concern was the teachers' desire for uninterrupted *nonteaching time* during which they could relax, eat lunch, and catch up on work. Teachers resented having this time controlled or withdrawn unexpectedly by administrators.

Sixth, teachers wanted *equitable treatment*. They resented favoritism and school politics, and they sought assurances that important decisions—such as transfers—and routine decisions—such as duty rosters—would be made in orderly, fair ways. One Mill City teacher characterized the favoritism that she believed was apparent in the practices of her principal:

> He runs things on a buddy-buddy system. There are always people in this building who have to be looking for an unfair advantage. They search for some crumb, so that they can be treated differently. . . . Teachers are treated differently—some are told that they can never leave their duty posts when they're supervising the hall while others are permitted to go into his office, put up their feet, and smoke.[19]

By contrast, teachers in the neighboring Mill City school were quite admiring of the principal's evenhandedness. One said, "He's very fair, one of the fairest men I've ever worked for."[20]

Seventh, teachers expected a modest amount of *influence over school policies and practices*, particularly those that affected their classrooms. They liked to be consulted about such things as textbook selection, budget decisions, discipline policies, and grading practices. They wanted the opportunity to initiate change. However, they did not want large-scale responsibility for school-wide matters; their attention centered on their classrooms. As the president of the Shady Heights union said, "We believe that someone has to run the school, and we're not interested in taking over the management responsibilities of the principal."[21]

Student discipline was one of teachers' most frequently mentioned concerns. They believed that order in their classrooms depended largely on the overall order of the school. Poor student attendance, fighting in the halls, and disrespect at recess were all viewed by teachers as evidence of administrative failings. Teachers wanted assurance of administrative support if they sent students to the office; some reported that their classroom success depended on students' awareness of that backing.

Security within the school was related to discipline. However, in urban schools where intruders had assaulted teachers and students, it was a larger issue, requiring more than firm discipline practices. Such incidents precipitated demands for locked entrances, assigned guards, and repaired intercoms. In one Metropolis school, where a teacher had been mugged in her classroom the day before my visit, teachers repeatedly complained about the poor security in the school.[22] In another school, the stabbing of a teacher by an outsider in 1979 had led to a faculty march on the principal's office.[23]

A tenth concern expressed by teachers in this study was about the lack of *parental support and public regard* for their work. If they could have regulated such things, teachers would have arranged for parents to emphasize the value of school with their children, to monitor homework, to endorse a teacher's expectations for good behavior, and to respect the teacher's expertise. One Mill City teacher characterized the lack of parental support as "a never-ending problem in the school. . . . There are so many kids here with no family backing."[24] Teachers were dissatisfied with their current low public esteem and believed that it affected both their classroom success and their sense of professional worth.

Finally, teachers said that they wanted to work with *effective principals*. As one Plantville teacher said, "An effective building has to be run from the top."[25] Effective principals were characterized as those who not only ensured the order, security, and maintenance of the school, but who also provided direction, leadership, and high standards for student and teacher success. These administrators, said to be neither functionaries nor paper pushers, were described as visible, active, and principled; and they expected teachers to be so as well. One Plantville teacher described the shortcomings of her principal:

> I really believe in the importance of a principal—everything you read and study seems to point to it. I think that Mr. ——— could take a more central role of leadership in the building. I think he should take more suggestions from the teachers, listen to them more closely, and act on them.[26]

A Metropolis teacher voiced concerns about her principal:

> He's scared. He is very fearful of his own position and he'll sway in whatever direction he feels most comfortable at the time. He doesn't take a leadership role in the school and is preceived by the teachers to be too wishy-washy. He doesn't plan for the entire school, or initiate programs for the good of the students. I believe he stays too close to his office and doesn't venture out enough to find out what is going on in the building—both what's good and what's bad.[27]

By contrast, this Shady Heights teacher approved of his principal:

> He's a Napoleon. He's forthright and professional. Teachers can participate as much as they choose, and they can actively influence the policies of the building. Anything that's for the betterment of the student, he's for 100 percent. But he'll also let you know if you're going down the wrong road.[28]

Some of the issues that concern teachers could be dealt with through collective bargaining; some could not. Many had been addressed in the contracts of this study, and in some cases teachers could readily enforce what had been won at the table. For example, when teachers gained the right to a duty-free lunch, they could simply refuse further cafeteria assignments. However, in other cases, teachers had to depend on administrative cooperation for the implementation of negotiated provisions; noncompliance was difficult to document or remedy. For example, teacher expectations of equity were included in contractual provisions calling for fair rosters; however, "fairness," being undefined, rested largely with the administrator. Teacher participation in school policymaking could be provided for by a contract provision establishing a building advisory committee, but the effectiveness of the committee could be subtly undercut by the principal. The standards for satisfactory student discipline were not easily defined in writing, and, while the teachers might have negotiated these issues, there was little assurance that they would achieve effective school discipline without the cooperation of a determined and respected principal.

Certain of these teacher concerns were not bargainable, including guarantees of parental support, public regard, and administrative leadership. The school department could not bargain what it could not provide. Yet, while these concerns were not negotiable and were not represented in contracts, they remained very prominent for teachers.

Teacher Views of Unionism / While unionized teachers are often portrayed as fervent and pugnacious in their pursuit of higher wages, job security, and improved working conditions, the teachers in this study were ambivalent about teacher unionism. Throughout the study, very few regarded themselves as union members who single-mindedly enforced the contract in their schools. Respondents were pleased that collective bargaining had improved their salaries, limited the size and number of their classes, and tempered administrative abuse. But they were also uneasy about its effects on their professional status, on the quality of their relationships with administrators, and on the competence and performance of their peers. Even though union membership levels were high and teachers in several districts overwhelmingly supported strikes during periods of strained negotiations, many teachers reported having strong reservations about both the notion of unionism and the conduct of their local organization.[29]

There were many teachers like this one who regretted the

necessity of collective bargaining: "I'm an idealist and I would like to believe that it would not be necessary, that these things could be settled without a formal organization, but I think that it's probably unrealistic at this time."[30] There were other teachers who firmly believed that virtually all educational gains were union accomplishments that would be swept away were it not for the continued presence and vigilance of the union. As one Vista teacher said, "Without a union, we'd be nowhere."[31] While there was overwhelming, if sometimes reluctant, agreement among teachers in all sample districts about the continued necessity of collective bargaining for teachers, few teachers reported full satisfaction with the contract or with the action of their organization.

Some teachers in each district were dissatisfied with the cost and the politics of their state or national affiliate. As one Mill City teacher said, "I feel I'm being used. I certainly feel my money is being used."[32] Many would have preferred to belong to a professional organization that confined its attention to local, narrowly educational issues.

There were teachers in each district who were dissatisfied with the adversarial relations that accompanied collective bargaining. They believed that it should be possible for teachers and administrators to work collaboratively in the interest of better schools. One Metropolis teacher said, "[The union] seems to cause a lot of problems out of poor diplomacy and a style of confrontation."[33] Another Metropolis teacher expressed concern about the combative relationship she believed unions promote:

> I think it's a common misconception that if you have a boss or a manager, then you have to do battle with that person on every issue. Historically, as a union, we have had elements of that. When a grievance had to be decided or a policy determined, we were always to loggerheads with the administration. There was not enough give and take.[34]

Some teachers repudiated the blue-collar image of unions—pickets, mobs, rigidity—which they considered inconsistent with professionalism. One teacher who described herself as "absolutely not active" joined the union out of an obligation to other teachers. She said: "I intensely dislike teachers' unions. My big fear in life is that my obituary will be headlined, 'AFL-CIO Member Dies.' I consider unions to be blue-collar, not professional organizations. I think that they have no place in education."[35] Many teachers whose families had been laborers before them were proud of their professional advancement and did not want to compromise that advancement by being identified with the union.

There were teachers who opposed specific positions taken by their local organizations. Some in Shady Heights argued that seniority-based promotions were wrong. One said, "I'm basically against promotion by seniority—the idea that the people who hang around the longest are the ones who are rewarded."[36] Several teachers in Metropolis opposed the union's pursuit of freezes on layoffs. One considered no-layoff provisions to be a waste of money. "That's not how you run a business, and education should be run as a business."[37] There were teachers in several districts who opposed strikes by bus drivers and secretaries. "If there's any excuse to strike," one man said, "then the members blindly follow."[38]

One of the most frequently voiced dissatisfactions was that unions, in meeting their obligations to fairly represent all teachers, protect poor teachers, or, as one teacher said, "the slouchers."[39] According to this view, which was expressed by both active and inactive union members, the union had so succeeded in guaranteeing due process for teachers that the school department had become incapable of terminating incompetent employees. Many expressed views like these of a Metropolis principal who had begun her career as an active member of the teachers' union:

> They no longer should have to defend the riff-raff. When they first organized, it was important for teachers to see that the Federation was strong and that they would defend people. But now they're plenty large. They could police their own instead of defending some teacher who can't teach himself out of a paper bag.[40]

Others said that the union should ensure procedural rights for teachers without fighting to save their jobs. In general, such teachers argued that public esteem for teachers was damaged by the successful defense of incompetents. Some further argued that in representing all teachers the union "encourages mediocrity. They endorse equality and the result is a leveling of all people."[41]

Some teachers objected to what they believed was the union's excessive concern for contract compliance. One Plantville teacher who expressed this view said, "I don't like certain picayune things that come up—when someone runs to look at the book and immediately files a grievance. I see that as kid stuff."[42]

Finally, while some teachers in all districts complained about low salaries, other teachers in all districts criticized the union for pursuing financial gains over educational objectives. As one Metropolis teacher said, "There's a lack of strength in educational policies. There's too much emphasis on 'me.'"[43] They criticized unions for seeking higher wages and reduced duties at the expense of well-maintained buildings, adequate supplies and equipment, and in-service training.

These were the recurring criticisms of unions and collective bargaining. Most teachers focused on one or two points of dissatisfaction that were offset by points of agreement. Few teachers expressed total disapproval, just as few voiced unconditional acceptance. Collective bargaining was viewed as a useful and necessary means to achieve narrow objectives rather than as a cause deserving constant and unconditional commitment. At the district level, where the voice of one teacher might be inaudible, teachers accepted the necessity of pursuing their interests collectively. However, at the school site, where teachers were known individually and where they had the opportunity to act on their own behalf with administrators, they were far less likely to stress their union identities.

It was apparent that teachers' decisions to ally with others as union members, to define teacher interests in opposition to administrative interests, and to pursue problems through formal procedures were highly dependent on their views of the principal. In most schools, if the principal was attentive to the broad range of teacher interests and was effective in supporting instruction, teachers were likely to endorse administrative prior-

ities, overlook occasional contract violations, avoid formal grievance procedures, and bend the contract in the interest of the
school. As one Mill City teacher said, "If we have to bend it to
make survival easier, then we'll do it."[44]

Principals Adapt to Reduced Formal Authority

The interdependence of teachers and principals, the breadth
of teacher concerns, and teachers' ambivalence about their union
membership all provided principals with the opportunity to avoid
or moderate labor relationships that were formal and adversarial
and thus to promote cooperation and elicit high levels of service
from their staff.

Principals reported that they could no longer rely primarily
on the formal powers of their positions. One Metropolis principal characterized the kind of authority that principals had lost
through collective bargaining:

> When I was in the Navy, I would work all day and then I would go
> hat in hand to my officer and say, "Please, sir, can I go ashore?" He
> always said "yes," but there was always the chance that he might
> say "no." That was the kind of authority principals had in the
> past.[45]

As a result of collective bargaining, principals' powers were more
closely defined and the rights of teachers clarified and legit-
imized.

However, the informal authority that principals held with
teachers—the authority made possible by the characteristics of
the school organization discussed above—had not been constrained in the same way. Principals in this study were regularly
asked whether they believed their authority had been undermined by collective bargaining. While some were adamant that it
had, most contended that it had not and, in explaining their
responses, made distinctions between formal and informal
authority similar to these made by a Shady Heights principal:

> Certainly the collective bargaining agreement doesn't add to the
> authority of the principal. However, power in a job is based on job
> performance, not on the authority of the position. This provides

> more potent power than you can use. When I think back to 1961
> and compare that with now, in many ways I can get more from my
> teachers than my principal could have gotten from me, and that
> was before collective bargaining. If you rely on the authority of
> the position, not on power that is based on confidence, then
> there's a problem.[46]

While collective bargaining had unquestionably complicated the work of principals, the organization of the school
provided them with the opportunity to achieve sufficient autonomy and influence to manage their schools well. One Shady
Heights principal assessed the constraints imposed on his administration by collective bargaining: "Principals do, in fact, have a
few restrictions. But we don't really understand how to use all
the power that we have. We don't even know where all the
buttons are that might be pushed."[47]

Aggressive Management / Principals responded to these
changes in their formal authority and to their new responsibilities
for contract administration in a variety of ways. A few used the
contract aggressively to manage their schools and achieve
administrative ends. Such principals typically knew the contract
in detail and were unintimidated by its constraints and procedures. One such principal explained, "My philosophy on labor
relations is to know the contract well. I try to squeeze out every
management prerogative available."[48] This Metropolis principal
was particularly effective in documenting the weaknesses of
incompetent teachers and moving them out of his school. He had
never lost a grievance over an unsatisfactory rating; he had
mastered the procedures and used them confidently and aggressively to improve the quality of teaching in his school.

This aggressive approach to contract management was
effective in achieving certain defined ends, such as transferring
incompetent teachers or maintaining adequate supervision, but
it also encouraged formalism, literal contract interpretation, and
retaliation by the union. It made it difficult to gain faculty
cooperation for noncontractual responsibilities such as spon-
soring clubs, covering classes of absent teachers, or monitoring
the halls between classes. One principal who used this strategy
speculated about the difficulty of assessing it:

Even though I would win there would then be periods of strife when the union would go after me for other things. I don't know whether this approach is good. I don't know what in the end is effective. I know there are principals who get along with all their teachers. I don't know if that is what's good.[49]

Defensive Management / Other principals complied with the contract carefully, but did so defensively, to avoid challenge and confrontation. Such principals were often better informed about how the contract limited them than about how it empowered them. While principals who managed the contract aggressively would test the limits of their administrative power, these principals would stay safely within its zones. One Shady Heights principal said, "I function defensively, in anticipation of the problems."[50] Another said, "I never put myself in a situation where I could come up with egg on my face."[51]

Not only did these principals make sure that they met all their contractual obligations, but they avoided asking teachers to bend the contract in any way, and in some cases they granted more concessions to the union than were contractually necessary. Some had tried to promote volunteer efforts among teachers, but had failed; they were reluctant to try again. One principal described this reaction:

> Some time ago, when I was stuck and when I needed teachers to cover special duties, I would ask the teachers to take those duties on a rotating basis. However, I was duly informed, "You're not supposed to do that." And so lunch, recess—it's a real mess. I'm hamstrung; I'm tired out. When I was informed of that, it was as much as to say, "You're not supposed to ask teachers to do anything." And the result of that—well, it's a little bit of intimidation.[52]

Reciprocal Management / A third group of principals, who took a reciprocal approach to contract management, were usually very aware of their contractural constraints and obligations, but intentionally deemphasized them with their teachers. They sought to have teachers regard the contract as a guide rather than a rulebook.

In some cases, there was a conscious trade of favors;[53] principals occasionally permitted teachers to violate the contract with the understanding that they eventually would reciprocate. A teacher in one school where the principal encouraged such a relationship said:

> The principal bends the contract on behalf of the teachers. For example, there's a three-day limit on prior notice for professional days. Sometimes people can't give that kind of notice. They've bent that one for me already. The administration here is not dogmatic and in response, teachers would respond with favors.[54]

The principal of another school characterized the administrative side of this trade-off: "If you do something for them and they're happy, then they will do something for you. Keep people happy if you can. Avoid confrontation."[55]

In other cases, the reciprocal agreement between teachers and principals was based less explicitly on traded favors than on the realization by both teachers and administrators that they needed each other to make the school work. In many schools, teachers and principals likened the reciprocal ties to those of the family. One principal emphasized that he did not think of his teachers as "union members. They are part of the family. There's nothing we can't work out among ourselves."[56] One Vista principal described the reciprocal process in his school:

> I believe that if rapport and communication are really, truly part of the educational process, then there is no conflict in the roles of teacher-educator and administrator-educator. As a principal I violate the negotiated agreement and the teachers know that I do. But they would never file a grievance because we have already discussed and agreed on what was right for the kids.[57]

A Metropolis principal who enjoyed an unusually high degree of faculty support explained how he was dependent on his teachers:

> I like the cooperative spirit. . . . I need others to share the feeling of responsibility for the school. But the trick is that I can't have all the authority yet share the responsibility. I have to be able to say, "Come join me and together we can attack the problem that's bugging both of us." If something's going on in the lunchroom, I can ask teachers to go in with me, but I can't ask them to go instead of me. I can't expect teachers to be in the hallways during the change of classes, yet stay in my office because I consider it too

noisy out there. There has to be this cooperation—this shared responsibility. It's a family here, but I want no father image, not even a big brother image. We ought to be able to share our problems, and if we don't—if I assume all the authority—then someday I'll have trouble. Someday there will be a fight in the lunchroom and the teachers won't help.[58]

Reciprocal strategies of contract management enabled administrators and teachers successfully to fend off formalism and literal contract enforcement, often to the advantage of the students. These principals retained more leverage with staff than did those who responded defensively, for this was an interdependent arrangement with obligations for both sides. However, because reciprocal strategies were based primarily on trust and allegiance, they occasionally created what one principal called "soft spots," where principals were reluctant to monitor performance closely and to hold teachers accountable for short-comings.

Principals, then, adapted to collective bargaining in a variety of ways. Some embraced the opportunity to involve teachers in school management, while others restricted teachers to advisory roles. A few used the contract to manage the school and insisted on literal compliance with its provisions, while most minimized its role and relied instead on reciprocal relations with teachers to get things done. While most carefully complied with the contract, some did so in order to preserve their right to exercise all available management prerogatives, while others did so only to avoid trouble. There were a small number of principals who actively opposed the union and a small number who abdicated to it. Some principals coped well, most managed, and a few did not cope.

Teacher Responses

There were a small number of schools in this study where the adversarial stances of teachers reportedly set the character of school site labor relationships. These schools were located in the strong union districts of Shady Heights and Metropolis. In most schools, however, it appeared that the principal was primary in establishing the tone of labor relations, whether they were cooperative or combative. As one Shady Heights teacher said, "Quite frankly, it depends on the principal. It depends on who's leading the parade."[59] Teachers were very responsive to the principals' actions, and school site labor relationships changed dramatically with changes in administration.

Overall, teachers in this study avoided literal contract enforcement. In part, they did so because they believed it to be educationally unsound. But they and their principals were also well aware that rigidly insisting on contract compliance was often not in either's best interest. To enforce one side of the contract fully was to invite similarly rigid expectations from the other side. As one Metropolis principal said, if there were a teacher "who made me walk the chalk line, then I'd make that teacher walk the chalk line."[60] Therefore, both sides saved room to adjust the force and detail of the contract to the particular needs of the school, the teachers, or the administrators.

Teachers Consult Principals First / Teachers widely reported preferring to work things out with their principals before turning to the union representative or resorting to formal, adversarial measures. All teachers interviewed for this study were asked how they would deal with a problem in the school: "Whom would you go to; how would you proceed?" In virtually all schools in all districts, teachers' prevailing response was that they would go first to the principal or assistant principal, whether the issue were contractual or noncontractual. In explaining their responses, many teachers said that they would do this because their principals were approachable and responsive. One teacher said, "Usually in this building we don't have to go any further than the principal."[61] Another said, "We can shoot from the hip with him."[62] A third reported:

> He's very reasonable. Anything that you present to him in a reasonable way will get some satisfactory reply. If the problem involved the contract, I would still go the the principal. What causes friction is calling on the formal processes when something might be settled informally. Only after I went to the principal and got no satisfactory answer would I go to the building rep.[63]

Even in schools where the administration was not well respected, teachers reported that they would try talking with the principal first, although many did not expect satisfactory responses. While teachers reported that they might consult building representatives about contractual rights or alternative courses of action, very few said that they would initially submit their problems to the building committee or building representative.

Teachers Grieve Contract Violations Selectively / In considering whether to file a grievance, teachers were again very attentive to the principal's motives and intentions. All teachers were asked to name issues that they might grieve, and only three reported that they would grieve every contract violation. Indeed, on further questioning, it became clear that while these three teachers believed that all contract violations should be grieved, even they had not and would not do so.

Other teachers reported being selective about the issues they would grieve. Threats to job security (job loss, unjust transfer, seniority violations, unfair evaluations), repeated assignment to noncontractual duties (cafeteria or lavatory supervision), and violations of class size limits were the most frequently named issues. Issues mentioned by a smaller group of teachers included being required to do something educationally wrong, harassment by an administrator, unusual and dangerous maintenance problems, and extreme supply shortages. Twenty-two teachers said that there was no issue they would grieve, either because it was not their style ("I'm not a fighter"),[64] because it would compromise cooperative relationships with the principal, or because they did not believe grievances could remedy the problems.

Most teachers noted that only extreme problems would precipitate grievances. One teacher explained that she would grieve supply shortages only if there were "no paper and no books."[65] Another said she would grieve only a permanent assignment to lunch duty, which would violate the contract. While teachers might complain about minor issues, they could imagine themselves grieving only major ones.

Also prominent in teachers' responses to these questions was their emphasis on fairness. They seemed to respond as much to the intention behind the contract violation as they did to the violation itself. "Unjust transfers," "unfair evaluations," "unjustifiable dismissals," or "unnecessary demands" might provoke grievances. However, if the violations were preceived to be reasonable, short-term, necessary for the good of the school, and equitable in their effects, teachers were often willing to accept the extra work or tolerate the inconvenience.

Allegiance to School and Principal May Supersede Allegiance to Union / Finally, teachers' allegiance to the school and to the principal often took precedence over their union affiliation and the contract. When teachers had cooperatively solved problems or established practices within the school, they would defend them against challenge by union officers. For example, in one Plantville school, the staff and principal had developed an arrangement by which teachers would supervise the cafeteria after their duty-free lunch. When the union president challenged the principal's right to administer such an arrangement, the teachers responded with a letter demanding that the union leader stop intervening in their school affairs. It said, in part:

> We feel that it should be known, that although we are not, at present, getting a thirty-minute duty free lunch, we have a system that is quite agreeable to us. Our lunch and recess duty is arranged so that at the end of the week, we average thirty minutes duty free per day, or approximately 150 minutes free time per week. We do not feel that another system would be as acceptable.

> We must consider the total needs of the children, and at our school it is more feasible to keep the system that we have, rather than to change it. A thirty-minute duty free lunch at the elimination of extracurricular activities which are afforded to the children during this period, hardly seems worth it.

> We are also writing this letter to let you know that we are totally behind the administrator of this school, and feel that in this instance we would like to resolve the problem of lunch duty among ourselves without the intervention of the union.[66]

Metropolis teachers in several schools reportedly had asked union staffers to leave their schools when they began to question various school practices or when they were rude or hostile to the principal. One principal said of the union staffer assigned to her school: "He does his dance a lot, but the teachers here will tell him to get out when they hear him raise his voice at me."[67]

The Limits of Compromise

The flexibility of the contract at the school site was not without limits. "There are," as Robert Frost wrote, "roughly zones"[68]—in this case zones of acceptable administrative discretion and teacher tolerance that were set by contract language, union strength, and union aggressiveness. For example, the contractually defined workday for teachers set the minimum time teachers had to spend in the school. Generally, teachers were seen to work longer hours, either arriving early or staying late. Yet these longer hours were always discussed in reference to the contractual language and local expectations rather than in reference to some optimal standard of teacher service and performance. Teachers and their principals often proudly said that they did "more" and stayed "later" than the contract required. But in Plantville, where the work day was five hours and forty minutes, "later" might mean 3:30 P.M., while in Mill City, where the work day was seven and one-half hours, "later" might mean 5:00 P.M.

While the principal and individual school staffs could significantly influence and regulate the implementation of contract language and the effects of collective bargaining on their schools, the range of possible outcomes was limited.

Most teachers reported being ready to compromise on behalf of the school, and most principals reported success in shaping school site labor practices. Yet there were instances where such efforts failed. In a small number of schools, teachers who advocated close enforcement of the contract exerted a great deal of influence over other teachers. In these circumstances, the principal could not exercise the same informal authority with staff that other principals did. This problem occurred in Metropolis, where principals retained little control over staff composition because of frequent seniority transfers and where district union staff members were active in monitoring contract compliance in the schools. One Metropolis district administrator remarked on the difficulty of maintaining constructive reciprocal relationships under these circumstances: "It requires a rare administrative skill to run a school in this way, and some of the principals have given up. Too many of them have been smashed when they tried to bend the contract, and so they live by the detail of the contract."[69]

One Metropolis administrator contended, "The kinds of principals who succeeded before collective bargaining succeeded after it."[70] But it seemed that these principals now needed a combative streak to survive. In addition to being responsive to teacher concerns, the Metropolis principal was expected by district adminstrators to be "imperturbable," to "have the courage of his convictions," and to be willing to take the "risky step and the flak that follows."[71] One administrator elaborated:

> He has to be a kind of Type A person who is able to say, "I have to set the limit here. I know that the union will raise hell; they will scream and yell and we will end up in grievances and even in arbitration and the union will make a fool of me out of that, but I must do it anyway."[72]

Some principals who cultivated cooperative relationships with teachers had never before been required to take this hard stand. As this administrator said, "There are a lot of principals who don't want to go through that, who will back off making decisions and take the path of least resistance."[73] Sometimes that path led out of education.

Conclusion

The picture of labor relations at the school site that emerged from this study had few fixed and many flexible features. Certain contract provisions, once negotiated, were fully implemented and limited the principal's control over faculty composition, the allocation of students to classes, and the supervision of the cafeteria. Other provisions, however, were reinterpreted and informally renegotiated at the school site, where such factors as teacher interests, educational consequences, administrative leadership, and staff allegiance were balanced and counterbalanced.

It was important to the teachers of this study that principals respect and honor their contract, but they also allowed for flexibility, amendment, and even mistakes when the principal's actions were believed to be responsible, well intentioned, and in the interest of a good school. They accepted authoritarian as well as democratic administrators and were critical of laissez-faire principals who relinquished too much power. They were tolerant, and often respectful, of principals who held high standards, monitored teacher performance, and expected more of teachers than the contract required. Teachers did not want to run the schools, but they were prepared to support a principal who demonstrated that their schools could be run well. For most teachers, being part of a good school took precedence over union membership or close enforcement of the contract. As one Metropolis administrator observed, "Teachers like to be part of a winning team."[74]

Conclusion

Collective bargaining has changed the schools. Principals have less formal authority, and teachers can exercise more power. School personnel practices are increasingly standardized, and grievance procedures reinforce the hierarchical structure of districts. Teachers, whose work obligations have been defined and often reduced, can rely on their contracts and unions to protect their jobs.

But the effects of collective bargaining on the school are neither as extreme nor as uniform as critics often suggest. Shifts in formal authority have rarely disabled administrators. Principals typically report that union building representatives and building committees are allies rather than adversaries. Grievance procedures are viewed by teachers and administrators alike as appropriate protections against administrative excesses. Personnel practices are more orderly, but not rigid. Teachers' responsibilities, which once were boundless and diffuse, now have limits that administrators usually say are reasonable. Teachers cannot be arbitrarily disciplined or dismissed, but administrators can and do terminate staff.

Collective bargaining has not been shown to have increased teachers' commitment to their work or enhanced their standing as professionals, but neither has it destroyed the schools. Caricatures of straitjacketed principals, Kafkaesque school bureaucracies, or schools under seige by militant teachers scarcely represent the experiences of these sample districts. Overall, the organizational effects of collective bargaining appear to be both moderate and manageable.

This is not to suggest, though, that labor relations practices look the same in all districts of all schools. In fact, negotiations, contract language, and administrative practices are remarkably diverse. District-level labor relationships are variously collaborative, cooperative, or contentious. Not only do negotiations yield different contracts in different districts, but similar contract provisions, such as those defining grievance procedures, lead to a variety of local practices. Union officers are aggressive in one district, cautious in another, and school district officials variously seek confrontation with or support from their teachers.

Within any one district, school site labor practices vary as well. In one school, the union is active, the contract is prominent, and administrator-teacher relationships are formalized. In another school within the same district, teachers and administrators maintain collegial relationships, minimize the role of the contract, and resolve problems informally. Few contract provisions are implemented fully throughout the schools of any district, most being subject to interpretation, amendment, or informal renegotiation at the school site.

Explaining the Outcomes

Why are the organizational effects of collective bargaining less extreme than many suppose? And what accounts for the great diversity in labor practices from district to district and from school to school? The answers to these questions lie in the nature of schools and the character of collective bargaining.

Those who have predicted that teacher unionism would transform the schools into hostile, rigid institutions expected that teachers would pursue their self-interests narrowly, that they would aggressively enforce the contract provisions negotiated on their behalf, and that traditional educational values—flexibility, responsiveness, and cooperation—would be abandoned for conformity, confrontation, and formality. Such commentators discounted the independence of teachers and the day-to-day realities of school work.

The school site is a place where teachers' values rather than union values prevail. Teachers' allegiance to their schools and to their principals often takes precedence over their allegiance to the union. Teachers resist having their schools subsumed as indistinguishable components of the larger district. They fiercely defend their autonomy and use the union and the contract as they see fit, invoking them in some cases, ignoring them in others.

There are, as well, special working relationships between teachers and principals that differ significantly from the traditional relationships of labor and management. Teachers' and principals' interests and concerns overlap, their work is interdependent, and each needs the cooperation and support of the other for success. Therefore, they promote reciprocal commitments and avoid formal, adversarial confrontations unless the circumstances are extreme. Despite their administrative positions, principals often act as advocates of "their" teachers, endorsing teachers' values and protecting teachers' professional autonomy.

Teachers' ambivalence about unionism also moderates the impact of unionism on the schools. Most teachers prefer to maintain what they perceive to be "professional" rather than "labor" relationships with school administrators. They seek to resolve differences with their principals in committee meetings rather than in grievance hearings, and they try to make collegiality work before citing the contract.

Teachers are also well aware that their contract can regulate only part of what matters to them in their work. The union cannot ensure effective discipline, a well-coordinated school schedule, and balanced student assignments, but without such assurances, teachers can scarcely do their jobs. If school administrators manage these matters well, teachers are often flexible in enforcing the contract. Union activists who are forceful and firm while bargaining about teacher interests at the district level can be moderate and cooperative when applying the contract to their schools.

There are, as well, no simple explanations for the great diversity in local labor practices, for this diversity results from a complex interaction of setting and people. No single factor determines the character of local labor practices, but many are relevant—history, past practices, local educational policies, prevailing community sentiments, and, most important, people, who are central to negotiations and contract management.

The personalities, styles, and relationships of key actors—union leaders, district administrators, principals, and building representatives—were repeatedly found to be very important in explaining local labor practices. If any of the central labor or management figures was combative, the labor relationship was consequently more formal and adversarial; confrontation provoked confrontation. However, where both sides preferred cooperation, the ongoing labor relationship reflected that preference, even in a strong union district such as Shady Heights. District administrators who favored centralized administrative practices used the opportunity presented by collective bargaining to reassert control over the schools, while those who preferred decentralized administration did little to standardize school practices.

Similarly, within the schools, building representatives who sought to work cooperatively with the school administration usually did so, while those who were more oppositional usually formalized the labor relationship. A few principals saw unions as a threat to their authority and intentionally ignored the contract or rejected the legitimacy of the building representatives, thus provoking the union. Other principals willingly honored the contract and successfully enlisted the support and cooperation of staff.

For all these individuals, at both the district and school site levels, the settings in which they worked influenced how much they could do and how freely they could act. Each individual proceeded with a different set of opportunities and encumbrances and, therefore, had different successes and failures. No one could expect to accomplish everything he or she set out to do, whether it be to settle a contract congenially, to teach the union a lesson, to win an arbitration, or to enlist teacher services beyond the requirements of the contract. But individuals still had considerable latitude within which to act, and their actions proved to be remarkably important in determining the role of unionism locally.

That individuals were regularly so important is not surprising when one considers how negotiations and contract management work. It is individuals who strike bargains, make concessions, interpret language, advise strategies, and act on the basis of what they think others will do. Typically, personalities predominate over roles, rules, and rituals. Collective bargaining is a people-centered process, just as schools are people-centered places.

This is not to say that all background factors were unimportant in explaining the diverse labor practices. Three deserve particular notice. First, district size seemed to influence the levels of cooperation and informality that might be maintained between labor and management at the district level. Trust, mutual understanding, and informal agreement seemed to be more possible in small districts than in large ones. Second, the labor tradition of the community appeared to influence the strength of the teachers' union and contract, with the strong labor city of Metropolis having a strong teachers' union and the antilabor community of Vista having a less militant teachers' organization. Third, the expansion or decline of school enrollments and the local economy seemed to influence the progress of negotiations and the prominence of the contract. Where there were fewer students and fewer dollars to divide among all local employees, negotiations became more strained and contract provisions tied to job security were enforced more stringently district-wide. By contrast, in districts where enrollments and the economy were growing, negotiations were intense, but not belligerent, and there was more flexible enforcement of contract provisions that, in other districts, were tied to job security.

But while these three factors appeared to be important, other local background factors explained little of the observed variation. The number of years that a district had been bargaining was not regularly reflected in the strength of its union or contract.[1] Whether a district was urban, suburban, or rural in itself told little about the character of its labor relations.[2] Surprisingly, even the number of strikes experienced by a district provided little insight into the character of ongoing labor relations, for, once settled, strikes were remarkably isolated from the routine matters of contract administration.[3]

The determinants of school site labor practices were no more clear-cut. None of the background factors, such as school size, level, or location, could in itself explain the quite diverse school site labor practices. For example, although in some cases the size of a school seemed to explain the formality of its labor relationship, there were large schools where informality prevailed and small schools where interactions were structured and rigid. Although the faculties of secondary schools were more militant overall than those of elementary schools, there were a number of schools where the pattern was reversed.[4]

It would have been nice to have derived a simple, neatly predictive model to explain the great diversity in educational labor practices, but none was to be found. That this variation cannot be expressed in a model may make these research findings less elegant, but it does not make them less useful. The very fact that the organizational outcomes of collective bargaining are not readily predictable and that personalities and administrative styles take precedence over background factors such as locale, socioeconomic status, or years of bargaining experience means that local teachers and administrators can intentionally influence the impact of teacher unionism on their schools. There is room for considerable discretion because surprisingly little is predetermined at any level of the school district. Negotiators, district administrators, union leaders, principals, building representatives, building committees, and teachers continually redefine what collective bargaining means for the schools of their district. Rules are often bent, compromise is ongoing, and changes in school or union leadership can dramatically alter the local labor relationship. At the school site, the principal and teachers mutually define the role of the union in their school. They may define that role cooperatively or through confrontation, but the definition they arrive at will probably differ from that reached by other staffs in other schools.

Assessing the Organizational Effects of Unionism

These schools' experiences suggest that the question, "Is collective bargaining good or bad for schools?" can only be answered equivocally, for collective bargaining, being a process rather than a product, can have both good and bad effects. In many cases, contract provisions appeared to affect schools favorably. Reductions in class size reportedly made classroom instruction easier and, many believed, better. Reduction-in-force procedures introduced order and equity into decisions that were potentially chaotic, demoralizing, and subject to administrative abuse. Reductions in teachers' supervisory duties enabled them to concentrate more professional time on instruction. Defining the teachers' workday protected teachers against excessive and capricious demands on their time. Building advisory committees often promoted staff participation in school policymaking.

But there were instances in the study where provisions addressing these same issues had been negotiated with detrimental effects. Rigidly enforced class size limits that included no allowances for subject or ability groupings diminished the schools' capacity to respond to student needs. A teachers' workday that coincided with the students' instructional day reduced the likelihood of after-school tutoring, emergency conferences, or in-service training. Layoff and transfer provisions that authorized frequent bumping of junior teachers or permitted a teacher with no experience in a particular subject to displace someone less senior disrupted the continuity of students' instruction. In these instances, the union had demanded, and management had granted, more constraints on administrative discretion and more rights for teachers than were warranted. Such contract provisions set limits on administrative expectations and teacher responsibilities that fell short of the complex needs of the school.

Whether collective bargaining works for or against good schools depends on a number of interrelated factors. It depends on the extent to which school site needs are taken into account when working conditions are negotiated. It depends on the amount of discretion reserved for principals and the degree of support provided them by the district office. It depends on the insight and ingenuity of principals as they administer the contracts. It depends on the concessions that teacher unions will make for the good of the schools and on the extent of teachers' commitment to their students, principal, colleagues, and school.

Implications

In thinking about the future of educational labor relations, it is useful first to consider collective bargaining in a somewhat broader context. For, as the findings of this research have demonstrated, collective bargaining is not simply a standardized set of practices, applied wholesale to the schools, but one of many educational policies that must be implemented by teachers and school administrators and that ultimately affect their roles as practitioners.

How We Think about the Policymaking Process / These findings about the diversity of local labor practices provide a new perspective on continuing discussions of schools and change. In this context, collective bargaining can be viewed as a locally derived regulatory policy similar to governmental policies designed to change school practices. Many who have studied the implementation of governmental programs have documented weak local commitment to federally defined goals and modest levels of local compliance with federal regulations.[5] The local renditions of programs such as Chapter I or Education for All Handicapped Children sometimes differ markedly from the programs originally conceived by state and federal policymakers. Many policy analysts consider such divergence to be problematic and attribute it to differences between federal goals and local objectives and to the infrequency of state and federal monitoring. Change is said to be slow, reform uncertain.

The provisions of teacher contracts are much like the regulations of federal programs, but they differ in two important ways. First, they are locally determined and, therefore, might be expected to be consistent with the priorities of local teachers. Second, because compliance can be monitored daily by union members, one might predict high levels of enforcement.

Interestingly, the implementation story of collective bargaining sounds much like the implementation story of federal programs. Here, too, there was considerable discrepancy between rules and practice. Identical contract language produced strikingly different outcomes even within the schools of the same district. Notably, such deviations were usually endorsed, even initiated, by the teachers on whose behalf the contract had initially been negotiated.

The experiences of these districts suggest that teachers and principals remake even this locally derived policy until it is their own—until it is consistent with past practices and current preferences. Contract implementation, like program implementation, demands ongoing mutual adaptation between the rules and local school practices.[6] In the process, each is changed by the other. Collective bargaining agreements are not fully enforced, contract provisions are modified and informally renegotiated by teachers and principals, and the unions' objectives are only partially realized. But the schools are changed too. Principals work amidst new constraints. Teachers' concerns are granted more attention.

The fact that school people do not readily and faithfully execute such blueprints for change is not surprising in light of what we know about schools as social organizations. Both program regulations and contract provisions are written for district-wide application rather than for school site interpretation. But the school site is a place apart from the district office, and the people who work there march to different drummers. Those outside the school who would transform or regulate its practice remain somewhat suspect, whether they be district officials, legislators, or even union leaders.

The failure of schools to implement programs and policies fully may seem problematic to some policy analysts and policymakers who analyze the snags and devise ways to avoid them. But this study suggests that it is misleading to regard incomplete or inexact implementation as a mistake to be fixed. "What went wrong?" is not the correct question. "What went right?" may be. For it appears that the adaptation of policies within schools is both inevitable and functional. The process by which teachers and principals reshape policies engages them in making the change their own; it assures that the policy is incorporated into ongoing practices; and it maintains continuity of instruction and administration over time. Ironically, incomplete compliance may be in the interests of long-term compliance.

The problem, of course, is in distinguishing between cases where incomplete implementation serves schools and children and cases where it does not. Sometimes noncompliance only prolongs injustice or perpetuates obsolete practices. But in the case of collective bargaining, this adaptive process seems to work on behalf of good schools, assuring teachers and principals the opportunity to moderate formalism, preserve professional autonomy, and adjust the contract to the particular needs of the school.

The Effects of Collective Bargaining on the Principal's Role / The process by which teacher contracts are constructively adapted to fit the needs of schools does not, of course, happen automatically. It requires that principals be both effective managers and leaders and that teachers be invested in the well-being of their schools. But as collective bargaining presents these new demands, it also alters the ways in which principals can manage and lead.

Collective bargaining has increased the importance of the principal's position as it has made the principal's work more difficult. It is the principal who must make the contract work at the school site, but this is by no means a routine administrative task. It requires an understanding of teachers' priorities, a familiarity with contract language, a judgment about school-wide needs, and a capacity both to compromise and to get things done. Principals cannot rely solely on their positional authority with teachers whose respect and support they need to do their jobs.

Currently, there is much talk about how principals are increasingly expected to act as managers and paper pushers rather than as educational leaders. Federal, state, and local policies, including collective bargaining, have introduced regulations, forms, standards, and legal language for today's principals that were unknown by their predecessors. But while it is true that principals now must attend to many more bureaucratic duties than in the past, it is also true that, more than ever, they must coordinate policies to serve students, foster support for school-wide goals, promote high standards for instruction, and increase teachers' commitment to a shared purpose. If principals cannot meet these varied demands, it is possible that eventually the policies will undermine the very schooling they are designed to improve, that teachers will define their responsibilities narrowly, and that the contract will indeed run the school. Collective bargaining and other educational policies have increased, not reduced, the demands on school administrators as leaders and, in some cases, exposed the failings of those who can not lead.

Constructive contract implementation depends as much on teachers as it does on principals. In order for teachers to make the kinds of concessions, adjustments, and extra efforts that are apparently necessary today to keep a school running well, they must, it seems, have a shared, sustained, and stable commitment to their schools. They must be willing to see beyond their personal interests and to cooperate with those outside their classroom doors. The principals' success in shaping the character of school site labor practices despite substantial reductions in their authority depends on establishing trust and winning the allegiance of teachers.

However, in this study, such reciprocal commitments were difficult to maintain when a school's staff was rapidly changing due to numerous layoffs and transfers. In Metropolis, where this was a growing problem, some teachers who had experienced several involuntary transfers reported being reluctant to invest much in the school. For them, teaching had been reduced to just another job—more akin to employment than a calling. I cannot conclude on the basis of this study that effective management of school site labor relations or other educational policies is jeopardized by rapid changes in staff assignments. But because principals were found to rely extensively on reciprocal relations with teachers, such a conclusion is plausible and deserves further inquiry.

Conjectures about the Future / Some might argue that it is simply a matter of time before the unions transform the schools into impersonal, unprofessional, adversarial institutions. While it is always risky to predict the future, it seems unlikely that this will be so, because of what we know both about the policymaking process and about the priorities of school practitioners. These two factors suggest that there will be few dramatic changes in the teacher contracts of the next decade and that we will see efforts by both teachers and administrators to correct for the extremes of the past. The data of this study support such a forecast.[7] There appear to be limits on what the unions can expect to achieve and on what management is willing to concede.

Throughout the study, local administrators reported that although they had made some unwise concessions to aggressive union negotiators during early bargaining, they were no longer doing so, having become more careful about anticipating the practical, long-range implications of union demands and having drawn the line about what changes might be bargained. Also, teachers were not ready actively to support union demands that would jeopardize their schools. Union leaders often reported that they could not expect to enlist broad teacher support for a strike over any issues but wages or job security. Overall, teachers expressed considerable satisfaction with the gains they had made in working conditions and did not anticipate that many more changes could be negotiated. The notable exceptions were in Mill City, where teachers pressed for the elimination of involuntary administrative transfers, and in Vista, Mill City, and Metropolis, where teachers sought class size limits below thirty.

Teachers wanted contracts that were protective but not prescriptive. As a group, they reported seeking negotiated agreements that ensured sufficient autonomy in their work, reasonable demands on their time, equitable treatment, and protection against abuse. They explicitly did not expect to run their schools. Given such responses, it seems unlikely that teachers' contracts will eventually prescribe the details of instructional or administrative policies or that teachers will insist on literal interpretation and application of each negotiated provision.

Although the teacher contracts of the next decade will probably not include major changes in working conditions, there is little evidence that teacher unionism is waning. Rather, collective bargaining has been incorporated into the routine of schools. In fact, there was virtually unanimous agreement among both teachers and administrators that collective bargaining continues to be necessary in today's schools—necessary to protect teachers from abuse, to ensure fair wages, to represent collective interests, and to defend educational budgets during a time of declining resources. Some saw it as a necessary evil, but nonetheless necessary.

Finally, then, collective bargaining has not, and probably will not, transform the schools into impersonal, rule-bound workplaces. It has introduced new ways of making routine decisions and setting long-range policy. It has required a new accountability for employers and employees. It has altered the relationships of teachers and administrators. But labor practices have also been adapted to fit the educational enterprise and the norms of those who work there. Educators' work is finally interdependent, educational values are hearty, and schools are resilient organizations.

Appendices

A. Interview Protocols

Superintendent, Assistant Superintendent for Personnel

1. Would you summarize your employment history in education and in this particular district.

2. What is the history of the teachers' union in this district?
   Were teachers organized prior to collective bargaining?
   When was the first representation election?
   When was the first contract negotiated?
   How would you characterize early bargaining?
   Have there been challenge elections?
   Have there been strikes? If so, when and over what issues?

3. How would you characterize current labor-management relations at the district level? What is the relation between the school board and the union?

4. How solidly are teachers in the district behind the union?
5. How would you characterize your style or strategy in dealing with the union?

6. Do you believe that administrator-teacher relationships have changed as a result of collective bargaining? Are they more collegial, adversarial, bureaucratic?

7. How would you characterize current teacher morale in the district? What affects it? Does the presence and activity of the union affect morale?

8. What do you see as the important current labor issues in this district?

9. Do you believe that the authority of management has been eroded as a result of collective bargaining? If so, what effect does that have on the ways schools work?

10. Do you think that there are advantages for management in having a collective bargaining agreement?

11. Is the contract implemented literally and policed closely? Are there, to your knowledge, provisions that are bent or ignored?

12. Has the length of the teachers' work day been affected by collective bargaining?

13. Have teacher services and performance been affected either positively or negatively by collective bargaining?

14. Have there been educational gains that have resulted from collective bargaining? Have there been educational losses?

15. How many grievances are processed annually? What percentage of these grievances would you estimate relate to building practices? How many reach the superintendent's level?

16. How many arbitrations are there annually? Is there any pattern to the kind of issues that reach arbitration?

17. What direction do principals receive from the district office about responding to grievances? Are they encouraged to settle them informally or formally?

18. Are there apparent differences in labor-management relations across schools within the district? If so, what accounts for those differences?

19. Do you believe teacher unions are necessary? Do you have reservations about the things that unions stand for?

Union Officers

1. Would you summarize your employment history in education and in this school district?

2. What is the history of the teachers' union in this district?
   Were teachers organized prior to collective bargaining?
   When was the first representation election?
   When was the first contract negotiated?
   How would you characterize early bargaining?
   Have there been challenge elections?
   Have there been strikes? If so, when, and over what issues?

3. How would you characterize current labor-management relations in this district? What is the relation between the school board and the union?

4. How solidly are teachers in the district behind the union?

5. How would you characterize your style or strategy in dealing with the district office administration?

6. Do you believe that administrator-teacher relationships have changed as a result of collective bargaining? Are they more collegial, adversarial, bureaucratic?

7. How would you characterize current teacher morale in the district? Do you believe that morale is related in any way to the union?

8. What do you see as the important current labor issues in this district?

9. Do you believe that the authority of management has been eroded as a result of collective bargaining? If so, what effect does this have on the way schools work?

10. Do you think that there are advantages for management in having a collective bargaining agreement?

11. Is the contract implemented literally and policed closely? Are there, to your knowledge, provisions that are bent or ignored?

12. Has the length of the teachers' work day been affected by collective bargaining? If so, how?

13. Have teacher service and performance been affected either positively or negatively by collective bargaining? If so, how?

14. Have there been educational gains that have resulted from collective bargaining? Have there been educational losses?

15. How many grievances are processed annually? What percentage of these grievances would you estimate relate to building practices? How many grievances reach the superintendent's level?

16. How many arbitrations do you have annually? Is there any pattern to the kinds of issues that reach arbitration?

17. What kinds of direction do building representatives receive from the union leadership about initiating grievances? Are they encouraged to settle grievances formally or informally?

18. Are there apparent differences in labor-management relations across schools within the district? If so, what accounts for those differences?

19. Do you believe teacher unions and collective bargaining are necessary? Do you have any reservations about the things that unions stand for?

Principals

1. Would you summarize your employment history in education and in this school district?

2. Are you a member of a union or association?

3. Are you in agreement with the things that teacher unions stand for and do?

4. Do you believe that teacher unions and collective bargaining are necessary?

5. How would you characterize union-management relations in this district?

6. How solidly are the teachers in the district behind the union?

7. How would you characterize labor-management relations in your school? What is your style or strategy in dealing with your faculty and labor issues? What role does the building representative play?

8. Do you think that the administrator-teacher relationships have changed as a result of collective bargaining? Are they more collegial, adversarial, bureaucratic?

9. Have teacher service and performance been affected, either positively or negatively by collective bargaining?

10. Has the length of the teachers' work day been affected by collective bargaining? Do teachers provide after-school help for students? What percentage of your faculty would you estimate meet only the minimum requirements for the length of the work day?

11. Is there adequate faculty supervision for extracurricular activities?

12. Does a faculty advisory committee function in your school? If so, what kinds of issues does it address?

13. Are teachers available for parental conferences? Is this an active parent community?

14. What are the issues of discontent among teachers in the district and within this school?

15. Is the contract policed closely in your building?

16. What grievances have you had in this school? What percentage of grievances are resolved informally? Does the district office provide direction for principals in responding to grievances?

17. Are there instances when the contract is bent to meet the particular needs of the schools?

18. How would you characterize your style as an administrator?

19. Are there ways in which the contract enables you to manage your school more effectively?

20. Are there any teachers in your school whom you believe should not be teaching? If so, is their failure to perform effectively due to the contract or the union? Are any measures being taken to terminate them?

21. Do you use seniority in making teaching and supervisory assignments?

22. What part of the contract is most troublesome for you in managing the building?

23. Does collective bargaining undermine your authority as a principal?

24. Do you see any relationship between teacher quality and union membership or non-membership?

Teachers

1. How long have you taught? in this district? in this school? grade?

2. Are you an active union member? Are you usually in agreement with the positions the union takes? Do you have any reservations about the things unions/associations stand for?

3. Do you believe a teachers' union or association is necessary?

4. How would you describe relations between the union and the district office administration? How do teachers view the superintendent? the school board? the union leadership?

5. How would you describe relations between the union and the principal in your school? Does the faculty advisory committee function? How do the union reps function?

6. How would you describe the principal's style as an administrator?

7. Are you satisfied with the influence you have over what happens in the schools? How do you influence school policy?

8. Over what kinds of issues is there discontent among teachers in the district and in this school?

9. How are supervisory responsibilities assigned?

10. How often are faculty meetings held? What issues are dealt with?

11. In what kinds of ways are teachers held accountable for their responsibilities in the school? e.g. sign-in, checking plan books.

12. Is the contract policed closely in the building? What sorts of issues receive the most attention? Do teachers know the details of the contract?

13. Is the contract ever bent to meet the particular needs of this school?

14. Has the length of the teacher's work day been affected by collective bargaining? Do teachers provide after-school help for students? What percentage of your faculty would you estimate meet only the minimum requirements for the length of the work day? How many extra hours per week do you spend on school-related work?

15. What kinds of volunteer activities go on in the building? What percentage of the faculty would participate in these extra activities?

16. If you have a problem about the way things are being done in this building, whom would you go to? If it seemed to be a violation of the contract, whom would you go to?

17. Are you familiar with any grievances that have been initiated in this building?

18. What kind of issue might you grieve?

19. Do you believe that collective bargaining has affected teacher service and performance either positively or negatively?

20. Are there teachers in your school whom you believe should not be teaching? Is their failure to perform effectively due to either the contract or the union?

21. What are the big union issues at this time? Are teachers satisfied with the gains that have been made through collective bargaining?

22. Are you satisfied being a teacher?

23. How does this school compare with others in the system?

Table A Distribution of Interviewees

School District	District administrators	Union officers and staff	Principals and assistant principals	Teachers	Community leaders	Totals
Metropolis	16	5	21	37	2	81
Mill City	2	2	13	29	0	46
Northwood	1	2	3	23	0	29
Plantville	3	1	7	33	0	44
Shady Heights	2	1	10	33	0	46
Vista	5	4	11	28	0	48
Totals	29	15	65	183	2	294

B. Data Analysis

Data analysis, like data collection, posed a number of new problems of method. I had dictated 2,500 pages of field notes from nearly 300 interviews at over twenty-five sites, and I intended to make sense of them responsibly and throughly. But there was no computer software package to assist me in sorting, coding, and storing the responses. There were no academically recognized procedures for analyzing multi-site qualitative data. There was, instead, prevailing skepticism about "soft" data and suspicion about conclusions unaccompanied by F ratios or regression coefficients. Therefore, in devising ways to sort, analyze, and report my research data, I had to rely on brief methodological accounts from a small number of similar studies, the good advice of colleagues, and my own ingenuity.

After site visits to three districts, I began to make a comprehensive list of the various topics that were emerging during the interviews. Eventually, I had sixty-nine topics, including such items as "history of union-management relations," "role of union building representative," and "teacher satisfaction with contractual gains." Using this list of numbered topics, I bracketed and coded the entire text of the field notes by topic numbers. At the edge of each segment of data, I also noted the identifying number of the respondent so that I could refer to the individual's employment history or union affiliation, if that became useful. I photocopied a second set of coded notes to be cut apart and reassembled by topic, so that I might review all references to a particular topic without searching through all 2,500 pages.

However, sorting the data by topic was not enough. For, as I studied them, I needed to have quick visual access to information about the respondents' roles, schools and districts so that I could readily compare their responses. I was finding considerable variation in policy and practice, both within districts and across districts and I wanted to recognize the patterns of that variation in the data. Therefore, before cutting the field notes, I color coded each page to designate the district and school site of origin. For example, all field notes from the grade school in Northwood were striped with purple, those from a Mill City high school were striped with green, and those from the district level in Metropolis were striped with pink. Finally, I noted the roles of the various respondents along the edge of each page. Principals' notes were punched with round holes, district administrators' notes were edged with pinking shears, union leaders' notes were punched with heart-shaped holes, and teachers' notes were left plain. Each piece of data, then, included easily retrievable information about the location, role, and identity of the interviewee.

Having prepared the field notes, I cut and reassembled them into notebooks by topic so that all responses about a single subject, such as "grievances at the school site," were grouped together and ordered by district, school, and role. Although slow, tedious, and somewhat primitive, this process of preparing the data made it possible to easily review the entire range of responses about any particular topic and to identify patterns of similarity and difference in those responses.

In analyzing the data, I first read through the data notebooks, listing tentative findings suggested by the field notes. Initially, I compiled this list of ideas and hunches without systematically confirming or disconfirming them. The list, which had 220 separate items, included such observations as

> Even those teachers who are active in the union are not uniformly committed to union positions;

> Collective bargaining may safeguard against arbitrary management, but the tradeoff may be more formal management;

> There is no apparent relationship between good or poor teachers and union membership;

> Teachers feel that their primary responsibility is to their clients, not their employers.

After again reviewing the data notebooks, I selected key findings from this initial list and wrote a short essay about each one, elaborating the argument and citing examples from the data that supported it. Examples of these key findings are:

> Although grievance procedures are seldom used in some schools, their presence has important, indirect effects on teacher and administrator behavior.

> Teachers regard instructional work as professional and super-
> visory work as custodial.

Critiques of these papers by two of my colleagues helped me to clarify these arguments and to reassess the data that supported them.

It was on the basis of these papers that I began to organize the chapters of the report. As I worked my way through the outline of each section, I read and reread the relevant portions of the data to test whether they were consistent with the conclusions and I revised the conclusions when they were not. Repeated reviews of the data revealed the similarities and differences in policy, practice, and opinion across roles, schools, and districts, and permitted me to incorporate this complexity into the discussion of findings.

In analyzing the data, I had to make many judgments about the reliability of the various respondents. The interviews had yielded many sorts of data—descriptions, opinions, explanations, facts, errors, and falsehoods. Throughout the periods of data collection and data analysis, I simultaneously served several roles—recorder, analyzer, synthesizer, and resident skeptic. In some cases, information offered by interviewees could be confirmed or disconfirmed in the field—for example, whether class size limits were actually enforced in the schools. Often, though I had to make judgments about the validity of various pieces of data. Some individuals had offered information on topics they knew little about, while others had spoken from direct and extensive experience. I weighed such responses accordingly. As I wrote, I regularly reviewed whether the available facts supported the generalizations offered and carefully considered the plausibility of competing explanations.

In reporting the data and conclusions throughout the text, I have made every effort to distinguish between facts, opinions, and explanations, and to convey how prevalent various views were. When I have written that "most" respondents expressed a particular view, I am referring to at least 80 percent of the relevant group. When there were conflicting opinions or competing explanations, I have presented those differences. Quotations are used throughout the text to illustrate the findings. The quotations that are included were selected either because they were typical of many similar responses or because they clearly expressed what other respondents said less elegantly.

I sent a copy of the penultimate draft of this report to each district office, union office, and school where I had conducted interviews. I encouraged respondents to send me their corrections, clarifications, or complaints so that I might incorporate them into the final manuscript. I heard from only two respondents, who said that the accounts of their districts were accurate. I am confident that the descriptions, accounts, and analysis reported here do match the experiences of these six sites. Whether they provide meaningful insights into the day-to-day labor relations of other districts, must be left to the reader to decide.

C. The Contracts

Contract Provision	Metropolis	Plantville	Shady Heights
DEFINITION OF GRIEVANCE	Complaint that there is lack of policy, improper or unfair policy or practice, deviation from, misinterpretation, misapplication, inequitable, or improper application of provision of agreement	Complaint that there is violation, misinterpretation, or inequitable application of provision of agreement	Complaint of unfair treatment, violation, misinterpretation, or misapplication of provision of agreement, or that health, safety, or liability is jeopardized
ALL GRIEVENCES SUBJECT TO BINDING ARBITRATION	Yes	Yes	Yes
AGENCY SHOP	Prohibited by statute	Yes	Yes
UNION PRIVILEGES IN SCHOOLS	Bulletin board space Use of mail boxes May schedule union meetings before or after school hours	Bulletin board space Use of mail boxes May schedule meetings before or after school hours	Bulletin board space Use of mail boxes May schedule meetings before or after school hours

Mill City	Vista	Northwood
Claim based on event or condition that adversely affects rights of teacher and for which solution lies within province of Board	Claim that there is violation, misinterpretation, or misapplication of established Board policy	Claim that dispute or disagreement exists involving interpretation or application of terms of agreement
Yes	Advisory arbitration only	Yes
No	No	No
Bulletin board space Use of mail boxes Right to meet with new teachers prior to school year	Bulletin board space Use of mail boxes May schedule meetings after school hours	May use school facilities and equipment Use of mail boxes May schedule meetings after school hours

(*continued*)

Contract Provision	Metropolis	Plantville	Shady Heights
UNION PRIVILEGES IN SCHOOLS (*continued*)	Given time for announcements in faculty meetings		Time for announcements at faculty meetings
BUILDING REPRESENTATIVE		Principal shall recognize building representative as official Federation representative. Secondary—1 period release time per week	
BUILDING COMMITTEE MEET WITH PRINCIPAL	Union committee maximum 5 teachers May meet during preparation periods Broad meet and discuss requirements Certain issues require consensus	Union committee Monthly meetings Consult on local school problems and policies	Faculty committee 5–10 members Strictly advisory Meet after school to discuss educational matters of concern to teachers and principal
REDUCTION IN FORCE	Seniority by law	Seniority	Seniority

Mill City	Vista	Northwood
May schedule meetings before or after school hours		May make announcements at faculty meetings
	Recognized as representative of members Release time for Association business	
(Superintendent mandated)	Faculty committee at least 4 teachers Meet every 2 weeks on request of teachers or principal To facilitate communication on matters about school	
Seniority by law		Criteria in order of priority: overall instructional program, qualifications and experience, seniority

(continued)

Contract Provision	Metropolis	Plantville	Shady Heights
INVOLUN-TARY TRANSFERS	Seniority used to achieve racial or experience balance Administrative transfers permitted for unsatisfactory ratings	Seniority	"On a fair basis"
PROMO-TIONS	Oral examinations Posted requirements of position	If qualifications are equal, seniority decides	If qualifications are equal, seniority decides
EVALUA-TIONS AND RATINGS	Observations may not be basis of unsatisfactory ratings unless written statement of evaluation given to teacher within 5 days of observation All ratings on basis of satisfactory, unsatisfactory only	Conducted with full knowledge of teacher Postevaluation conference at request of teacher or evaluator Official evaluation signed by teacher in personnel file Copy to teacher Teacher has right to written reply	Teachers who are rated unsatisfactory must be observed once each quarter at least 20 min., notified of observer's evaluation, and offered constructive criticism Teachers may request conference

Mill City	Vista	Northwood
No stated criteria "Teachers may not refuse an administrative-initiated transfer"	Relevant factors including seniority	Area of competence, major/minor fields, grade or subject matter from which transfer contemplated, and other relevant factors
Criteria will be included in posting	Professional experience (includes seniority), competence, qualifications, other relevant criteria	
Nontenured annual, tenured—4 year intervals Teacher or principal may initiate appraisal out of rotation Postevaluation conference required Teachers may respond in writing up to 20 days after signing evaluation	Defined by Board Policy	

(*continued*)

Contract Provision	Metropolis	Plantville	Shady Heights
EVALUA-TIONS AND RATINGS (*continued*)	Nontenured teachers rated semi-annually; tenured teachers rated annually. Interim ratings are progress reports, not in personnel file Teachers receive copy of evaluation. Within 10 days may (1) submit self-evaluation for file; (2) invoke grievance for improper rating If principal wants to hold disciplinary conference with teacher must advise teacher in writing of right to have union rep present and, except in emergency, give 24-hr. notice	Dissatisfied teacher may discuss evaluation with superintendent	All teachers observed on regular basis. Abnormally excessive evaluations shall be explained. Never used to pressure or harass Evaluations signed by teacher and evaluator No evaluations for competence in subject matter without prior notice

Mill City	Vista	Northwood
When deficiencies noted, recommendations for improvement must be included, observer must confer with teachers and give copy of report. Same observer does follow-up		
Every effort made to do 2 observations, 1 by Jan. 1, 1 by April 1		

(continued)

Contract Provision	Metropolis	Plantville	Shady Heights
PERSONNEL FILES	No derogatory material except pertaining directly to work, performance, or matters that are cause for dismissal or suspension All such materials signed Teacher can examine file, respond to all materials Material not in file cannot be used against teacher for any purpose Unfavorable anecdotal reports destroyed after 18 months if no similar record	Teacher can inspect and make copies of any materials Only one official file per teacher Those who inspect file must sign log	One official file No anonymous letters or material based on hearsay Teachers must read, date, sign, derogatory material File available to teacher within 7 days of request Grievances are not included in file
PERSONAL LEAVE	3 days per year for urgent personal business. May not extend holidays	Teachers may use sick leave for unavoidable absence to conduct personal business 5 days funeral leave	1 day per year for urgent financial or legal transactions 1 day to participate in graduation exercises

Mill City	Vista	Northwood
Teachers can review file and make additions of pertinent rebuttal material	1 file in personnel office—principals may have copies of materials Teachers can inspect files Teachers must read and sign all derogatory material	File must contain complete copies of all relevant materials Teachers may review files with Association representative Teachers can copy materials at cost and add written comments
3 days per year for religious, court, graduation, weather, moving, business 3 day notice required	2 days per year, cumulative 1 day notification of principal required	1 day per year 2 days per year after accumulation of 20 sick days Not cumulative

(*continued*)

Contract Provision	Metropolis	Plantville	Shady Heights
PERSONAL LEAVE (*continued*)	At termination of employment, teachers compensated for all unused days	Religious holidays specified	1 day to attend family graduation 3 days for religious holidays
SICK LEAVE	10 days per year Cumulative without limit Teacher compensated for 25% unused sick leave upon termination	15 days per year accumulated to 150 days plus 1 day per year after 10 years of service (not cumulative) Sick leave bank established Teacher may draw after 5 days of unpaid leave	District allots 5 days per year per teacher. Teachers draw from fund up to 90 days. If fund insufficient, deductions according to formula from each absent teacher's salary
DUTY-FREE LUNCH	Elementary: 45 min. Secondary: 40 min.	30 min.	Elementary: 40 min. Secondary: 1 period
LUNCH DUTY	Teachers shall be relieved "to the extent possible"		Senior high— present practice Junior high—1 period every 2 weeks

Mill City	Vista	Northwood
	Principal approval required before or after holidays	Approval needed before or after holidays
15 days per year cumulative to 210 days Severence pay for 25% unused sick leave up to 35 days	10 days per year, cumulative without limitation If misuse suspected, medical certificate required	10 days per year 4 or more consecutive days or suspected abuse, may require medical certificate
30 min.	30 min.	30 min.
No required lunch supervision	The Board will make an effort to reduce such duties	Elementary: scheduling shall be done in consultation with the staff

(*continued*)

Contract Provision	Metropolis	Plantville	Shady Heights
MEETINGS	All meetings on school time except 2 per month may extend 30 min. beyond school day with permission of district superintendent Teachers may submit agenda items Printed materials shall not be read aloud	10 inservice or curricular meetings per year—1½ hrs. 10 building meetings per year—1 hr. 48-hr. notice except in emergencies	3 meetings per month—1 hr. (faculty, department, curricular)
EXTRACUR-RICULAR ASSIGN-MENTS	Elementary: 220 paid hrs. per school Secondary: 400 paid hrs. per school	Specified activities compensated Dance proctoring is unpaid and voluntary Sunday commencement is voluntary	Strictly voluntary Specified activities compensated

Mill City	Vista	Northwood
1 meeting per week. Meetings may extend 1 hr. beyond the workday	1 meeting per week before or after school—1 hr. Agenda available 24 hrs. in advance	
	Teachers are responsible to advise 1 student organization	Teachers must sponsor 1 club or activity All other participation voluntary. If volunteers are unavailable, may be appointed and compensated at $8.75 per hr. No police duties

(continued)

Contract Provision	Metropolis	Plantville	Shady Heights
PERFOR-MANCE MONI-TORING	Teachers with satisfactory rating can only be required to submit outlined lesson plans If classroom performance declines detailed plans may be required		
TEACHER ASSIGN-MENT	May be assigned 5 periods per week outside area of appoint-ment—more with teacher's consent		Teachers can refuse assign-ment outside of certifica-tion area
LENGTH OF WORKDAY	Elementary: 6 hrs., 45 min. Secondary: 6 hrs., 45 min.	Elementary: 6 hrs., 10 min. Secondary: 6 hrs., 45 min.	Elementary: 6 hrs., 30 min. Secondary: 6 hrs., 45 min.
EVENING MEETINGS	2 night activit-ies per year scheduled by principal in consultation with teachers	2 parent visit-ing nights per year	Voluntary

Mill City	Vista	Northwood
Lesson plans must be prepared each week Grade books must be kept up to date		
	Teachers shall not be assigned outside certi-fication areas or major or minor fields of study	New teachers are to be assigned within area of appointment
Elementary: 7 hrs., 30 min. Secondary: 7 hrs., 30 min.	Length unspecified except on Fridays, when coincides with school day	8 hrs.

(continued)

Contract Provision	Metropolis	Plantville	Shady Heights
PREPARA-TION PERIODS	Elementary: 225 min. per week, no less than 30 min. at once. Lost preparation time paid back in time or money Secondary: payback for lost time after 4 periods per year	Elementary: 1 period per week (30–45 min.) in addition to periods of specialists' instruction "Shall be used for unassigned professional work" Teachers may leave school with principal's permission for "valid educational reasons"	Elementary: 15 min. before and after school must be used for preparation Junior high: 5 periods per week Senior high: 4 periods per week Teachers may be called for coverage on equitable, rotating basis After 10 coverages, paid $5 per class May leave building with principal's permission
EXTRA DUTIES	Teachers to be relieved "to extent possible" No duty on street corners unless immediately adjacent to school, police unavailable, and duty performed in that school in past	There will be computerized class registers High school teachers schedule own after-school help	Teachers shall not be required to collect insurance Detention compensated at teachers pro rata salary High School Department Day—45 min. per week for after-school tutoring

Mill City	Vista	Northwood
Elementary: 25 min. contiguous to lunch Secondary: coverage for absent teachers may be rotated	Elementary: 150 min. per week Minimum 15 min. per day. Teachers not required to be present with specialists Secondary: Teachers may be asked to cover classes during emergencies Teachers expected to "normally devote themselves to preparation"	Elementary: 45 min. per day Secondary: 1 period per day If teachers have no preparation periods, they receive extra pay at 1/6 salary Coverage of absent teachers' classes at $10 per class
	The Board shall make an "effort to reduce non-teaching duties"	Teachers expected to supervise bus students, lunchroom, playground, study halls, "and other like functions." Scheduling to be done in consultation with staff

(*continued*)

Contract Provision	Metropolis	Plantville	Shady Heights

TEACHING LOAD	Elementary:
	  no split roster required
	Secondary:
	  no more than 3 grade levels or 4 preparations
	Junior high:
	  24 major subject periods with 6 classes or 25 periods with 5 classes
	Secondary:
	  no more than 3 consecutive teaching periods
		Elementary:
		  no split classes required
		Secondary:
		  25 teaching periods, 5 administrative periods, 5 preparation periods
			Secondary:
			  not more than 2 subject matter areas
			Junior high:
			  not more than 25 periods per week
			Senior high:
			  not more than 21 periods per week

CLASS SIZE	33 per class except special education
	Superintendent must approve classes over 33
		Elementary:
		  system-wide average—23
		  Class limit—28
		Secondary:
		  system-wide—10% may exceed 28. Class limit—35
		  English—28
			Goal: 25 per class

Mill City	Vista	Northwood
	Secondary: 5 teaching periods, 1 preparation period, and 160 student contacts per day (175 if assignment includes study hall) Middle School: 1 preparation period. 165 student contacts	
	High school: 38 maximum. Remedial classes: 22 Middle school: 22.5 average in school Elementary: district-wide averages: K: 25 1–3: 28 4–6: 30	

(*continued*)

Contract Provision	Metropolis	Plantville	Shady Heights
CLASS SIZE *(continued)*			
DISCIPLINE DISRUPTIVE STUDENT	Teachers have immediate recourse to administrators who shall give teachers effective and consistent support	Discipline code to be developed	Policy for responding to "chronically disruptive student"

Mill City	Vista	Northwood
	When grade enrollment in school exceeds district-wide average by 50% new teacher employed if possible	
Discipline code included in appendix	Teacher may exclude disruptive student for 1 period Students suspended only by principal	

Notes

Introduction

1. The first teachers' contract was signed in Cicero, Illinois, in 1944 (William Edward Eaton, *The American Federation of Teachers, 1916–1961: A History of the Movement* [Carbondale: Southern Illinois University Press, 1975], pp. 141–42).

2. Throughout the text, the terms "teacher unions" and "unionism" will be used to refer to the National Education Association and its affiliates as well as to the American Federation of Teachers and its affiliates. While the sample sites were drawn from both organizations, no conclusions can or should be made about the national affiliates on the basis of this small sample.

3. Nearly two decades ago, Myron Lieberman set forth both sides of the case in *Education as a Profession* (Englewood Cliffs, N.J.: Prentice-Hall, 1965), pp. 334–53.

More recently, Marshall O. Donley, Jr., predicted favorable outcomes from collective bargaining: "Where will all this collective bargaining lead? In the long run, it will lead, among other things, to fewer strikes by teachers, greater professionalism of educators, higher teacher morale, an enlarged role in the school for the teacher, and higher salaries for school personnel" (*Power to the Teacher* [Bloomington: Indiana University Press, 1976], p. 207).

By contrast, a feature story about education in *Newsweek* magazine reviewed prevailing criticisms about the effects of teacher unionism: the "unseemly blue collar image," the prevalence of strikes, the "demeaning" effects of collective bargaining on teacher professionalism, and the unions' protection of incompetents. "The unions," it said, "are the source of considerable friction within and without the profession" (Dennis A. Williams et al., "Teachers Are in Trouble," *Newsweek* [April 27, 1971]).

Currently, Myron Lieberman and Albert Shanker continue the polarized debate. Myron Lieberman, "Teachers Bargaining: An Autopsy," *Phi Delta Kappan* 63, no. 4 (Dec. 1981): 231–34; and Albert Shanker, "After Twenty Years Lieberman's Vision Is Failing," *Phi Delta Kappan* 63, no. 4 (Dec. 1981): 236, 278.

4. Stephen K. Bailey, "Foreword" in *Faculty and Teacher Bargaining: The Impact of Unions on Education*, ed. George W. Angell (Lexington, Mass.: Lexington Books, 1981), p. ix.

5. Bureau of National Affairs, *Special Report: Teachers and Labor Relations, 1979–1980* (Washington, D.C.: Bureau of National Affairs, 1980), p. 412.

6. See, e.g., Ronald J. Perry, "Reflections on a School Strike: The Superintendent's View," *Phi Delta Kappan* 57, no. 9 (May 1976): 587–90; and Ellen Hogan Steele, "Reflections on a School Strike: A Teacher's View," *Phi Delta Kappan* 57, no. 9 (May 1976): 590–92.

7. Charles M. Rhemus and Evan Wilner, *The Economic Results of Teacher Bargaining: Michigan's First Two Years* (Ann Arbor, Mich.: Institute of Labor and Industrial Relations, 1965); Herschel Kasper, "The Effects of Collective Bargaining on Public School Teachers' Salaries," *Industrial and Labor Relations Review* 24 (Oct. 1970): 57–72; Robert Thornton, "The Effects of Collective Negotiations on Teachers' Salaries," *Quarterly Review of Economics and Business* 2 (Winter 1971): 37–46; Robert N. Baird and John H. Landon, "The Effects of Collective Bargaining on Public School Teachers' Salaries: Comment," *Industrial and Labor Relations Review* 25 (April 1972): pp. 410–17; W. Clayton Hall and Norman E. Carroll, "The Effects of Teachers' Organizations on Salaries and Class Size," *Industrial and Labor Relations Review* 26 (Jan. 1973): 834–41; David B. Lipsky and John E. Drotning, "The Influence of Collective Bargaining on Teachers' Salaries in New York State," *Industrial and Labor Relations Review* 27 (Oct. 1973): 18–35; Donald E. Frey, "Wage Determination in Public Schools and the Effects of Unionization," Working Paper 42E (Princeton, N.J.: Princeton University, Industrial Relations Section, 1973); Jay G. Chambers, *The Impact of Bargaining and Bargaining Statutes on the Earnings of Public School Teachers: A Comparison in California and Missouri* (Stanford, Calif.: Stanford University, Institute for Research on Educational Finance and Governance, 1980).

8. Charles R. Perry and W. A. Wildman, *The Impact of Negotiations in Public Education: The Evidence from the Schools* (Worthington, Ohio: Jones Publishing Co., 1970) p. 214.

9. Charles R. Perry, "Teacher Bargaining: The Experience in Nine Systems," *Industrial and Labor Relations Review* 33, no. 1 (Oct. 1979): 17.

10. Lorraine McDonnell and Anthony Pascal, *Organized Teachers in American Schools* (Santa Monica, Calif.: Rand Corp., 1979), p. 78.

11. Charles T. Kerchner and Douglas E. Mitchell, *The Dynamics of Public School Bargaining and Its Impacts on Governance, Administration and Teaching* (Washington, D.C.: National Institute of Education, 1981).

12. I use the term "power" to refer to the capability of an individual or group to overcome the resistance of another individual or group in achieving a desired outcome. This use is consistent with other interactive definitions of the term that are found in the literature. See, for example, Peter M. Blau, *Exchange and Power in Social Life* (New York: Wiley, 1964); R. A. Dahl, "The Concept of Power," *Bahaviorial Science* 2 (1957): 201–18; Jeffrey Pfeffer, *Power in Organizations* (Marshfield, Mass.: Pitman Publishing, 1981). As Samuel Bacharach and Edward Lawler observe, the source of power may be formal authority, informal influence, or both. *Power and Politics in Organizations*, (San Francisco: Jossey-Bass Publishing Co., 1980).

13. The works of Charles Kerchner and Douglas Mitchell and of Lorraine McDonnell and Anthony Pascal provide important exceptions here. Both reports of field work findings detail differences in outcomes among several districts.

14. S. Slichter et al., *The Impact of Collective Bargaining on Management* (Washington, D.C.: Brookings Institution, 1960), pp. 954–57.

15. Perry, p. 5.

16. Charles T. Kerchner, "The Impact of Collective Bargaining on School Governance," *Education and Urban Society* 11, no. 2 (Feb. 1979): 182.

17. Susan Moore Johnson, "Performance-based Staff Layoffs in the Public Schools: Implementation and Outcomes," *Harvard Educational Review* 50, no. 2 (May 1980): 214–33.

18. Ibid., pp. 217–19. For a more general discussion of schools as "loosely structured" and "loosely coupled" organizations, see Charles Bidwell, "The School as a Formal Organization," in *Handbook of Organizations*, ed. James G. March (Chicago: Rand McNally, 1965), pp. 927–1022; Terrence E. Deal and Lynn Colatti, "Loose Coupling and the School Administrator," mimeographed, (Stanford, Calif.: Stanford University, Stanford Center for Research and Development in Teaching, 1975); and Karl E. Weick, "Educational Organizations as Loosely Coupled Systems," *Administrative Science Quarterly* 21 (March 1976): 1–19.

19. McDonnell and Pascal conclude: "The principal plays a central role in determining whether collective bargaining works in the school building" (p. 81). Van Cleve Morris et al. document the wide range of principals' administrative styles in *The Urban Principal: Discretionary Decision-making in a Large Educational Organization* (Chicago: University of Illinois at Chicago Circle, 1981).

20. Dan C. Lortie observes, "Uncertainty is the lot of those who teach" (*Schoolteacher: A Sociological Study* [Chicago: University of Chicago Press, 1975], p. 133).

Barak Rosenshine and Norma Furst conclude that a "complete

list of educational 'shoulds' can only be guessed at . . . research in this area has barely begun" ("The Use of Direct Observation to Study Teaching," in *The Second Handbook of Research on Teaching*, ed. Robert M. W. Travers [Chicago: Rand McNally, 1973], p. 162).

James March writes: "Educational technology is poorly understood; asserted educational objectives tend to be vague, contradictory, or not widely shared; participants in educational organizations include individuals and groups who move in and out of activity in the organization sporadically" ("American Public School Administration: A Short Analysis," *School Review* 86 [Feb. 1978]: 223).

21. Lortie, pp. 181, 197, and 200.

22. Ibid., pp. 109–33.

23. Philip W. Jackson, *Life in Classrooms* (New York: Holt, Rinehart & Winston, 1968), p. 165.

24. Richard B. Freeman and James L. Medoff argue that unionism can be assessed differently depending on the outcomes one considers. Considering only bargaining outcomes from "the monopoly view" can lead to a negative assessment, while considering the organizational effects from "the collective voice/institutional response view" can lead to a favorable assessment ("The Two Faces of Unionism," *Public Interest* 57 [Fall 1979]: 70).

25. e.g., Public school enrollments have declined 12 percent since 1971 and are projected to continue to decline through 1984. (National Center for Education Statistics, *Projections of Education Statistics to 1990–91*, Vol. 1 [Washington, D.C.: U.S. Department of Education, 1983], p. 15). 2. The Consumer Price Index has risen to 217.7, an increase of 111.7 percent over the base year of 1967 (Newspaper Enterprise Association, *The World Almanac of Facts, 1981* [New York: Newspaper Enterprise Association, 1981]). 3. Scholastic Aptitude Test scores dropped steadily for fourteen years (*Report on Educational Research* 12, no. 1 [October 15, 1980]). 4. Court orders to desegregate students and staff have been handed down in many major school districts. 5. The average annual school energy costs of $20 per child in 1973 have been projected to reach $280 per child in 1985 (*Education U.S.A.* 23, no. 19, [January 5, 1981]: 138). 6. Thirty-eight states have instituted minimum competency testing (National Center for Education Statistics, *The Condition of Education, 1980* p. 92). 7. Ninety-four percent of all public schools have participated in some federal categorical program (ibid., p. 61). 8. Proposition 13 in California and Proposition 2½ in Massachusetts have limited municipal tax rates and reduced public school revenues.

26. Robert E. Doherty, "Does Teacher Bargaining Affect Student

Achievement?" *Faculty and Teacher Bargaining: The Impact of Unions on Education,* ed. George W. Angell (Lexington, Mass.: Lexington Books, 1981), p. 64.

27. Site selection procedures were designed to reduce the problems of having a small sample. For a further discussion of the issues of sample size in qualitative research, see Jerome T. Murphy, *Getting the Facts: A Fieldwork Guide for Evaluators and Policy Analysts* (Santa Monica, Calif.: Goodyear Publishing Co., 1980), pp. 38–47.

Chapter 1

1. The information included in this description of Metropolis comes from interviews, observations, and documents gathered during July, October, and November 1980.

2. The information included in this description of Mill City comes from interviews, observations, and documents gathered during November and December 1979.

3. The information included in this description of Plantville comes from interviews, observations, and documents gathered during June and July 1979.

4. The information included in this description of Shady Heights comes from interviews, observations, and documents gathered during July, August, September, and October 1979.

5. The information included in this description of Vista comes from interviews, observations, and documents gathered during January and February 1980.

6. The information included in this description of Northwood comes from interviews, observations, and documents gathered during September 1980.

7. An agency shop provision requires that all nonunion teachers in the district pay fees to the union for bargaining on their behalf. Typically such fees are little less than full membership dues.

8. Although principals in Metropolis and Vista also bargained collectively, only in Plantville were principals represented by the same organization as the teachers.

9. James G. March writes: "A student can go from almost any school in the country to almost any other school and find a curriculum that is understandable. Students transfer easily from one school to another, from schools in the East to schools in the West, from rural schools to urban schools, from progressive schools to conservative. A

teacher or administrator can transfer from almost any school district to almost any other and find a bureaucratic structure that is easily recognizable" ("American Public School Administration: A Short Analysis," *School Review* 86 [Feb. 1978]: 221-21).

Chapter 2

1. Howard S. Becker, "The Teacher in the Authority System of the Public School," *Journal of Educational Sociology* 27 (Nov. 1953): 133.

2. R. Theodore Clark, Jr., "Commentary," in *Faculty and Teacher Bargaining: The Impact of Unions on Education*, ed. George W. Angell (Lexington, Mass.: Lexington Books, 1981), p. 87.

3. Robert P. Moser, "Administrator's Clinic: Principals: Shock Absorbers and Stimulators," *Nation's Schools* 94 (Aug. 1974): 11.

4. Frank W. Lutz and William E. Caldwell discuss the exclusion of the principal from negotiations. They write, "One repeatedly hears the cry of the principal: 'We never know what's going on in negotiations until we read it in the papers.'" "Collective Bargaining and the Principal," in *The Principal in Metropolitan Schools*, edited by Donald A. Erickson and Theodore L. Reller (Berkeley, Calif.: McCutchan Publishing Corp., 1979), p. 257.

Lorraine McDonnell and Anthony Pascal found that when principals participated in teacher negotiations, their roles were "ambiguous" (*Organized Teachers in American Schools* [Santa Monica, Calif.: Rand Corp., 1979], p. 49).

5. Interview with Shady Heights assistant superintendent for personnel, July 26, 1979.

6. Interview with president of Metropolis principals' association, July 9, 1980.

7. Interview with Metropolis principal, Oct. 23, 1980.

8. Interviews with Mill City principals, Nov. 6, 7, and 8, 1979.

9. Interviews with Metropolis principals, Oct. 22 and 23, 1980, and Nov. 4, 1980.

10. Interview with Northwood principal, Sept. 21, 1980.

11. Interview with Metropolis principal, Nov. 4, 1980.

12. It is important to emphasize that teacher contracts regulate only parts of school operations. Notably, many matters of instructional and organizational policy are not usually included—e.g., the structure of the school day, the selection of course offerings, the instructional content or organizational format of classes, the assignment of teachers to classes, or the testing and evaluation of students.

13. Interview with Mill City principal, Nov. 7, 1979.

14. Douglas E. Mitchell et al., *The Impact of Collective Bargaining on School Management and Policy* (Claremont, Calif.: Claremont Colleges, 1980).

15. Interview with Vista principal, Jan. 7, 1980.

16. Interview with Shady Heights principal, Aug. 9, 1979.

17. *Agreement between the Plantville School Committee and the Plantville Federation of Teachers, Unit A, September 1, 1979, to August 31, 1981*, p. 49.

18. *Bargaining Agreement between the Vista Education Association and the Board of Education of the Vista Unified School District, 1979–1982*, p. 58.

19. *Agreement between the Board of Education of the School District of Metropolis and the Metropolis Federation of Teachers, September 1, 1980, to August 31, 1981*, p. 5.

20. Interview with Mill City teacher, Dec. 3, 1979.

21. Interview with Mill City principal, Nov. 6, 1979.

22. Interview with Shady Heights teacher, Oct. 17, 1979.

23. Interview with Metropolis principal, Oct. 22, 1980.

24. Interview with Metropolis principal, Oct. 21, 1980.

25. Interview with Northwood superintendent, Sept. 21, 1980.

26. Interview with Metropolis principal, Oct. 22, 1980.

27. Interview with Metropolis principal, Oct. 23, 1980.

28. Interview with Metropolis principal, Oct. 22, 1980.

29. Interview with Shady Heights principal, Aug. 14, 1979.

30. Interview with Shady Heights principal, Aug. 14, 1979.

31. Interview with Metropolis principal, Nov. 4, 1980.

32. Interview with Metropolis teacher, Nov. 18, 1980.

33. Interview with Metropolis principal, Oct. 21, 1980.

34. *Agreement between the Board of Education of the School District of Metropolis and the Metropolis Federation of Teachers, September 1, 1980, to August 31, 1981*, p. 3.

35. This is consistent with the findings of McDonnell and Pascal, who report: "School-site committees also vary greatly in schools even within the same district. In one district with contractually mandated committees, a central office administrator noted that they are 'all over the map' in terms of effectiveness, ranging from adversarial to cooperative working relationships. Some actually co-administer the building while others have no influence" (p. 77).

36. Interview with Vista principal, Jan. 9, 1980.

37. Interview with Vista principal, Jan. 7, 1980.

38. Interview with Vista principal, Jan. 7, 1980.

39. Interview with Vista principal, Jan. 8, 1980.

40. Interview with Metropolis principal, Oct. 21, 1980.

41. Interview with Metropolis principal, Nov. 5, 1980.

42. Interview with Metropolis principal, Oct. 23, 1980.

43. Interview with Metropolis principal, Oct. 23, 1980.

44. Interview with Mill City teacher, Dec. 5, 1979.

45. Interview with Mill City teacher, Dec. 6, 1979.

46. Interview with Vista teacher, Feb. 13, 1980.

47. Interview with Metropolis principal, Oct. 23, 1980.

48. Interview with Shady Heights teacher, Oct. 4, 1979.

49. Interview with Plantville teacher, Oct. 11, 1979.

50. Interview with Metropolis principal, Nov. 4, 1980.

51. Interview with Metropolis subdistrict administrator, June 26, 1980.

52. Interview with Metropolis principal, Oct. 20, 1980.

53. *Master Agreement Between the Board of Education, Mill City, and the Mill City Education Association, 1978*, p. 61.

54. Interviews with Shady Heights teachers, Oct. 16, and 17, 1979.

55. Interview with Mill City principal, June 26, 1979.

56. Observations at Vista school board meeting, Jan. 10, 1980; interviews with Vista teachers, Feb. 11 and 12, 1980.

57. Interviews with Shady Heights principal and teachers, Aug. 4, 1979, and Oct. 4 and 5, 1979.

58. Interview with Metropolis principal, Oct. 21, 1980.

59. Interview with Metropolis principal, Oct. 20, 1980.

60. Interviews with Shady Heights principal and teachers, Aug. 14, 1979, and Oct. 16, 1979.

61. Interview with Vista principal, Jan. 10, 1980.

62. Interview with Shady Heights principal, Aug. 2, 1979.

63. Interviews with Vista teachers, Feb. 13 and 14, 1980.

64. Interview with Metropolis principal, Oct. 21, 1980.

65. Interview with Mill City principal, Nov. 8, 1979.

66. Interview with Shady Heights principal, Aug. 2, 1979.

67. Interview with Plantville principal, June 26, 1979.

68. Interview with Plantville principal, June 26, 1979.

69. Interview with Shady Heights principal, Aug. 9, 1979.

70. Interview with Metropolis principal, Oct. 22, 1980.

71. Interview with Metropolis principal, Oct. 23, 1980.

72. Interview with Shady Heights principal, Aug. 14, 1979.

73. Interviews with union presidents in Shady Heights, Sept. 24, 1979, and Plantville, July 11, 1979.

74. Interview with Northwood teacher, Sept. 23, 1980.

75. Interview with Mill City superintendent, Nov. 5, 1979.

76. Interview with Mill City principal, Nov. 6, 1979.

77. *Agreement between the Board of Education of the School District of Metropolis and the Metropolis Federation of Teachers, September 1, 1980, to August 31, 1981*, p. 2.

78. Interview with Metropolis union staff member, July 9, 1980.

79. Interview with Metropolis principal, Oct. 23, 1980.

80. Interview with Metropolis subdistrict superintendent, July 8, 1980.

Chapter 3

1. James G. March writes: "The situation is masked sometimes by considerable panoply of hierarchical artifacts—plans, memoranda, meetings, rules, deference, annoyance, organization charts, evaluations; but most observers agree that direct administrative leverage over education is relatively small and distributed widely through a large number of only loosely coordinated administrative positions." "American Public School Administration: A Short Analysis" *School Review 86* [Feb. 1978]: 229–30. See also Van Cleve Morris et al., *The Urban Principal: Discretionary Decision-making in a Large Educational Organization* (Chicago: University of Illinois at Chicago Circle, 1981), p. 143.

2. Arthur E. Wise, *Legislated Learning: The Bureaucratization of the American Classroom* (Berkeley: University of California Press, 1979), p. 200.

3. Ibid., p. 212.

4. Interview with Metropolis Labor Relations Office administrator, July 10, 1980.

5. Interview with Metropolis Labor Relations Office administrator, June 24, 1980. The influence of these institutionalized advocates of collective bargaining is similar to that Paul T. Hill oberved in state and local officials who administer federal programs and thus constitute part of an informal regulatory system.

(*Enforcement and Informal Pressure in the Management of Federal Categorical Programs in Education* [Santa Monica, Calif.: Rand Corp., 1979]).

6. Ronald G. Corwin found "a high positive correlation between the number of levels of authority in a school system and organizational conflict." He argues that "if social hierarchies limit conflict by establishing zones of authority, they also promote it to the extent that people at each level feel obligated to defend their domains from challenge by

subordinate levels." ("The Organizational Context of School Board–Teacher Conflict," *Understanding School Boards: Problems and Prospects*, ed. Peter J. Cistone [Lexington, Mass.: D. C. Heath, 1975], p. 138).

7. Interview with Metropolis Labor Relations administrator, July 9, 1980.

8. Charles T. Kerchner writes: "Collective bargaining places great reliance on uniformity. Indeed, one of the stated purposes of labor relations is to avoid capriciousness in the treatment of employees. The objective reality behind this goal is that uniform rules for the treatment, payment and discipline of employees are part of every labor agreement" ("The Impact of Collective Bargaining on School Governance," *Education and Urban Society* 11, no. 2 [Feb. 1979]: 195).

9. These findings are consistent with those of Douglas E. Mitchell et al., who write: "Our data indicate, for example, that bargaining has produced a trend toward more homogeneous and consistent interpretation and application of work rules among all the schools within any given district. Central office managers are noticeably sensitive to the potential problems in contract administration which can arise if contract clauses are interpreted or applied in different ways in different schools. In most of our sample districts, central office managers warn middle managers that there are hazards in allowing divergent practices" (*The Impact of Collective Bargaining on School Management and Policy* [Claremont, Calif.: Claremont Colleges, 1980]).

10. Interview with Metropolis Labor Relations Office administrator, June 24, 1980.

11. Interview with Shady Heights principal, Aug. 9, 1979.

12. Interview with Mill City teachers' union president, Nov. 6, 1979.

13. Interview with Northwood superintendent, Sept. 21, 1980.

14. Interview with Plantville principal, July 5, 1979.

15. Interview with Shady Heights principal, Aug. 2, 1979.

16. Interview with Mill City personnel director, Nov. 5, 1979.

17. Interview with Metropolis principal, Oct. 22, 1980.

18. Interview with Metropolis principal, Oct. 20, 1980.

19. Interview with Metropolis principal, Oct. 23, 1980.

20. Interview with Shady Heights principal, Aug. 9, 1979.

21. Interview with Metropolis principal, Oct. 23, 1980.

22. Interview with Metropolis principal, Nov. 4, 1980.

23. Interview with Shady Heights principal, Aug. 9, 1979.

24. Interview with Shady Heights principal, Aug. 9, 1979.

25. Interview with Shady Heights principal, Aug. 9, 1979.

26. Interview with Shady Heights principal, Aug. 2, 1979.

27. Interview with district administrators in Metropolis, Shady Heights, and Plantville, July 7 and 26, 1979; July 8, 9, and 10, 1980; and Oct. 21, 1980.

28. Interview with Metropolis subdistrict superintendent, June 26, 1980.

29. Interview with Metropolis union staff member, Nov. 4, 1980.

30. Interview with Vista principal, Jan. 10, 1980.

31. The state attorney general subsequently ruled that the practice conflicted with the evaluation process that was already in place, which had been developed in response to state requirements.

32. Interview with Metropolis Labor Relations Office administrator, July 9, 1980.

33. Interview with Metropolis Labor Relations Office administrator, June 24, 1980.

34. Interview with Metropolis subdistrict administrator, June 25, 1980.

35. Interview with Metropolis subdistrict superintendent, June 26, 1980.

36. Interview with Mill City district administrator, Nov. 5, 1979.

37. Interview with Mill City superintendent, Nov. 5, 1979.

38. See Gertrude H. McPherson, "What Principals Should Know about Teachers," in *The Principal in Metropolitan Schools*, ed. Donald A. Erickson and Theodore L. Reller (Berkeley, Calif.: McCutchan Publishing Corp., 1979), pp. 233–55; and Dan C. Lortie, "The Balance of Control and Autonomy in Elementary School Teaching," in *The Semi-Professions and Their Organizations*, ed. Amitai Etzioni (New York: Free Press, 1969), pp. 1–53.

39. Interestingly, Morris et al. found that district administrators did not even try to directly control principals' practices: "Although elementary and secondary school principals find themselves following organizational rules and regulations (most of which are promulgated by their superiors), it is rare for a principal at either level to be directly instructed to do something or to refrain from doing something by echelons above him" (p. 198).

40. Interview with Northwood teachers' union president, Sept. 24, 1980.

41. Interview with Mill City personnel director, Nov. 5, 1979.

42. Interview with Mill City union president, Nov. 6, 1979.

43. The union leader was more aggressive in his approach to teacher negotiations and strike preparations than he was in resolving in-

school disputes. (interview with Mill City union president, Nov. 6, 1979).

44. Interviews with Mill City district office administrators, Nov. 5, 1979.

45. Interview with Plantville assistant superintendent, June 7, 1979.

46. Interview with Plantville union president, July 11, 1979.

47. Interview with Vista superintendent, Jan. 9, 1980.

48. Interview with Vista principal, Jan. 7, 1980.

49. Interview with Vista teachers' union president, Jan. 8, 1980.

50. Interview with Shady Heights assistant superintendent for personnel, July 26, 1979.

51. There was considerable discrepancy in the reported numbers of arbitrations. The Labor Relations Office records showed that there were 270 grievances and 6 arbitrations during the 1979 calendar year. However, a Labor Relations Office administrator reported that thirty to forty arbitrations are heard each year (interview, July 9, 1980). The union chairman of grievances estimated that twenty grievances are arbitrated each year (interview, June 25, 1980).

52. Interview with Metropolis union officers, June 25, 1980.

53. Interview with Metropolis subdistrict superintendent, July 8, 1980.

54. Interview with Metropolis Labor Relations Office administrator, June 25, 1980.

55. Interview with Metropolis principal, Oct. 23, 1980

56. Interview with Shady Heights union president, Sept. 24, 1979.

57. Interview with Shady Heights assistant superintendent for personnel, July 26, 1979.

58. Interview with Shady Heights principal, Aug. 2, 1979.

59. Interview with Mill City teacher, Dec. 3, 1979.

60. Interview with Plantville teacher, Sept. 20, 1979.

61. Interview with Metropolis union staff member, Nov. 4, 1980.

62. Interview with Shady Heights teacher, Oct. 4, 1979.

63. Interviews with Mill City teachers, Dec. 4, 1979.

64. Interview with Vista principal, Jan. 8, 1980.

65. Interview with Shady Heights principal, Aug. 9, 1979.

66. Interview with Plantville principal, June 27, 1979.

67. Interview with Plantville principal, June 28, 1979.

68. Interviews with Plantville teachers, Sept. 20 and 21, 1979.

69. Interviews with Metropolis principals, Oct. 10 and 21, 1980.

70. Interviews with Shady Heights teachers, Aug. 14, 1979.

71. Interview with Shady Heights principal, Aug. 2, 1979.

72. National public school enrollments peaked at 46.0 million in 1971–72 and then began to decline, reaching 41.6 million in 1979–80 (W. Vance Grant and Leo J. Eiden, *Digest of Education Statistics, 1980* [Washington, D.C.: National Center for Education Statistics, 1980], p. 34).

73. George C. Kyte, *The Principal at Work* (New York: Ginn & Co., 1952), p. 106; Harry F. Wilcott, *The Man in the Principal's Office: An Ethnography* (New York: Holt, Rinehart & Winston, 1973), p. 194; Susan Moore Johnson, "Performance-based Staff Layoffs in the Public Schools: Implementation and Outcomes," *Harvard Educational Review* 50, no. 2 (May 1980): 214.

74. Interview with Mill City principal, Nov. 7, 1979.

75. Interview with Metropolis Labor Relations Office administrator, June 24, 1980.

76. A 1979 survey of high school principals revealed that 97 percent of them had the power either to select teachers, who would then be endorsed by the district office, or to select teachers from limited options provided by the district office (Lloyd E. McCleary and Scott D. Thomson, *The Senior High School Principalship. Vol. 3. The Summary Report* [Reston, Va.: National Association of Secondary School Principals, 1979], p. 19).

77. Interviews with Plantville June 7, 1979, and Shady Heights district office administrators, July 26, 1979.

78. Interviews with Mill City principals, Nov. 7 and 8, 1979.

79. Interview with Metropolis principal, Nov. 4, 1980.

80. Interview with Mill City principal, Nov. 8, 1979.

81. Interview with Mill City principal, Nov. 6, 1979.

82. Interview with Metropolis principal, Nov. 4, 1980.

83. Interview with Metropolis principal, Nov. 4, 1980.

84. Interview with Shady Heights principal, Aug. 9, 1979.

85. Interview with Mill City principal, Nov. 6, 1979.

86. Interview with Shady Heights union president, July 26, 1979.

Chapter 4

1. A systematic investigation of prebargaining practices was not included in this study. These generalizations about principals' former discretionary powers are based on respondents' recollections of the past.

2. Interview with Vista principal, Dec. 21, 1980.

3. R. Theodore Clark, Jr., "Commentary," in *Faculty and Teacher Bargaining: The Impact of Unions on Education*, ed. George W. Angell (Lexington, Mass.: Lexington Books, 1981).

4. John E. Dunlop asserts: "The workday, workweek, and workyear in education are products more of tradition and interdistrict comparisons than of any other factors. . . . Collective bargaining has for the most part confirmed existing practices in these matters or merely moved with already existing trends" "Commentary," in *Faculty and Teacher Bargaining: The Impact of Unions on Education*, edited by George W. Angell [Lexington, Mass.: Lexington Books, 1981]). p. 80.

Clark concludes differently: "While I do not have the solid documentation . . . , I know that collective bargaining has resulted in substantial pressures to reduce the minutes of instruction per day" (p. 86).

Charles R. Perry found that three of his five sample districts had negotiated shorter school days. ("Teacher Bargaining: The Experience in Nine Systems," *Industrial and Labor Relations Review* 33, no. 1 [Oct. 1979]: 13).

5. *Bargaining Agreement between the Vista Education Association and the Board of Education of the Vista Unified School District, 1979–1982*, p. 35.

6. Interview with Metropolis principal, Oct. 23, 1980.

7. Interview with Vista principal, Jan. 10, 1980.

8. Interviews with Plantville teachers, Oct. 10, and 11, 1979.

9. Interview with Mill City principal, Nov. 6, 1979.

10. Interviews with Plantville teachers, Sept. 20, and 21, 1979.

11. I was interviewing a teacher when I was told that the school would be locked in five minutes (Oct. 10, 1979).

12. Interview with Plantville principal, Aug. 17, 1979.

13. Interview with Plantville teacher, Sept. 21, 1979.

14. Teachers' rights to participate on many district-wide committees had been won through collective bargaining.

15. Interview with Shady Heights principal, June 26, 1979.

16. Interview with Metropolis principal, Nov. 4, 1980.

17. In part, school districts have equalized the pay for athletic activities in response to federal requirements for sex equity; e.g., the girls' basketball coach is no longer expected to volunteer.

18. Interview with Mill City principal, Nov. 6, 1979.

19. *Agreement between the Shady Heights School Committee and the Shady Heights Teachers' Union, February 1, 1979, to January 31, 1981*, p. 21.

20. Interviews with Shady Heights teachers, Oct. 4 and 5, 1979.

21. Interviews with Metropolis principals, Oct. 22 and 23, 1980.

22. Interview with Metropolis teacher, Nov. 6, 1980.

23. Interview with Metropolis principal, Nov. 4, 1980.

24. Charles T. Kerchner and Douglas E. Mitchell report similar findings in *The Dynamics of Public School Bargaining and Its Impact on Governance, Administration, and Teaching* (Washington, D.C.: National Institute of Education, 1981).

25. Interview with Mill City teacher, Dec. 6, 1979.

26. Interview with Northwood principal, Sept. 21, 1980.

27. Interview with Metropolis principal, Oct. 23, 1980.

28. Interview with Plantville district administrator, June 7, 1979.

29. Interview with Vista principal, Jan. 10, 1980.

30. Interview with Metropolis principal, Nov. 4, 1980.

31. *Agreement between the Shady Heights School Committee and the Shady Heights Teachers' Union, February 1, 1979, to January 31, 1981*, p. 19.

32. *Agreement between the Plantville School Committee and the Plantville Federation of Teachers, Unit A, September 1, 1979, to August 31, 1981*, p. 15.

33. *Bargaining Agreement between the Vista Education Association and the Board of Education of the Vista Unified School District, 1979–1982*, p. 43.

34. *Agreement between the Board of Education of the School District of Metropolis and the Metropolis Federation of Teachers, September 1, 1980, to August 31, 1981*, p. 57.

35. Interviews with Metropolis subdistrict administrator, Oct. 21, 1980, and Metropolis principal, Nov. 4, 1980.

36. Interview with Metropolis union president, June 9, 1980.

37. Interview with Metropolis teacher, Nov. 5, 1980.

38. Interview with Shady Heights principal, Aug. 2, 1979.

39. Interview with Metropolis subdistrict superintendent, Oct. 21, 1980.

40. Interview with Metropolis principal, Oct. 23, 1980.

41. Interview with Metropolis principal, Oct. 20, 1980.

42. Interview with Metropolis principal, Oct. 20, 1980.

43. Interview with Shady Heights principal, Aug. 14, 1979.

44. *Master Agreement between the Board of Education, Mill City, and the Mill City Education Association, September 1, 1977, to December 31, 1979*, p. 57.

45. *Agreement between the Board of Education of the School District of Metropolis and the Metropolis Federation of Teachers, September 1, 1980, to August 31, 1981*, p. 29.

46. *Bargaining Agreement between the Vista Education Association and the Board of Education of the Vista Unified School District, 1979–1982*, p. 34.

47. The president of the Shady Heights teachers' union reported that the union had not pressed for a full period of duty-free lunch for

high school teachers because such a change would have made it impossible to manage the cafeteria (interview, Sept. 24, 1979).

48. Interview with Metropolis principal, Oct. 20, 1980.

49. Interview with Metropolis principal, Oct. 21, 1980.

50. Interview with Plantville principal, Aug. 17, 1979.

51. Interview with Metropolis district office administrator, June 26, 1980.

52. Interview with Metropolis principal, Oct. 22, 1980.

53. Interview with Shady Heights principal, Aug. 9, 1979.

54. Interview with Vista principal, Jan. 10, 1980.

55. Interview with Plantville principal, June 28, 1979.

56. Interview with Shady Heights principal, Aug. 9, 1979.

57. Interview with Mill City principal, Nov. 6, 1979.

58. Interview with Shady Heights principal, Aug. 9, 1979.

59. Interview with Mill City principal, Nov. 8, 1979.

60. Interview with Mill City principal, Nov. 8, 1979.

61. Interview with Shady Heights teacher, Oct. 2, 1979.

62. Interview with Metropolis principal, Oct. 21, 1980.

63. Interview with Metropolis principal, Oct. 23, 1980.

64. Interview with Northwood teachers' union president, Sept. 24, 1980.

65. Interview with Metropolis subdistrict administrator, June 26, 1980.

Chapter 5

1. Robert Benjamin, *Making Schools Work* (New York: Continuum Publishing Corp., 1981), p. 54.

2. Since 1977, fifteen states have mandated such testing for teacher certification (Education Commission of the States, "Issuegram: Teacher Competency" [Denver, August 1981]).

3. Susan Moore Johnson, "Performance-based Staff Layoffs in the Public Schools: Implementation and Outcomes," *Harvard Educational Review* 50, no. 2 (May 1980): 215.

4. Interviews with Plantville district office administrator, June 6, 1979, and union officer, July 11, 1979.

5. Interviews with Mill City teachers and principal, Dec. 3, 1979.

6. Interviews with Mill City teachers, Dec. 4, 1979.

7. Interview with Mill City principal, Nov. 6, 1979.

8. Interview with Metropolis teacher, Nov. 20, 1980.

9. Interview with Shady Heights principal, Aug. 14, 1979.

10. Interview with Plantville principal, June 28, 1979.

11. Interview with Metropolis teacher, Nov. 5, 1980.

12. Interview with Plantville teacher, Sept. 28, 1979.

13. Interview with Vista union leader, Feb. 12, 1980.

14. Interview with Mill City teacher, Dec. 6, 1979.

15. Interview with Plantville teacher, Oct. 10, 1979.

16. Interview with Mill City principal, Nov. 6, 1979.

17. Interview with Mill City teacher, Dec. 5, 1979.

18. Interview with Mill City teacher, Dec. 6, 1979.

19. Interview with Mill City district administrator, Nov. 5, 1979.

20. Interview with Mill City superintendent, Nov. 5, 1979.

21. *Agreement between the Shady Heights School Committee and the Shady Heights Teachers' Union, 1978–1979*, p. 10.

22. Ibid.

23. Interview with president of Metropolis principals' association, July 9, 1980.

24. Interview with Metropolis subdistrict administrator, July 8, 1980.

25. Interview with Metropolis principal, Oct. 21, 1980.

26. Interview with Metropolis principal, Nov. 4, 1980.

27. Interview with Vista union building representative, Feb. 14, 1980.

28. Interview with Shady Heights principal, Aug. 14, 1979.

29. The report is consistent with my previous findings (Johnson, p. 220).

30. Interview with Mill City principal, Nov. 6, 1979.

31. Others have documented how rarely teaching performance is evaluated. (Sanford M. Dornbush and W. Richard Scott, *Evaluation and the Exercise of Authority* [San Francisco, Calif.: Jossey-Bass Publishing Co., 1975]; John W. Meyer and Brian Rowan, "The Structure of Educational Organizations," in *Environments and Organizations*, ed. Marshall W. Meyer, et al. (San Francisco, Calif.: Jossey-Bass Publishing Co., 1978), p. 81

32. Interview with Metropolis principal, Nov. 5, 1980.

33. Interview with Shady Heights principal, Aug. 14, 1979.

34. Interview with Metropolis teacher, Nov. 6, 1980.

35. Steele V. Louisville and Nashville Railroad Company, 323 U.S. 192, 65 Sup Ct. 226, 89 L.Ed. 173 (1944).

36. Belanger V. Matteson, 346 A.2d 124 (1975).

37. Interview with Metropolis district administrator, June 25, 1980.

38. Interview with Vista union building representative, Feb. 13, 1980.

39. Interview with Mill City principal, Nov. 8, 1979.

40. Interview with Metropolis principal, Oct. 20, 1980.

41. Interview with Metropolis principal, Oct. 21, 1980.

42. Interview with Mill City principal, Nov. 6, 1979.

43. Interview with Mill City principal, Nov. 7, 1979.

44. Interview with Metropolis subdistrict superintendent, July 8, 1980.

45. Interviews with Metropolis district office administrator, June 24, 1980, and Labor Relations Office administrator, June 25, 1980. These reports are consistent with the findings of Van Cleve Morris et al.: "Even in the case of gross incompetence, the principal is required to spend weeks and months in carefully staged observations, teacher conferences, consultations with the district superintendent, not to mention the piece-by-piece accumulation of supporting documents—the "paper trail"—to prosecute the case. And these long hours, personally unpleasant and emotionally draining, customarily lead nowhere: the impossibly incompetent teacher is simply transferred to another school by central headquarters to inflict his or her stupidity on another group of unsuspecting students" *The Urban Principal: Discretionary Decision-making in a Large Educational Organization* [Chicago: University of Illinois at Chicago Circle, 1981], p. 61).

46. Interview with Metropolis district office administrator, June 25, 1980.

47. Interview with Shady Heights principal, Aug. 14, 1979.

48. Interview with Metropolis district administrator, Aug. 24, 1980.

49. Interview with Metropolis district administrator, Aug. 24, 1980.

50. Interview with Metropolis subdistrict administrator, Oct. 21, 1980.

51. Interview with Metropolis principal, Nov. 4, 1980.

52. Interview with Shady Heights principal, Aug. 14, 1979.

53. Interview with Mill City principal, Nov. 6, 1979.

54. Interview with Plantville principal, Aug. 17, 1979.

55. Interview with Metropolis principal, Oct. 23, 1980.

56. Interview with Plantville teacher, Nov. 11, 1979.

57. Interview with Shady Heights principal, Aug. 2, 1979.

58. Interview with Vista principal, Jan. 10, 1980.

59. Interviews with Vista teachers, Feb. 12, 1980.

60. Interview with Mill City teacher, Dec. 5, 1979.

61. Interview with Shady Heights teacher, Oct. 2, 1979.

62. Interviews with Shady Heights teachers, Oct. 5, 1979.

Chapter 6

1. All data for the description of Metropolis High School No. 1 were gathered during interviews with the principal and teachers of this school on Oct. 23 and Nov. 6, 1980.

2. A data for the description of Metropolis High School No. 2 were gathered during interviews with the principal and teachers of this school on Oct. 23 and Nov. 5, 1980.

3. All data for the description of Plantville Elementary School No. 1 were gathered during interviews with the principal and teachers of this school on Aug. 17 and Sept. 20 and 21, 1979.

4. All data for the description of Plantville Elementary School No. 2 were gathered during interviews with the principal and teachers of this school on June 28 and Sept. 27 and 28, 1979.

5. All data for the description of Vista High School were gathered during interviews with the principal and teachers of this school on Jan. 10 and Feb. 13 and 14, 1980.

6. All data for the description of Shady Heights High School were gathered during interviews with the principal and teachers of this school on Aug. 14 and Oct. 4 and 5, 1979.

7. Others have found the role of the principal to be central in successful school programs. See, e.g., Paul Berman and Milbrey McLaughlin, *Federal Programs Supporting Educational Change, Vol. VIII, Implementing and Sustaining Innovation* (Santa Monica, Calif.: Rand Corp., 1978), pp. 30–31; Ronald Edmonds, "Effective Schools for the Urban Poor," *Educational Leadership* 37, no. 1 (Oct. 1979): 15–24; and Donald R. Moore et al., *Student Classification and the Right to Read* (Chicago, Ill.: Designs for Change, 1981), p. 115.

8. Dan C. Lortie likens the relationship between teachers and principals to that between vassals and lords during medieval times: "The Superordinate is expected to use his power to protect and help those of lesser rank; they, in turn, are bound in fealty to return the appropriate deference and respect" (*Schoolteacher: A Sociological Study* [Chicago: University of Chicago Press, 1975], p. 200).

9. Ibid., pp. 196–97; see also Gertrude H. McPherson, "What Principals Should Know about Teachers," in *The Principal in Metropolitan*

Schools, ed. Donald A. Erickson and Theodore L. Reller (Berkeley, Calif.: McCutchan Publishing Corp, 1979), pp. 235–36 and 242–43.

10. Lortie, pp. 15–17; see also Richard Weatherly and Michael Lipsky, "Street-Level Bureaucrats and Institutional Innovation: Implementing Special Education Reform," *Harvard Educational Review* 47, no. 2 (May 1977): 171–96); and Seymour B. Sarason, *The Culture of the School and the Problem of Change* (Boston: Allyn & Bacon, 1971), pp. 118–20.

11. Seymour Sarason writes: "The tendency to think in terms of, and to over-evaluate, the power of the principal is no less mistaken in the case of principal than it is when we think of the power of the President of our country." (p. 119).

12. Lortie, pp. 201–2.

13. Interview with Shady Heights principal, Aug. 9, 1979.

14. Such questions included: What do you need to do your job well? Are you satisfied with the gains in working conditions that have been made through collective bargaining? What kind of issue might you grieve?

15. Interview with Vista teacher, Feb. 13, 1980.

16. Interview with Plantville teacher, Sept. 28, 1979.

17. Interview with Mill City teacher, Dec. 6, 1979.

18. Interview with Mill City teacher, Dec. 4, 1979.

19. Interview with Mill City teacher, Dec. 6, 1979.

20. Interview with Mill City teacher, Dec. 4, 1979.

21. Interview with Shady Heights union leader, Sept. 24, 1979.

22. Interviews with Metropolis teachers, Nov. 18, 1980.

23. Interview with Metropolis principal and teachers, Oct. 23, 1980.

24. Interview with Mill City teacher, Dec. 4, 1979.

25. Interview with Plantville teacher, Sept. 28, 1979.

26. Interview with Plantville teacher, Sept. 28, 1979.

27. Interview with Metropolis teacher, Nov. 18, 1980.

28. Interview with Shady Heights teacher, Oct. 4, 1979.

29. R. Theodore Clark, Jr., explains teachers' ambivalence about being union members: "Teaching is a profession, and professional employees, at least in this country, tend not to desire unionization unless it is necessary for defensive reasons. It should come as no big surprise then that many teachers and would be teachers embrace collective bargaining with less than total enthusiasm. Moreover, the highly adversarial nature of collective bargaining in public education, including strikes, picketing, and name calling, is hardly designed to enhance the reputation or attractiveness of the teaching profession"

("Commentary," in *Faculty and Teacher Bargaining: The Impact of Unions on Education*, edited by George W. Angell [Lexington, Mass.: Lexington Books, 1981], p. 89).

30. Interview with Mill City teacher, Dec. 5, 1979.
31. Interview with Vista teacher, Feb. 12, 1980.
32. Interview with Mill City teacher, Dec. 4, 1979.
33. Interview with Metropolis teacher, Nov. 20, 1980.
34. Interview with Metropolis teacher, Oct. 23, 1980.
35. Interview with Plantville teacher, Sept. 21, 1979.
36. Interview with Shady Heights teacher, Oct. 5, 1979.
37. Interview with Metropolis teacher, Nov. 19, 1980.
38. Interview with Shady Heights teacher, Oct. 17, 1979.
39. Interview with Shady Heights teacher, Oct. 17, 1979.
40. Interview with Metropolis principal, Oct. 20, 1980.
41. Interview with Shady Heights teacher, Oct. 4, 1979.
42. Interview with Plantville teacher, Oct. 10, 1979.
43. Interview with Metropolis teacher, Nov. 18, 1980.
44. Interview with Mill City teacher, Dec. 4, 1979.
45. Interview with Metropolis principal, July 9, 1980.
46. Interview with Shady Heights principal, Aug. 14, 1979.
47. Interview with Shady Heights principal, Oct. 5, 1979.
48. Interview with Metropolis principal, Nov. 4, 1980.
49. Interview with Metropolis principal, Nov. 4, 1980.
50. Interview with Shady Heights principal, Aug. 2, 1979.
51. Interview with Shady Heights principal, Aug. 2, 1979.
52. Interview with Shady Heights principal, Aug. 2, 1979.
53. Alvin W. Gouldner sets forth "two interrelated minimal demands of the norm of reciprocity: (1) People should help those who have helped them, and (2) People should not injure those who have helped them" ("The Norm of Reciprocity: A Preliminary Statement," *American Sociological Review* 25, no. 2 [April 1960]: p. 171).
54. Interview with Vista teacher, Feb. 13, 1980.
55. Interview with Mill City principal, Nov. 6, 1979.
56. Interview with Metropolis principal, Oct. 22, 1980.
57. Interview with Vista principal, Jan. 7, 1980.
58. Interview with Metropolis principal, Oct. 23, 1980.
59. Interview with Shady Heights teacher, Oct. 2, 1979.
60. Interview with Metropolis principal, Oct. 10, 1980.
61. Interview with Shady Heights teacher, Oct. 2, 1979.
62. Interview with Shady Heights teacher, Oct. 2, 1979.
63. Interview with Shady Heights teacher, Oct. 4, 1979.

64. Interview with Plantville teacher, Sept. 27, 1979.

65. Interview with Vista teacher, Oct. 4, 1979.

66. Letter from Plantville teachers to former union president (Jan. 12, 1973).

67. Interview with Metropolis principal, Oct. 23, 1980.

68. "That though there is no fixed line between wrong and right,/There are roughly zones whose laws must be obeyed" (Robert Frost, "There are Roughly Zones," in *Complete Poems of Robert Frost* [New York: Holt, Rinehart & Winston, 1949], p. 401).

69. Interview with Metropolis district office administrator, July 10, 1980.

70. Interview with Metropolis subdistrict superintendent, July 8, 1980.

71. Interviews with Metropolis district administrators, June 24 and 26 and July 10, 1980.

72. Interview with Metropolis district administrator, June 26, 1980.

73. Interview with Metropolis district administrator, June 26, 1980.

74. Interview with Metropolis district administrator, July 9, 1980.

Conclusion

1. Plantville, where teachers had been bargaining but seven years, had one of the strongest contracts in the study. Similarly, Lorraine McDonnell and Anthony Pascal found that the "weakest contract in our fieldwork sample has been bargaining ten years, as long as the district with the strongest contract." They conclude, "Our evidence on bargaining agendas indicates that most teacher organizations will obtain future contractual provisions to the point where they reflect the average district in our sample" (*Organized Teachers in American Schools* [Santa Monica, Calif.: Rand Corp., 1979], p. 80).

2. E.g., Plantville and Mill City did not fulfill the expectation that urban districts have more strident unions or less amicable labor relations. Nor did Shady Heights confirm the view that suburban districts have weak teacher organizations or contracts.

3. I visited the Metropolis schools just two weeks after the conclusion of a major teachers' strike and found the recent work stoppage to have affected school site labor relations only slightly. Reports from Mill City, Shady Heights, and Metropolis indicated that the first strikes

experienced in each of those districts had seriously disrupted teacher-teacher and teacher-administrator relations within the schools. However, during subsequent strikes, principals had been careful not to take rigid management stands, and thus they had managed to avoid alienating their teachers and jeopardizing ongoing labor practices in their schools.

4. Respondents in Plantville usually reported that secondary teachers were more militant than elementary teachers, and they provided several plausible explanations: e.g., elementary teachers work more closely with their principals, more secondary teachers are men with families to support. Respondents in Northwood usually reported that teachers there were more militant in the elementary schools, and several speculated that this was so because, without extracurricular responsibilities, elementary staff had more time to organize union efforts.

5. Jerome T. Murphy, "Title I of ESEA: The Politics of Implementing Federal Education Reform," *Harvard Educational Review* 41 (1971): 35–63; Milbrey McLaughlin, "Implementation as Mutual Adaptation: Change in the Classroom," *Teachers College Record* 77 (1976): 337–51; Jeffrey L. Pressman and Aaron B. Wildavsky, *Implementation* (Berkeley: University of California Press, 1973); Walter Williams and Richard F. Elmore, eds., *Social Program Implementation* (New York: Academic Press, 1976).

6. Milbrey McLaughlin et al. first wrote of "mutual adaptation" in reference to school improvement programs. This research suggests that the term is applicable as well to regulatory policies (*Federal Programs Supporting Educational Change. Vol. 3. The Process of Change* [Santa Monica, Calif.: Rand Corp., 1975], p. vii).

7. This refers to nonwage items. Teachers who expected that there would be few changes in working conditions often anticipated that they would agressively pursue higher salaries.

Bibliography

Aaron, Benjamin; Grodin, Joseph R.; and Stern, James L. *Public-Sector Bargaining*. Washington, D.C.: Industrial Relations Research Association, 1979.

Angell, George W., ed. *Faculty and Teacher Bargaining: The Impact of Unions on Education*. Lexington, Mass.: Lexington Books, 1981.

Argyle, Nolan. "The Impact of Collective Bargaining on Public School Governance." *Public Policy*, 28, no. 1 (Winter 1980): 117–41.

Austin, Gilbert R. "Exemplary Schools and the Search for Effectiveness." *Educational Leadership* 37, no. 1 (Oct. 1979): 10–21.

Bacharach, Samuel B. and Lawler, Edward J. *Power and Politics in Organizations*. (San Francisco: Jossey-Bass Publishing Co., 1980.

Bailey, Stephen K. "Foreword." In *Faculty and Teacher Bargaining: The Impact of Unions on Education*, edited by George W. Angell. Lexington, Mass.: Lexington Books, 1981.

Baird, Robert N., and Landon, John H. "The Effects of Collective Bargaining on Public School Teachers' Salaries: Comment." *Industrial and Labor Relations Review* 25 (April 1972): 410–17.

Bardach, Eugene. *The Implementation Game*. Cambridge, Mass: MIT Press, 1979.

Becker, Howard S. "The Teacher in the Authority System of the Public School." *Journal of Educational Sociology* 27 (November 1953): 128–41.

Benjamin, Robert. *Making Schools Work*. New York: Continuum Publishing Co., 1981.

Berman, Paul, and McLaughlin, Milbrey. *Federal Programs Supporting Educational Change. Vol. 4. The Findings in Review*. Santa Monica, Rand Corp., 1975.

———. *Federal Programs Supporting Educational Change. Vol. 8. Implementing and Sustaining Innovations*. Santa Monica, Rand Corp., 1978.

Bidwell, Charles. "The School as a Formal Organization." In *Handbook of Organizations*, edited by James G. March. Chicago: Rand McNally, 1965, pp. 927–1022.

Blau, Peter M. *Exchange and Power in Social Life*. New York: Wiley, 1964.

Bridges, Edwin M. *Job Satisfaction and Teacher Absenteeism*. Project No. 79–A13. Stanford, Calif.: Stanford University, Institute for Research on Educational Finance and Governance, December 1979.

Bureau of National Affairs. *Special Report: Teachers and Labor Relations, 1979–1890*. Washington, D.C.: Bureau of National Affairs, 1980.

Callahan, Raymond E. *Education and the Cult of Efficiency*. Chicago: University of Chicago Press, 1962.

Capitol Publications. *Report on Educational Research*. 12, no. 21 (October 15, 1981). Arlington, Va.: Capitol Publications.

Chambers, Jay G. *The Impact of Bargaining and Bargaining Statutes on the Earnings of Public School Teachers: A Comparison in California and Missouri*. Project No. 80–B6. Stanford, Calif.: Stanford University, Institute for Research on Educational Finance and Governance, 1980.

Clark, R. Theodore, Jr. "Commentary." In *Faculty and Teacher Bargaining: The Impact of Unions on Education*, edited by George W. Angell. Lexington, Mass.: Lexington Books, 1981.

Cohen, Michael D., and March, James G. *Leadership and Ambiguity: The American College President*. New York: McGraw-Hill, 1974.

Cooper, Bruce S. "The Future of Middle Management in Education." In *The Principal in Metropolitan Schools*, edited by Donald A. Erickson and Theodore L. Reller. Berkeley, Calif.: McCutchan Publishing Corp., 1979, pp. 272–99.

Cooper, Bruce S., and Bussey, John C. *Collective Bargaining in Public Education—and Other Sectors: A Comparative Review of Research*. Dartmouth, N.H.: Dartmouth College, 1980.

Corwin, Ronald G. *Militant Professionalism: A Study of Organizational Conflict in High Schools*. New York: Appleton-Century-Crofts, 1970.

———. *Education in Crisis: A Sociological Analysis of Schools and Universities in Transition*. New York: John Wiley & Sons, 1974.

———. "The Organizational Context of School Board-Teacher Conflict." In *Understanding School Boards: Problems and Prospects*, edited by Peter J. Cistone, Lexington, Mass.: D.C. Heath, 1975, pp. 131–58.

———. "Patterns of Organizational Control and Teacher Militancy: Theoretical Continuities in the Idea of 'Loose Coupling.'" In *Research in Sociology of Education and Socialization*, edited by Ronald G. Corwin, 2: 261–91. Greenwich, Conn.: JAI Press, 1981.

Cresswell, Anthony M., and Murphy, Michael J. *Teachers, Unions, and Collective Bargaining in Public Education*. Berkeley, Calif.: McCutchan Publishing Corp., 1980.

Crowson, Robert L., and Porter-Gehrie, Cynthia. "The Discretionary

Behavior of Principals in Large-City Schools." *Educational Administration Quarterly* 16, no. 1 (Winter 1980): 45–69.

Dahl, R. A., "The Concept of Power," *Behavioral Science* 2, no. 2, (March 1957): 201–18.

Darling-Hammond, Linda, and Wise, Arthur. *A Conceptual Framework for Examining Teachers' Views of Teaching and Educational Policies.* Santa Monica, Calif.: Rand Corp., 1981.

Deal, Terrence E., and Colatti, Lynn. "Loose Coupling and the School Administrator." Mimeographed. Stanford, Calif.: Stanford University, Stanford Center for Research and Development in Teaching, 1975.

Doherty, Robert E. "Public Interest at Stake." *American School Board Journal* 155, no. 4 (October 1967): 11–14.

———. "Does Teacher Bargaining Affect Student Achievement?" In *Faculty and Teacher Bargaining: The Impact of Unions on Education*, edited by George W. Angell. Lexington, Mass.: Lexington Books, 1981, pp. 63–77.

Donley, Marshall O., Jr. *Power to the Teacher.* Bloomington: Indiana University Press, 1976.

Dornbush, Sanford M., and Scott, W. Richard. *Evaluation and the Exercise of Authority.* San Francisco: Jossey-Bass Publishing Co., 1975.

Dunlop, John E. "Commentary." In *Faculty and Teacher Bargaining: The Impact of Unions on Education*, edited by George W. Angell. Lexington, Mass.: Lexington Books, 1981, pp. 77–85.

Duke, Daniel L.; Showers, Beverly; and Imber, Michael. *Teachers as School Decision Makers.* Project No. 80–A7. Stanford, Calif.: Stanford University, Institute for Research on Educational Finance and Governance, May 1980.

Eaton, William Edward. *The American Federation of Teachers, 1916–1961: A History of the Movement.* Carbondale: Southern Illinois University Press, 1975.

Eberts, Randall W., and Pierce, Lawrence C. *The Effects of Collective Bargaining in Public Schools.* Eugene: University of Oregon, Center for Educational Policy and Management, December 1980.

Edmonds, Ronald. "Effective Schools for the Urban Poor." *Educational Leadership* 37, no. 1 (October 1979): 15–24.

Education Commission of the States. *"Issuegram: Teacher Competency."* Denver, August 1981.

Ehrenberg, Ronald. *An Economic Analysis of Local Government Employment and Wages.* Washington, D.C.: U.S. Department of Labor, 1973.

Elmore, Richard F. *Complexity and Control: What Legislators and Administrators*

Can Do about Implementation. Seattle: University of Washington, Institute of Governmental Research, April 1979.

Fisher, Roger, and Ury, William. *Getting to Yes: Negotiating Agreement without Giving In.* Boston: Houghton-Mifflin Co., 1981.

Frederiksen, John, and Edmonds, Ron. "Identification of Instructionally Effective and Ineffective Schools." Mimeographed. Cambridge, Mass.: Harvard University, Search for Effective Schools Project, n.d.

Freeman, Richard B., and Medoff, James L. "The Two Faces of Unionism." *Public Interest* 57 (Fall 1979): 69–93.

Frey, Donald E. "Wage Determination in the Public Schools and the Effects of Unionization." Working Paper 42E. Princeton, N.J.: Princeton University, Industrial Relations Section, 1973.

Gouldner, Alvin W. "The Norm of Reciprocity: A Preliminary Statement." *American Sociological Review* 25, no. 2 (April 1960): 161–78.

Grant, W. Vance, and Eiden, Leo J. *Digest of Education Statistics, 1980.* Washington, D.C.: National Center for Education Statistics, 1980.

Grimshaw, William J. *Union Rule in the Schools.* Lexington, Mass.: Lexington Books, 1979.

Gross, Neal, and Herriott, Robert E. *Staff Leadership in Public Schools: A Sociological Analysis.* New York: John Wiley & Sons, 1965.

Hall, W. Clayton, and Carroll, Norman E. "The Effects of Teachers' Organizations on Salaries and Class Size." *Industrial and Labor Relations Review* 26 (January 1973): 834–41.

Hill, Paul T. *Enforcement and Informal Pressure in the Management of Federal Categorical Programs in Education.* Santa Monica, Calif.: Rand Corp., 1979.

Hirschman, Albert O. *Exit, Voice and Loyalty: Responses to Decline in Firms, Organizations, and States.* Cambridge, Mass.: Harvard University Press, 1970.

Horowitz, Donald L. *The Courts and Social Policy.* Washington, D.C.: Brookings Institution, 1977.

Jackson, Philip W. *Life in Classrooms.* New York: Holt, Rinehart, Winston, 1968.

Jessup, Dorothy. "Teacher Unionization: A Reassessment of Rank and File Motivations." *Sociology of Education* 51 (January 1978): 44–55.

Johnson, Susan Moore. "Performance-based Staff Layoffs in the Public Schools: Implementation and Outcomes." *Harvard Educational Review* 50, no. 2 (May 1980): 214–33.

Kasper, Herschel. "The Effect of Collective Bargaining on Public School Teachers' Salaries." *Industrial and Labor Relations Review* 24 (October 1970): 57–72.

Kaufman, Herbert. *Administrative Feedback: Monitoring Subordinates' Behavior.* Washington, D.C.: Brookings Institution, 1973.

Kerchner, Charles T. "The Impact of Collective Bargaining on School Governance." *Education and Urban Society* 11, no. 2 (February 1979): 182.

Kerchner, Charles T. and Mitchell, Douglas E. *The Dynamics of Public School Bargaining and Its Impacts on Governance, Administration and Teaching.* Washington, D.C.: National Institute of Education, 1981.

Kyte, George C. *The Principal at Work.* New York: Ginn & Co., 1952.

Lieberman, Ann, and Miller, Lynn. "The Social Realities of Teaching." *Teachers College Record* 80, no. 1 (September 1978): 54–68.

Lieberman, Myron. *Education as a Profession.* Englewood Cliffs, N.J.: Prentice-Hall, 1965.

——. "Teachers Bargaining: An Autopsy." *Phi Delta Kappan* 63, no. 4 (December 1980): 231–34.

Lipsky, David G., and Drotning, John E. "The Influence of Collective Bargaining on Teachers' Salaries in New York State." *Industrial and Labor Relations Review* 27 (October 1973): 18–35.

Lipsky, Michael. *Street-Level Bureaucracy.* New York: Russell Sage Foundation. 1980.

Lofland, John. *Analyzing Social Settings: A Guide to Qualitative Observation and Analysis.* Belmount, Calif.: Wadsworth Publishing Co., 1971.

Lortie, Dan C. "The Balance of Control and Autonomy in Elementary School Training." In *The Semi-Professions and Their Organizations,* edited by Amitai Etzioni. New York: Free Press, 1969, pp. 1–53.

——. *Schoolteacher: A Sociological Study.* Chicago: University of Chicago Press, 1975.

Lutz, Frank W., and Caldwell, William E. "Collective Bargaining and the Principal." In *The Principal in Metropolitan Schools,* edited by Donald A. Erickson and Theodore L. Reller. Berkeley, Calif.: McCutchan Publishing Corp., 1979, pp. 256–71.

March, James G. "American Public School Administration: A Short Analysis." *School Review* 86 (February 1978): 217–50.

——. *Footnotes to Organizational Change.* Project No. 80-A6. Stanford, Calif.: Stanford University, Institute for Research on Educational Finance and Governance, April 1980.

McCall, Morgan W., Jr., and Lombardo, Michael M. *Leadership: Where Else Can We Go?* Durham, N.C.: Duke University Press, 1978.

McCleary, Lloyd E., and Thomson, Scott D. *The Senior High School Principalship. Vol. 3. The Summary Report.* Reston, Va.: National Association of Secondary School Principals, 1979.

McDonnell, Lorraine, and Pascal, Anthony *Organized Teachers in American Schools.* Santa Monica, Calif.: Rand Corp., 1979.

McLaughlin, Milbrey. "Implementation as Mutual Adaptation: Change in the Classroom," *Teachers College Record* 77, (February 1976): 337–51.

McLaughlin, Milbrey; Greenwood, Peter; and Mann, Dale. *Federal Programs Supporting Educational Change. Vol. 3. The Process of Change.* Santa Monica, Calif: Rand Corp., 1975.

McPherson, Gertrude H. "What Principals Should Know about Teachers." In *The Principal in Metropolitan Schools,* edited by Donald A. Erickson and Theodore L. Reller. Berkeley, Calif.: McCutchan Publishing Corp., 1979, pp. 233–55.

Methé, David T., and Perry, James L. "The Impacts of Collective Bargaining on Local Government Services: A Review of Research." *Public Administration Review* 40, no. 4 (July/August 1980), pp. 359–71.

Metz, Mary Haywood. *Classrooms and Corridors: The Crisis of Authority in Desegregated Secondary Schools.* Berkeley: University of California Press, 1978.

Meyer, John W., and Rowan, Brian. "The Structure of Educational Organizations." In *Environments and Organizations,* edited by Marshall W. Meyer and Associates. San Francisco: Jossey-Bass Publishing Co., 1978.

Meyer, Marshall W. and Associates. *Environments and Organizations.* San Francisco: Jossey-Bass Publishing Co., 1978.

Mitchell, Douglas E.; Kerchner, Charles T.; Erck, Wayne; and Pryor, Gabrielle. *The Impact of Collective Bargaining on School Management and Policy.* Claremont, Calif.: Claremont Colleges, 1980.

Moore, Donald R.; Hyde, Arthur A.; Blair, Kathy A.; and Weitzman, Sharon M. *Student Classification and the Right to Read.* Chicago: Designs for Change, 1981.

Morris, Van Cleve; Crowson, Robert L.; Hurwitz, Jr.; Porter-Gehrie, Cynthia. *The Urban Principal: Discretionary Decision-making in a Large Educational Organization.* Chicago: University of Illinois at Chicago Circle, 1981.

Moscow, Michael; Loewenberg, Joseph J.; Koziara, Edward C. *Collective Bargaining in Public Employment.* New York: Random House, 1970.

Moser, Robert P. "Administrator's Clinic: Principals: Shock Absorbers and Stimulators." *Nation's Schools* 94 (August 1974): 11.

Murnane, Richard J. *Seniority Rules and Educational Productivity: Understanding the Consequences of a Mandate for Equality.* Project Report No. 80-A17.

Stanford, Calif.: Stanford University, Institute for Research on Educational Finance and Governance, 1980.

Murphy, Jerome T. "Title I of ESEA: The Politics of Implementing Federal Education Reform." *Harvard Educational Review* 41 (1971): 35–63.

————. *Getting the Facts: A Fieldwork Guide for Evaluators and Policy Analysts.* Santa Monica, Calif.: Goodyear Publishing Co., 1980.

Murphy, Michael J., and Hoover, David. "Negotiations at the Crossroads: Increased Professionalization or Reinforced Bureaucracy." In *Education and Collective Bargaining: Readings in Policy and Research*, edited by Anthony M. Cresswell and Michael J. Murphy. Berkeley, Calif.: McCutchan Publishing Corp., pp 476–83.

National Center for Education Statistics. *The Condition of Education, 1980.* Washington, D.C.: U.S. Department of Education, 1981.

————. *Projections of Education Statistics to 1990–91, Vol. 1.* Washington, D.C.: U.S. Department of Education, 1983.

National School Boards Association. *Collective Bargaining—Practices, and Attitudes of School Management*, Research Report 1977-2. Washington D.C.: National School Boards Association, 1977.

National School Public Relations Association. *Education U.S.A.* 23, no. 19 (January 5, 1981): 138. Washington D.C.: National School Public Relations Association.

Newspaper Enterprise Association. *The World Almanac of Facts, 1981.* New York: Newspaper Enterprise Association, 1981.

Perry, Charles R. "Teacher Bargaining: The Experience in Nine Systems," *Industrial and Labor Relations Review* 33, no. 1 (October 1979): 3–17.

Perry, Charles R., and Wildman, W. A. *The Impact of Negotiations in Public Education: The Evidence from the Schools.* Worthington, Ohio: Jones Publishing Co., 1970.

Perry, Ronald J. "Reflections on a School Strike: The Superintendent's View." *Phi Delta Kappan* 57 no. 9 (May 1976), 587–90.

Pfeffer, Jeffrey. *Power in Organizations.* Marshfield, Mass.: Pitman Publishing, 1981.

Phi Delta Kappa. *Why Do Some Urban Schools Succeed?* Bloomington, Ind.: Phi Delta Kappa, 1980

Pressman, Jeffrey L., and Wildavsky, Aaron B. *Implementation.* Berkeley: University of California Press, 1973.

Rhemus, Charles M., and Wilner, Evan *The Economic Results of Teacher Bargaining: Michigan's First Two Years.* Ann Arbor, Mich.: Institute of Labor and Industrial Relations, 1965.

Rosenshine, Barak, and Furst, Norma. "The Use of Direct Observation to Study Teaching." In *The Second Handbook of Research on Teaching*, edited by Robert M. W. Travers. Chicago: Rand McNally, 1973.

Ross, Doris, Flakus-Mosqueda, Patricia. *Cuebook II: State Education Collective Bargaining Laws*. Denver: Education Commission of the States, 1980.

Rutter, Michael; Maughan, Barbara; Mortinore, Peter; Ouston, Janet. *Fifteen Thousand Hours: Secondary Schools and Their Effects on Children*. Cambridge, Mass.: Harvard University Press, 1979.

Sanzare, James. *A History of the Philadelphia Federation of Teachers, 1941–1973*. Philadelphia: Philadelphia Federation of Teachers, 1977.

Sarason, Seymour B. *The Culture of the School and the Problem of Change*. Boston: Allyn & Bacon, 1971.

Shanker, Albert. "After Twenty Years Lieberman's Vision Is Failing." *Phi Delta Kappan* 63, no. 4 (December 1980): 236, 278.

Shils, Edward B., and Whittier, C. Taylor. *Teachers, Administrators, and Collective Bargaining*. New York: Thomas Y. Crowell, 1968.

Slichter, S.; Healy, J.; and Livernash, E. R. *The Impact of Collective Bargaining on Management*. Washington, D.C.: Brookings Institution, 1960.

Steele, Ellen Hogan. "Reflections on a School Strike: A Teacher's View." *Phi Delta Kappan* 57, no. 9 (May 1976), pp. 590–92.

Talbert, Joan E. *School Organization and Institutional Change: Exchange and Power in Loosely Coupled Systems*. Project Report No. 80-A9. Stanford, Calif.: Stanford University, Institute for Research on Educational Finance and Governance, 1980.

Thorton, Robert. "The Effects of Collective Negotiations on Teachers' Salaries." *Quarterly Review of Economics and Business* 2 (Winter 1971): 37–46.

U.S. Bureau of the Census. *Labor Management Relations in State and Local Governments, 1975*. Washington, D.C.: U.S. Bureau of the Census, 1977.

van Geel, Tyll. *Authority to Control the School Program*. Lexington, Mass.: Lexington Books, 1976.

Watson, Bernard C. "The Principal against the System." In *The Principal in Metropolitan Schools*, edited by Donald A. Erickson and Theodore L. Reller. Berkeley, Calif.: McCutchan Publishing Corp., 1979.

Weatherly, Richard, and Lipsky, Michael. "Street-Level Bureaucrats and Institutional Innovation: Implementing Special Education Reform." *Harvard Educational Review* 47, no. 2 (May 1977): 171–96.

Webb, Eugene J.; Campbell, Donald T.; Schwartz, Richard D.; Suchrest,

Lee. *Unobtrusive Measures: Nonreactive Research in Social Sciences.* Chicago: Rand McNally, 1966.

Weick, Karl E. "Educational Organizations as Loosely Coupled Systems." *Administrative Science Quarterly* 21 (March 1976): 1–19.

Williams, Dennis A.; Coppola, Vincent; Howard, Lucy; Huck, Janet; King, Patricia; Monroe, Sylvester. "Teachers Are in Trouble." *Newsweek*, April 27, 1971.

Williams, Walter, and Elmore, Richard F., eds. *Social Program Implementation.* New York: Academic Press, 1976.

Wise, Arthur E. *Legislated Learning: The Bureaucratization of the American Classroom.* Berkeley: University of California Press, 1979.

Wilcott, Harry F. *The Man in the Principal's Office: An Ethnography.* New York: Holt, Rinehart & Winston, 1973.

————. *Teachers versus Technocrats: An Educational Innovation in Anthropological Perspective.* Eugene: University of Oregon, Center for Educational Policy and Management, 1977.

Index